'A *Canterb...* ...Lee

...as
...at.'

...ke
...pt.
...tus

...sic

...re

...he

...l

...of
...as.
...st,

THE
FALLEN

Dave Simpson writes on music and the arts for the *Guardian* from an isolated base in the north of England. He has been a fan of The Fall since 1979, and once admitted to hating The Beatles.

THE
FALLEN

*Life In and Out of
Britain's Most Insane Group*

DAVE SIMPSON

CANONGATE

Edinburgh · London · New York · Melbourne

First published in Great Britain in 2008 by
Canongate Books Ltd, 14 High Street,
Edinburgh, EH1 1TE

This paperback edition first published by
Canongate Books in 2009

1

For photography credits and permissions acknowledgments please see
p.309. Every effort has been made to contact copyright holders where
appropriate, but please contact the publisher if there are any errors or
omissions.

British Library Cataloguing-in-Publication Data
A catalogue record for this book is available on
request from the British Library

ISBN 978 1 84767 144 8

Typeset by Palimpsest Book Production Ltd,
Grangemouth, Stirlingshire

Printed and bound in Great Britain by Clays Ltd, St Ives plc

www.meetatthegate.com

To my late parents, Reginald and Florence Olive Simpson.
Thanks for the words, Dad.

There is variety in genius as there is talent and beauty. Some geniuses are innovators, some are deep thinkers and some are people of extraordinary skill; most are a volatile mixture of intellectual gifts and character traits. The intellectual gifts are an ability to see things from highly unusual angles, to overlook what is not essential, and to understand the true significance of the obvious. The character traits are persistence, obduracy, capacity for taking great pains, and indifference to ridicule.

A C Grayling, Professor of Philosophy, University of London, 2007

That's my fucking aim in life, to keep it going as long as I can.

Mark E Smith, 1979

IN LOVING MEMORY OF THE FALLEN

Priest: Brethren, we are called upon to pay the last tributes of respect to brothers and sisters who have now gone. Places once filled are now vacant. Chairs once occupied are now empty. Hands, whose helpful clasp cheered us in days gone by, are folding in everlasting rest. It is fitting, therefore, that we should pause, no matter how engrossing our duties, and pay to our departed brothers and sisters the tribute due their memory.

Suggested music: 'Hey! Luciani' by The Fall

Brother scribe, the roll call.

Steve aka Dave ('the unknown drummer', 1976) 'No longer with us'

Tony Friel (bass, 1976 – December 1977) 'No longer with us'

Una Baines (keyboards, 1976 – March 1978) 'No longer with us'

Martin Bramah (guitar/backing vocals, 1976 – April 1979; July 1989 – July 1990) 'No longer with us'

Karl Burns (drums/guitar/bass/keyboards) (May 1977 – December 1978; October 1981 – June 1986; January 1993 – December 1996; May 1997 – April 1998) 'No longer with us'

Kay Carroll (backing vocals, management 1977 – April 1983) 'No longer with us'

Jonnie Brown (bass, January – March 1978) 'No longer with us'

Eric McGann aka Rick Goldstraw aka Eric Echo aka Eric the Ferret (bass, March – June 1978) 'No longer with us'

Yvonne Pawlett (keyboards, May 1978 – June 1979) 'No longer with us'

Steve Davies (percussion/drums, 30 May 1978 and again in June 1980) 'No longer with us'

Marc Riley (guitar, then bass, June 1978 – December 1982) 'No longer with us'

Steve Hanley (bass, April 1979 – April 1998) 'No longer with us'

Craig Scanlon (guitar, April 1979 – December 1995) 'No longer with us'

Mike Leigh (drums, January 1979 – March 1980) 'No longer with us'

Dave Tucker (clarinet, 1980–1) 'No longer with us'

Paul Hanley (drums, March 1980 – March 1985) 'No longer with us'

Brix Smith (guitar/backing vocals, September 1983 – July 1989; August 1994 – October 1996) 'No longer with us'

Simon Rogers (bass/keyboards/guitar, March 1985 – October 1986) 'No longer with us'

Simon Wolstencroft (drums/keyboards, June 1986 – August 1997) 'No longer with us'

Marcia Schofield (keyboards, October 1986 – July 1990) 'No longer with us'

Charlotte Bill (flute/oboe, 1990) 'No longer with us'

Kenny Brady (violin/keyboards, July 1990 – June 1991) 'No longer with us'

Dave Bush (keyboards, August 1991 – November 1995) 'No longer with us'

Mike Bennett (backing vocalist, late 1994 – late 1996) 'No longer with us'

Julia Nagle (keyboards/guitar, November 1995 – August 2001) 'No longer with us'

Lucy Rimmer (vocals, December 1995 – October 1996) 'No longer with us'

Adrian Flanagan (guitar, December 1996 – February 1997) 'No longer with us'

Keir Stewart (guitar, early 1997) 'No longer with us'

Tommy Crooks (guitar, August 1997 – April 1998) 'No longer with us'

Kate Themen (drums, April – May 1998) 'No longer with us'

Stuart Estell (guitar, 30 April 1998) 'No longer with us'

Karen Leatham (bass, August 1998 – December 1998) 'No longer with us'

Tom Head aka Thomas Patrick Murphy (drums, August 1998 – November 2000) 'No longer with us'

Neville Wilding (guitar, November 1998 – February 2001) 'No longer with us'

Adam Helal (bass, December 1998 – February 2001) 'No longer with us'

Nick Dewey (drums, 27 August 1999) 'No longer with us'

Steve Evets (backing vocals/bass, 2000–2) 'No longer with us'

Ed Blaney (guitar/backing vocals/management/'brokering', 2000–4) 'No longer with us'

Spencer Birtwistle (drums, November 2000 – November 2001; July 2004 – May 2006) 'No longer with us'

Ben Pritchard (guitar, February 2001 – May 2006) 'No longer with us'

Jim Watts (guitar/bass/keyboards/computers, February 2001 – March 2003; July – December 2004) 'No longer with us'

Brian Fanning (guitar, mid to late 2001) 'No longer with us'

Dave Milner (drums/backing vocals, November 2001 – June 2004) 'No longer with us'

Ruth Daniel (keyboards, 22 September 2002) 'No longer with us'

Simon Archer (bass, April 2003 – April 2004) 'No longer with us'

Steven Trafford (bass, April 2004 – May 2006) 'No longer with us'

Chris Evans (drums, 3 December 2004) 'No longer with us'

Rob Barbato (bass, 9 May 2006 – 1 June 2007) 'No longer with us'

Orpheus McCord (drums, 9 May 2006 – 1 June 2007) 'No longer with us'

Tim Presley (guitar, 9 May 2006 – 1 June 2007) 'No longer with us'

Mark Edward Smith (vocals, 1976 to date) 'Still with us. ALWAYS with us.'

This book documents a two-year period (2005–7) which I spent tracking down the dozens of people who had once played in The Fall. By the time the journey was over, what I refer to as 'the current line-up' had also departed, joining the ranks of The Fallen. After the book was originally published I tracked them down, which can be read about in the epilogue.

www.thefallenbook.co.uk

PROLOGUE: REMEMBERING THE FALLEN

It was a Tuesday morning in December, and I was ringing people in Rotherham, all of them called Brown.

'Hello,' I began, for the fifth time that day, 'I'm trying to trace Jonnie Brown who used to play in The Fall. I know he came from Rotherham and wondered if you might be a relative.'

'The Who?' asked the latest Mr Brown on the end of the line.

'No. The Fall . . . the band from Salford. Jonnie played bass for three weeks in 1978.'

'Is this some kind of joke?'

First I had become an internet stalker, now I was a telephone pest, all because of The Fall. Why was I doing this?

It started on 4 September 2005 when I drove to Manchester to interview Mark E Smith. I am a journalist and I've been interviewing pop stars for years but this encounter was different. Before the interview, even casual observers seemed to have a cautioning word. 'You'd better take a crash helmet,' joked one mate, aware of Smith's colourful reputation – in particular, stubbing a cigarette out on a pesky journalist's forehead. Days before my interview, I received a call from the paper's photographer, who found the singer so 'blotto' at the photo session he'd come away with hundreds of shots of the venerable vocalist having to be held upright by bewildered passers-by.

I'd met Smith years before, in 1981. I had approached the notoriously opinionated frontman on the steps of Leeds University, where The Fall were about to play. Considering that even then he had a spiky public image,

Smith was surprisingly polite, but I didn't get the autograph I craved. Neither of us could produce a pen – instead the singer rather charmingly took a bite mark out of my ticket, leaving a lasting impression of his 1981 dental work and a DNA sample which remains in my possession in case any Fall-mad scientists ever wish to make a clone of Mark E Smith.

As I drove the 70 miles along the M62 to the interview, passing signs for Smith's beloved Prestwich and Salford, something nagged at me all the way. What had happened in the intervening 24 years to transform the cheery ticket chomper into a character with a life seemingly as unique as his song-book and one of the true legends of British music?

If you're reading this, there's every chance you know a lot about The Fall. But if not, you should know the following:

The Fall are one of the most revered and influential bands in British pop, one who more than most lend themselves to obsession.

In John Peel's Record Box – which contained the late DJ's favourite records – Fall records had an entire section to themselves. Peel called them The Mighty Fall: 'the band against which all others are judged'. Their audiences still include fans who don't follow other bands, who never listen to anything else. Smith's inspired, social sci-fi songs are beloved of everyone from comedians Frank Skinner (who uses 1981 Fall song 'Jaw Bone and the Air Rifle' to open his TV show) and Stewart Lee, to the designer Calvin Klein, artist Grayson Perry, and authors Irvine Welsh and the late Philip K Dick. Musicians and music critics love them, too. Julian Cope estimates he saw them 28 times in 1978 alone. David Bowie, Bo Diddley, Thom Yorke and Alex Kapranos all claim to be fans, and Fall albums still regularly receive rave reviews for their paint-stripping riffs, blood-racing rhythms and what one writer has called their 'head-turning quality . . . a hail of one-liners, withering put-downs and bewildering images'.

Despite this acclaim, The Fall have never been a household name. They have had more hit singles that haven't penetrated the Top 20 than any other band – 16 in total. I love this fact. It signifies The Fall's complex relationship with pop and our culture in general: never quite in, but never quite out, maintaining a disaffected, opinionated presence on whatever landscape the music scene – and Britain's social make-up – is occupying at the time.

When the Sex Pistols were taking 'punk' onto *Top of the Pops*, an embryonic

Fall were taking pot shots at socio-culture from the unglamorous, un-pop environment of working men's clubs. During the synthesiser boom of the early to mid 1980s, Smith hectored wildly over walls of guitars. In the 1990s, when Britpop brought a return to straightforward rock anthems, Smith, contrarily, added everything from violins to complex computerised sounds. Along the way, they have produced an enormous body of work. *Reformation Post-TLC*, the band's 2007 studio album, was probably their twenty-seventh, although there have been so many nobody seems entirely sure.

The sheer longevity of The Fall is an achievement in itself. Through times when many bands have been lucky to make it to a second album, they have outlasted five prime ministers, the rise and decline of both Thatcherism and New Labour, the fall of the Berlin Wall, the Falklands conflict, Bosnia, two Iraq wars, the fluctuating fortunes of many of England's bigger football clubs – including Smith's treasured Manchester City – and some terrifying vagaries of fashion. When Smith embarked on his mission in 1976 – sporting an anti-fashion tank top – many people wore flares and few households had a car or a colour television. Now we have the internet and rabid globalisation, although people still wear flares, which may suggest to Smith his work is far from done. The Fall have moved with their times but have sounded, as Peel once suggested, 'always different, always the same'.

Throughout it all, Smith has maintained a fiercely uncompromising 'no sell-out' stance towards the music business that has survived apparent anomalies such as an advertising campaign for Vauxhall Corsa (featuring 'Touch Sensitive''s 'Hey hey hey hey!' refrain), ironic given that Smith doesn't hold a driving licence.

My own obsession with The Fall started that night, 17 March 1981 – I know the date because I still have the gaudy orange poster I ripped off the uni walls. Back then, the fact that they were playing the Riley-Smith Hall with a singer called Smith and a guitarist called (Marc) Riley seemed to bestow an almost mystical significance on the event. The gig was unlike anything I'd seen: the music was uncategorisable – Was it punk? Was it rockabilly? Was it experimental? All three? – but had a hypnotic tension that seemed to draw me in. Smith stalked the stage, radiating charisma and baffling but important-sounding words which seemed to convey urgent truths. Around the same time, I encountered other Fall fans who were convinced Smith was psychic.

From that day on, major developments in my life have seemed peculiarly bound up with The Fall. I had my first pint of bitter over the road from my first Fall gig. I lost my virginity – resulting in carpet burns from an orange nylon carpet, a feature of many a council semi at the time – to a girl called Carol, who also gave me my first Fall album, the 1980 master-piece, *Grotesque (After The Gramme)*, which contained 'The Container Drivers', a rollercoasting blast of Northern rockabilly that's still my favourite Fall song of all time. In the mid 1980s, when The Fall scored a big hit with a cover of The Kinks' 'Victoria', I was dating a girl called Victoria. I'm not saying her being called Victoria made the relationship any more desirable, but it did give things a certain *je ne sais quoi*. Sorry, Victoria.

I've found most Fall fans have similar tales – as if Smith, pop's ultimate ringmaster and provocateur, were wielding the same supernatural control over his audiences as he seems to hold over his group.

In fact, to call The Fall a group – a term Smith prefers to the apparently derogatory 'band' – is misleading. Apart from the erstwhile frontman, the line-up has endured so many upheavals that broadcaster Paul Morley, another Fall fanatic, has suggested there have been many different groups called The Fall, all fronted by Mark E Smith, all either wildly dark or wildly funny depending on the day of the week.

I should state now that like most Fall fans I regard Smith as a genius, although I've never been entirely sure just what his genius is. His splenetic observations and surreal, often slurred insights on everything from MI5 conspiracies to mythical Mancunian 'city hobgoblins' to the travails of British people in hot weather (and their resemblance to beached whales) – have earned him the tag of master lyricist and even seer for the way his songs seem to contain uncanny prophecies. For example, the song 'Powder Keg' – containing references to Manchester city centre – was released just weeks before the IRA bombing of central Manchester in 1996.

However, for me, the deeper aspect of Smith's genius is somehow entwined with the way he runs his group. Smith is a 'musical genius' who is not a musician. He certainly has an ear for a tune but it's debatable whether he can actually play a note. Smith distrusts musicians to the point of contempt but one of the many paradoxes in The Fall is that he is reliant on them to produce his lifetime's work.

For years, Smith – whose father, a plumber, ran his own small business – has maintained The Fall using industrial techniques that were on their way out when the group formed in 1976. The Fall operate like an old-fashioned factory: Smith is the site manager, responsible for hiring and firing workers and overseeing their performances. This is the most precious and secretive area of his art. Smith somehow coaxes performances from musicians – most of them found in his local pub – who shouldn't logically be up to the task of playing in a legendary group. Once musicians have outlived their useful-ness, or, perhaps, become too bolshie, they are discarded and left to fend for themselves.

In this way, the Fall factory has been able to produce at least one unit – an album, and often more – a year. However, in recent years the revolving door has almost spun off its hinges. What I didn't realise in 1981 was that, even then, The Fall had already seen off eleven musicians. But in more recent years, line-ups have imploded before gigs, after gigs and even during gigs, with accompanying tales of fist-fights and appalling behaviour. Even Paul Morley has pondered, 'What if he wasn't a genius, he was just an old drunken tramp that when he got really drunk started to spout phrases that made a kind of sense, and we read too much into it, you know?'

And yet, after each seemingly terminal session of public *hara-kiri*, Smith has got up, dusted himself down, assembled yet another Fall and continued, to the bafflement of many, to reshape the band and make even more great music.

By the time I interviewed Smith in 2005, I'd become fascinated both by his guarded doctrine of 'creative tension' but also by the curious lives and fates of the former members. Because Smith has always maintained a Goebbels-like iron grip over The Fall's interviews, little is heard from Fall musicians even where they're in the group, and certainly not afterwards.

As I prepared for my interview, I found myself wondering where they were, not least the line-up I encountered all those years ago in 1981.

The guitarist, Marc Riley, had become a famous DJ on Radio One. Steve Hanley, the bassist, had remained alongside Smith from 1979 until 1998, when he'd departed after a particularly infamous New York punch-up which landed Smith in jail. Craig Scanlon – perhaps the band's most revered guitarist – had been mysteriously sacked in the mid 1990s and was rumoured to be a broken man, grinding out his days working in the dole office.

Most perplexing of all was the mysterious fate of Karl Burns. Burns had been the band's high-profile drummer for 20 years – fired and rehired on numerous occasions – but since the New York incident had vanished as effectively as Lord Lucan. Even Peel had been moved to ponder, 'I don't know if Smith is killing them all or what?'

The more I totted up the number of people who were active members of The Fall (as opposed to producers, girlfriends or wives who added backing vocals, or saxophonists who contributed 15 seconds to a track in 1982), the more mysterious it seemed. Inevitably, Smith was unwilling to shed light – suddenly clamming up or changing the subject whenever we veered towards the topic of ex-workers. Each time I asked about Karl Burns, he swiftly changed the subject, summoning the barman to supply us with more lager.

So, I set myself the task of finding them, dead or alive, imagining that the former members not only held the key to the legends of The Fall, but that The Fallen musicians were themselves a piece of social history: 30 years of music seen through the eyes of the foot soldiers.

Which is why, on a Tuesday morning in December, I was ringing people in Rotherham called Brown. When I started my mission, there were 42 ex-members of The Fall on my list. When I ended it, there were 45. I had to find Jonnie Brown, and the rest, before MES 'killed' any more of them. Or me.

CHAPTER 1

'It's like football. Every so often you've got to replace the centre-forward.'

The first thing you notice when you have any sort of dealings with The Fall is that even in the most cursory functions they don't operate like any other group. There are no armies of publicists, marketeers or stylists, or even something as customary as a manager. What there is, is a very nice lady called Dorothy who acts as something like a go-between The Wonderful and Frightening World of The Fall (the title of their cracking 1984 album) and everybody else. Requests for interviews and such like are batted on to Elena, the third Mrs Smith and at time of writing the current keyboard player in The Fall, who then forwards them to Smith himself.

'How about getting Mark to talk about the former members and then some of the former members to talk about Mark?' I ask Dorothy.

She seems unsure, but she has a suggestion: 'Why not interview Mark, see how you get on, and then hopefully he'll put you in touch with some former members?'

Thus, I find myself hurtling in the Fiat Punto to Manchester's Malmaison, wondering which Smith – born 5 March 1957, whose name, Mark, is Hebrew for 'warlike' – I'll get today. My only previous interview with him took place in 1997, when *Melody Maker* had the idea to put Smith together with New Order bassist Peter Hook and The Beautiful South's singer Paul Heaton to debate the burning issues of the day. Smith turned up complaining of an attack of tinnitus, caused by a bang on the head sustained in the course of sacking his latest line-up two nights previously, and with a limp he suggested was the result of being mis-sold some 'corrective shoes'. It then transpired we'd have difficulty finding a venue for the interview because Smith was at the time barred from most of Manchester's city centre pubs. We finally found a suitable, if insalubrious, bar where I felt a tiny bit apprehensive regarding Smith's grouchy reputation. However, Smith was nice as pie with me, perhaps because he was more preoccupied with hilariously destroying Heaton, who had made the grievous mistake of confessing to be a huge fan of The Fall.

The session went on for hours and hours, during which we somehow managed to tackle subjects as diverse as the Spice Girls, the Teletubbies, the IRA and why electioneering Conservative politicians in Smith's native Salford have to don balaclavas if they dare to knock on doors, before I passed out on the train home.

The interview had already been postponed twice. Ominously, we were supposed to meet on the Friday, but Dorothy phoned to say Smith had suddenly had to dash off for some 'urgent business' in Austria. Whatever could that mean? Then I got halfway across the M62 to Manchester when Elena called to say Smith had been 'unavoidably detained' a second time. Two days, two hours and ten minutes later, he cascades through the Malmaison revolving doors – it's a chic establishment, suggesting the ban no longer applies – wearing a leather jacket that seems to be struggling to stay on his shoulders. When he sits down with the inevitable pint of their strongest lager, I notice his blue shirt is peppered with iron burns. Smith may be a musical genius, but he has clearly yet to master the more demanding domestic tasks. Later, when I mention the shirt to a friend, the friend comments, 'That sounds quite trendy.'

So how was Austria?

Smith looks bemused, then erupts in laughter. He hasn't been to Austria at all.

It wasn't planned, he explains. The thing was, he'd met some football fans on the Friday who ran a fanzine and they'd included a chart of all-time favourite Fall songs and 'Paranoia Man in Cheap Sh*t Room' – one of Smith's personal favourites – had made it to Number 5. He'd originally planned to nip out for an hour, but one thing led to another and he was enjoying himself so much he hadn't realised he'd been out with them most of the weekend.

Smith admits he's 'a bit hazy'. However, he wastes no further time in setting up one of his favourite pre-interview gambits: the erection of barbed-wire fences between The Mighty Fall and all those Other Groups.

'They've started manufacturing "alternative" groups now,' he begins, in his inimitable Salford slur. 'The last two awards ceremonies I went to, the arse licking when they went onstage was intolerable. Thanking the publisher, the manager, the record company, the one who started us off . . . and they're supposed to be alternative groups. It was sickening, actually. We were like "Shut up!"

'They all want careers in music. You'd think they'd be up for a party, but my mates who are builders have more fun than half these bands.'

He pauses, then explodes. 'And make more money, arrarrarr!'

This seems to be a recurrent feature of Smith's interview technique: establish camaraderie between artist and interviewer, and align us both against everybody else. He has been known to take a similar combative approach both with and against his own musicians. He soon reveals there's been yet more turmoil in the camp.

Spencer Birtwistle – a long-lost drummer who Fall fans had thought lost to the mists of time (or wherever Fall drummers go when they suddenly disappear) – is back in the band.

'He left a year or two back, having a hard time with his wife or something. When I rang him up he'd just packed his drum kit away for good that morning. He wasn't in a good state, actually. I said "I'm not doing this for therapy. I need you now!"'

And that was that. More curiously, guitarist Ben Pritchard – who after four years is a relative Fall veteran – has apparently resigned and been re-instated in the space of the last three days.

'He took three days to write the resignation letter,' explains Smith, trying hard to stifle a cackle.

Almost imperceptibly, we're onto the major topic of the interview: the hiring and firing of musicians, and Smith's seemingly lifelong philosophy of 'freshening up' The Fall, which he compares to managing a football team: 'Every so often you've got to replace the centre-forward.'

There seems to be quite a lot of this in Fall world. People exit, usually amid much rancour, then suddenly come back. The oddest instance of this was in the mid 1990s, when Brix Smith, Smith's long-suffering first wife and Fall guitarist, didn't let divorce or the fact she'd been out of the band for six years stop her popping up onstage, unannounced, in York.

'I call it the "two-year gap",' says Smith, pondering his lager. 'They think I'm a dictator. But after two years they come back and say they never had as much freedom.' Smith admits he can be 'a bit of a sod sometimes' but insists he's on 'fairly good terms' with most of the ex-members – the more recent ones anyway – even someone like former guitarist Neville Wilding, who Smith says 'could really be a nutcase'.

Smith goes on to explain that at one point – shortly before going onstage at the prestigious 1999 Reading Festival, no less – he and Wilding had been 'at it with knuckle-dusters' backstage, eventually taking to the stage covered in each other's blood. And now?

'We phone each other every month. All forgiven.'

A likely story? In The Wonderful and Frightening World, you never really know what's real.

I stare across the table. The crow's feet he sang about two decades ago in the song 'Living Too Late' are even more entrenched now, telling their own story of a life fronting The Fall. But when he smiles – and today he smiles surprisingly often – the years seem to melt away and he looks for all the world like a mischievous schoolboy.

Do people get too comfortable in The Fall?

'In the past very much so,' he says. 'Job for fuckin' life, you know. It's not like that in this business.' He says he sees membership of The Fall as a 'two- or three-year cycle' and he has two principal requirements of musicians. They should not 'think they're it', nor should they be 'fans of the bloody group!' because that always 'backfires'. He rightly insists turnover is common in orchestras or Northern Soul bands, but those organisations tend to be full of session players performing old material, not hungry young musicians making edgy music and having punch-ups.

When people leave The Fall – or even when they are in The Fall – they often say it's responsible for the best times of their lives and also the most terrifying. Whatever do they mean?

'There's been some big fights,' he confesses, lighting up a fag before he goes into the particular perils of foreign tours. 'You get to America and people pull a gun out. That's happened in Europe too. Someone jumps onstage and goes for the bass player, and he's never been out of Manchester before, it's his second gig. Welcome to The Fall!'

Projectiles are common at Fall gigs. Microphone stands were particularly popular for a while.

'Us throwing them at people or them throwing them at us?' Smith chortles. 'Both? Hahhahahhha, call it a draw.' And yet, over the years, it has often seemed the greatest threat to a Fall musician's wellbeing or sanity can come from the man employing them. Fall gigs routinely see Smith jostling one of his musicians, standing over them like an intimidating schoolmaster as they play.

In recent years, a favourite trick has been to dismantle the band's equipment – while they are playing. 'When you're playing five or six nights a week, the group get slick,' Smith says in his defence. Some of this is tongue-in-cheek but Smith is deadly serious when he points out that for him, and thus The Fall, routine is 'the enemy of music'.

Thus, Smith has become not just a director of musicians but some kind of experimental psychologist. In the past, he's admitted to giving musicians the wrong address to the studio, on the grounds that by the time they arrive they'll be so flustered they'll play better. His onstage instructions range from the sternly encouraging 'Give it some guts' and

'Fucking get it together and stop showing off' to a simple, bossy 'Hit it harder'.

'What's wrong with that?' he protests. 'It works. Admittedly it can be a problem if you're the guitarist.'

Another pint is drained and he describes his employment of the 'European phrasebook', sending guitarists to say things like 'I am a flower' in German.

'In Germany, when they're ordering breakfast you'll get them to shout the German for "Excuse me, stick it up your arse, will you?"' He is laughing so much he can barely speak.

Then, suddenly, he looks sad. '[The musicians] are getting wise to it now.'

On tour, he says, he sits at the back of the bus, like a manager with his players, to retain 'detachment'. 'That's the key to it, really. You can be matey and have a pint but you don't want to be round their houses.'

However, he suggests he's mellowing, talking benevolently of the latest line-up as 'my lads'. This means bassist Steven Trafford has been allowed the rare privilege of his own band on the side, which would never have happened before because he used to have 'that thing where if you played with any other group yer dead'.

Except it wasn't always like this. In fact, the original Fall line-up – Smith, Tony Friel, Una Baines and Martin Bramah – was a quartet of pals who spent a lot of time at each other's houses, listening to music and talking about the future. But at some point, fairly quickly, Smith became a ringmaster.

He ponders this for what seems an age.

'It wasn't . . . well, it was sort of intentional,' he finally concedes. 'But I wasn't thinking on those terms. I don't really plan though. I can't really plan ahead of next week. I certainly don't plot sackings like they say.' He looks wounded.

Perhaps the most vulnerable position in The Fall is the drum stool, and over the years there have been more incidents involving drummers than any other members.

Smith is a connoisseur of percussion – 'It's like Captain Beefheart said, "If you can't hear the drums, it's not there",' – and has a strong idea of how Fall drums should sound – not 'flashy'. He describes how the mysterious Karl Burns used to receive a five-pound fine 'every time he hit the tom tom'.

Have you never considered a drum machine?

He chokes on his pint. 'The first thing I have to do in every studio is get the bloody click track off,' he spits, sounding like a manic Victor Meldrew. 'Every bloody engineer, whoever they are, they think you don't notice, y'know, 'cause Mark Smith's the singer and he's had a few, you know. They'll go, "It wasn't quite in time, Mark, so I added a bit of drum machine."

'It's bloody stuff like that,' he rages, aghast. The other thing that drives him mad is when producers make the drums all sound in time; drummers love this 'because it makes them sound technical'. He suggests a lot of 'revered' groups only use machines because the drummers are rubbish and insists he could do better on a 'bloody typewriter'. That's debatable – and if it were true, Smith would surely have done it by now – but what is certain is that Fall musicians are never allowed to forget they are replaceable. If they forget it, Smith will less than subtly ram the point home. Once, when the rhythm section were late for a gig, he brought on players from the support band and was delighted when the errant drummer and bassist walked in to see their replacements on stage.

Perhaps the only certainty of being in The Fall is the knowledge that one day you will be out – although musicians are never privy to the knowledge of when this might happen. Members have even been fired during gigs, which Smith sheepishly says he is trying not to do now because it gets 'a bit tricky'.

Once, onstage in Stourbridge – the sort of off-the-beaten-track location that often features on Fall tours – a guitarist, Ed Blaney, was booted offstage by Smith after just two songs.

Smith roars with laughter. 'It wasn't working, was it?' He splutters. 'Some people are brilliant in rehearsals, they go onstage and they crack up.'

So you usher them off?

'It's for their own good,' he insists. 'People get nervous.' It's worth pointing out that Blaney had been in The Fall for four years at the time. However, Smith suggests he too gets nervous: 'After all these years, I do.'

This is an intriguing statement. It suggests that, for all the hiring and firing in the group, the person most feeling the pressure of carrying a legend like The Fall is Smith – because, after all, it's his reputation on the line.

As we touch on the stresses of fronting The Fall, he suddenly changes the subject, but interviewing Smith is often like this: ask one question, you'll get another answered. Often, he'll deliver his thoughts on something unrelated. Over the course of three alcohol-fuelled hours, Smith's train of thought careers like The Fall's line-up. Subjects covered range from his distrust of gadgets – 'I have these things lying around the house. They're useless!' – to why people in Hull think the singer from AC/DC is a 'fucking singing gnome' – Humberside is an unforgiving place, where fools are not suffered gladly – to the fact that Smith is under the impression Morecambe is in Yorkshire, whereas it lies on the coast of Lancashire, unless the site manager has recently had it moved. After two hours he spies my tape machine a foot in front of him and asks, 'Are we recording this? I thought it was your portaphone.'

More surprisingly, he often veers into the relatively uncharted waters of his personal life. I have followed this man's music since 1980 but know very little about him, which is probably how he likes it. Today I discover a few things. He's lived in the same house in Prestwich for 'a very long time'. He has thought of moving but says, 'By the time you think about it seriously, you've got something else to do.'

He hasn't taken a holiday for 'a very long time', although he eventually mutters something about 'a couple of trips to the Lakes'.

His front lawn is tended every fortnight by a local Irishman who calls him 'Mr Smith'.

He has no children, saying, 'It's enough with the bloody group!' This hasn't stopped various people hitting him with parentage claims. 'I must have seven around the world, all trying it on!'

He met Elena – née Poulou, some 20-odd years his junior – in Berlin, where she was working as a DJ, promoting a gig by The Fall. He courted her by touring not graves of former drummers but Northern fish-and-chip shops. He remembers a particular establishment in my hometown, Leeds. 'She said, "This is great. Can we live here?"'

Intriguingly, Poulou moved to Prestwich and joined The Fall before she married Smith. Somehow, we were back to the group. With Smith, everything seems to revolve around the group.

'I try to take some time off from The Fall,' he muses. 'I don't get very far. I try to keep Saturday clear!'

More pints appear and suddenly we're talking about one of the cornerstones of The Fall: Smith's formidable work ethic.

'I suppose it is a result of my upbringing,' says Smith (first job, meat factory; second job, docks clerk; third job, this one). 'When I started work – left school – you had to fight for your Saturdays off. It was a five-and-a-half-day week. They were just getting down from six.' But, ironically, most people work longer hours now than they did then.

'I could see that coming,' insists Smith, pointing out a parallel with record companies: in the 1980s, you'd get six sheets of royalties statements, how many records sold, how much money due. Whereas now, 'You get reams and reams of paper, designed to confuse you'. Bizarrely, he insists he receives royalties intended for The Cure's Robert Smith.

'There's more paper in my house than ever. I spend more time in studios just ploughing through sheets of paper.'

What's your house like?

'Modest . . . I throw things out.'

Like musicians?

He doesn't flinch.

'You wouldn't believe the things I throw out. You know, when you're a bit depressed and you see the *NME* from 1986 . . . you need a clear mind.'

This loathing – or even fear – of the past is fundamental to Smith. Today's music is fuelled by nostalgia. He knows this, he's had the offers – to re-form a certain line-up of The Fall or perform a certain 'classic' album. He's been tempted, when the band were really broke, but he'll always fight it. He learned very quickly that the business is 'full of people who live in the past'. Surely he can't mean me?

However, the Fall factory must roll on. The means to the end – and perhaps the end in itself – is production. Without production, The Fall would cease to exist and Mark E Smith, as everyone has known him for as long as he can remember, would cease to exist. And that notion must be truly terrifying.

We're getting strangely melancholy now. Have you ever thought it was all over, that the group was going to finish?

'Lots of times,' he says. 'About once every three years. No, seriously! But what would I do?'

He genuinely doesn't know. There have been offers, for magazine columns and short stories. Short-story writing interests him and he's written a few, two-and-a-half pages long, examples of what he considers the 'great British short story'. But he says the publishers don't want them; they want books like, 'what they think Fall lyrics are like, y'know, alcohol, violence, industrial estates'. Which is about one per cent of the picture. In this moment, he sounds truly depressed.

We talk a bit more about his personal life and he reflects that, for all the chaos around The Fall, he likes some things to be solid: 'a settled back four, if you like'. He agrees he probably makes his best music when his personal life is settled and thus marriage to Elena in 2000 – 'third time lucky, it's going marvellous, touch wood' – had to be a good thing from every perspective. But it wasn't always like that.

In 1998, when The Fall fought each other in New York and split up, he came very, very close to losing everything.

'I wouldn't go through it again,' he says candidly. The calls from London stopped. The business he loathes shunned him. But it was an 'eye opener'. His friends, his few real friends, from before the group, rallied around him.

'It was builders or people who've been on the dole all their life that said, "You've got to get a meal inside you, Marky Parky".' Perhaps the experience cemented his distrust of musicians.

'It makes you think.'

Did you ever think you were losing it?

'Me personally? A little bit . . . I was fed up.' There's a long and silent pause, but just as Smith frequently hauls The Fall back from the abyss, he brightens, explaining how The Fall were having financial trouble and he was depressed because he couldn't afford to take 'the girl' out for a drink. And then he broke his leg.

'I fell out with The Fall one year, then broke my hip the next,' he chuckles. He spent five hours in "Cheetham Hill Hospital" (North Manchester General).

'You can't walk out because you can't walk!' He is laughing like a drain. A week later, Smith led yet another Fall line-up onstage and opened with 'Walk like a Man'.

I tell him I don't think a lot of people get the humour in The Fall and he agrees. He even saw the humour in the infamous cigarette incident, pointing out the journalist 'had an attitude' and 'the bloke in the newsagent said it was one of the funniest things he'd read in ages'.

Do you ever read stuff about yourself and think, who is this man?

'All the time,' he sighs. 'I sometimes think there's a Mancunian or Northern sense of humour that doesn't travel. They don't get the glint in your eye. But you've got to watch it,' he scolds. 'All that professional Northerner stuff, you know, "Aye up mate". That's the end of the line. I'd rather walk the streets. You get these professional Mancs, fuckin' professional people like the *Guardian*.'

I feel a rapier slip beneath my Yorkshire born-and-bred shoulders.

'The accent's false! They say now you can get on in the media if you have a regional accent.'

He's smiling. The rapier is removed.

Regrets?

He pauses. 'About once a week.'

We'd touched on the New York fracas, but it's time to get into specifics. When he became a solo artist overnight, was that one of the 'regrets'?

'Nah . . .' Deep breath. 'Nah.'

So, conversely, was it planned? Another Machiavellian way of jettisoning the band?

'Not by me,' he insists, adding that it was the other musicians who planned it. 'I'm not joking. They had studio time booked by themselves, I found that out later. They engineered it, not me. They had another band, The Ark, that was their great idea. Mark without the M. Sank without trace, The Ark! But I'm too much of a gentleman to respond.'

I realise the room is silent, the barman hanging on Smith's every word like a Fall audience. I remember an open-air gig at the Phoenix Festival in Stratford-upon-Avon in the mid 1990s where I stood on the front row watching Smith pour out his vocals in the pelting rain, as if relishing unleashing his words in such a charged environment. His face was gnarled but twisted in some distant, knowing pleasure. Then – like today – it felt like him and me. It often feels like that when you watch the man perform.

But what we are discussing seems poignant. It resulted in Smith losing Steve Hanley, a bassist of almost 20 years' service whom Smith had once said 'defined' the sound of The Fall.

Did you not trust him, after all that time?

'To a certain extent, I suppose. You trust some . . . but you keep 'em on a short leash.'

But you yourself said he 'defined' the sound of The Fall.

'Correct. But it was coming.'

Smith says when he got back to Britain he phoned the newly departed members to give them a mouthful for leaving him in prison, but they'd 'changed all their fuckin' numbers'.

However, Julia Nagle – the keyboardist whom Smith was charged with assaulting – subsequently rejoined the band and stayed for another three years. Was a mountain made out of a molehill?

'Yeah. No regrets at all.'

Smith has been uncharacteristically open, but becomes defensive on the subject of Karl Burns, the now AWOL drummer who initiated the New York punch-up by walloping Smith onstage.

'Can we have two more beers here, sir?' he shouts to the watching barman.

Smith is evasive.

Burns attacked you first?

'Two more beers, please!'

Then he suddenly answers the question. 'I thought it [the attack] was very good. Best bit of the gig.'

I seize my chance. I ask about some of the former members, people like Una Baines and Martin Bramah, who were Smith's close friends many years ago. He insists they won't talk to him.

'I can never get hold of any of them. I think it's guilt. See, most of them left me, not the other way round.'

Then it dawns on me. Despite Dorothy's best intentions, there won't be any contacts given for former members. Nor does Smith want to talk about them. However amicably, he has controlled the boundaries of the interview as effectively as he controls The Fall. I feel he has told me a lot yet no more than he wanted to.

But we part on good terms. He buys me more beer in a pub over the road and even gives me the autograph I didn't get in 1981 – for my Fall-loving partner, Suzanne. Always a gentleman, Mark E Smith.

But after walking around Manchester for a while to sober up, I end up driving home to be met with a problem. My editor is keen to stick with the original idea, to talk not just to Smith but also to former members.

He's given me hours of his time, I don't want it to be all for nothing.

So, I realise I'm just going to have to find them. All of them.

CHAPTER 2

'The night it all went apeshit.'

At first I'm excited about the possibility of tracking down the entire Fallen, but this feeling is soon dampened by the enormity of the task.

I'm staring at a list of over 40 names. For my purposes at least, I'm going to have to have some limits. I decide that to qualify as a Fallen, a musician will have to have played an instrument live with the group. This rules out Adrian Niman, who played saxophone for 15 seconds on the *Room to Live* album in 1982, but includes Stuart Estell, who 'joined' The Fall from the audience for an encore in Reading in 1998.

However, finding them isn't easy without Smith, even if he did keep track of clarinet players who left in 1981. The numerous record companies The Fall have had over the years have only ever dealt with Smith. So you could be in The Fall for 19 years, like Steve Hanley, the group's most venerable bassist, and the music business would have no idea where you are. So what happens to any royalties? Do they all just go to Smith? I haven't even found anyone yet and already I'm facing a stream of nagging questions.

I contact the Musicians' Union, a complete non-starter. They claim to have 'no information relating to anybody who was ever in The Fall'. Of course.

I do have another lead, however. Sixteen years ago I interviewed a man called Grant Showbiz, who was in a band called Moodswings, and during the interview it transpired that Showbiz often produced or mixed The Fall. Inevitably, I stopped asking about Moodswings to probe him about The Fall, although he didn't give much away except to say Smith was a friendlier character than the grumpy public image and The Fall's greatness had come at the cost of 'periods of ill health'.

I manage to get in contact with Showbiz and he gives me some numbers, though, sadly, most of them are dead – the numbers, not the ex-members. But I do reach former guitarist/sleeves man Tommy Crooks, now an artist in East Lothian. There are worse places to start.

The craggy Scots guitarist played on 1997's *Levitate*. It's not exactly the best Fall album – it may even be the worst – but for me, Fall albums are like children: although they may have their faults, you gradually grow blind to them until you love them dearly. In any case, even a relatively mediocre album, by Fall standards, has innumerable strengths. *Levitate* took the group's sound into left-field dance music and spawned the terrifically catchy single, 'Masquerade'. Smith's lyrics are particularly idiosyncratic, although my favourite track, 'I'm a Mummy', is a cover of a song originally written for music halls by cabaret artist Douglas Byng in 1930. It was adapted in 1959, as simply 'The Mummy', by voice-over artist Bob McFadden and Dor (a pseudonym for Rod McKuen); their version is closest to The Fall's. Quite why Smith chose this particular song is unknown, but the words seem quite in keeping with his barmy public image: 'I was born one thousand, nine hundred and fifty-nine years ago/ Look what happens when I walk up to somebody/ I don't try to scare people/ I'm a Mummy!' For much of the album, Smith sounds half-cut, which perhaps also makes *Levitate* one of the more revealing albums in the canon.

Crooks took the sleeve photos, obtuse/arty, but more significant to me is that he was involved in the onstage New York punch-up in 1998. Over a crackling phone line, Crooks recounts what will soon become a familiar theme. He describes being in The Fall as 'the pinnacle of creativity', speaks of 'enormous pride' to have played within the group . . . but admits there was 'a lot of madness'.

It appears that even the process whereby someone joins The Fall is not normal. There are no advertisements in music papers and nothing so traditional as an audition. Smith just seems to somehow find them. In Crooks' case, he was walking around Edinburgh at 8.30 in the morning. Two people headed towards each other like gunslingers at dawn. One was Crooks, on his way to renovate a house. The other was Mark E Smith, on his way to renovate Tommy Crooks.

'I think he was up with a TV crew from Liverpool,' Crooks begins, his Edinburgh accent roughened and given a certain colour by something that may or may not have been his two years in The Fall. 'They were doing a thing about cities that had been nominated for City of Culture – Liverpool and Edinburgh. Of course Mark had a good laugh about that.'

Crooks was 'sidling up the road . . . our eyes met'.

Suddenly, the Scotsman found himself telling this person whom he'd never met before about his work as an artist. Smith was intrigued enough to request he send some artwork (images that would end up on *Levitate*). And very quickly after, he was in The Fall, despite living 200 miles away from Smith's patch and having only limited ability on guitar. Not that this was a problem – technical flamboyance is the very last quality you need to join The Fall – and he would simply commute 200 miles to Salford and stay with bassist Steve Hanley.

On arrival, Hanley ominously informed Crooks he was joining in 'the eye of the storm'. The phone crackles again as Crooks remembers the first rehearsal, which he describes as 'taking the biscuit' but was a reasonable indication of what he could expect.

'It was in Longsight, a squat in some shitty part of Manchester,' he recalls. The rehearsal room had been acquired because 'Mark had met some guy at the railway station' who'd said they could use his place to rehearse. The basement had mattresses all over the walls. Simon Wolstencroft [drummer] walked in, I met Steve. It was really weird seeing these guys.

'Eventually, Mark turned up,' says Crooks, who remembers the singer wore black gloves and that keyboardist Julia Nagle, briefly Smith's girlfriend, wore white gloves.

'We began . . . It was just bloody crazy!' He pauses. 'But really good.' He remembers lights coming on and off, and Smith unplugging his amplifier and holding the microphone up to the guitar. 'No chance of getting a sound out, y'know,' he grinned darkly. The object, Crooks believes, was to 'freak him out'.

We've only been talking minutes and already we're tapping into Smith's ability to use a psychological approach to motivate, or goad, average musicians. I mention that I've often thought of Smith as being as much a psychological conductor of his bands as the people who stand in front of classical orchestras waving a stick. Crooks isn't sure.

'I don't know if it was part of the psychology or just part of Mark!' he laughs, going on to recall 'good times and hard times'. The hardest was almost certainly the fateful American tour of 1998. Almost a decade later, there's still palpable emotion in his voice as he recalls events unfolding like on a battlefield. For starters, The Fall themselves were divided into 'battalions'.

The first was 'the group' – Crooks, Hanley and Karl Burns (on drums for the seventh time, having been fired and rehired on six previous occasions – Simon Wolstencroft, who was drummer when Crooks joined, had already joined the massed ranks of The Fallen). The other battalion was Smith, in cahoots with Julia Nagle, who Crooks remembers as being 'pretty vague. She'd walk on and do a gig, and that was it, or not do a gig . . . or walk off halfway in.' The notion of two battalions seems consistent with what has always seemed to be The Fall's creative dynamic: on the one hand, Smith, the leader or lightning conductor, usually with a lieutenant; on the other, the musicians, the cannon fodder.

'I remember the bus driver one day saying, "So what's this lot like then?"' remembers Crooks. 'The sound guy replied, "This is as weird as it gets".'

As the stress of the tour increased, the band had all been drinking heavily, but were desperately trying to stay 'professional'. But by the time they got closer to New York, things were becoming increasingly 'berserk'. Smith's mood was not helped by being trailed by 'some weird guy from Texas', who'd been stalking them across the States and was constantly phoning to get on the guest list. Crooks remembers the gig at Brownies as 'the night it all went apeshit': 'I think Mark had been threatened at gunpoint by a taxi driver . . . and had given him a mouthful of abuse. Mark arrived in a pretty bad mood. The rest is history.'

An excellent choice of words.

Peter Messiaen, an American eyewitness writing on the internet, remembers events at Brownies like this:

MES [Smith] handed me the mic and I took turns singing. Which was a lot of fun, but within two minutes of getting on stage, Mark decided to smack Karl's cymbal to the floor and fuck up his drum mics. Karl stopped playing and patiently readjusted his equipment, a look of perplexion [sic] and anger on his face . . . Resumed playing. Two songs later Mark attempted the same thing and that's when Karl snapped . . . jumped out from behind the drums and grabbed Mark's head, which he looked like he was completely capable of crushing if he felt like and screamed at him . . . Hanley, protective as always, pushed Karl away and got between the two . . . thereby saving Mark's life.

I think most of the crowd were shocked . . . there were a few assholes who thought it was all a big joke . . . I guess at a certain point after the Karl incident . . . after the Tommy incident . . . I forget what exactly was being played, MES tried to make everyone smile or ingratiate himself back into the band's good graces and the band seemed to respond a little bit . . . but then he went right back into asshole mode and flicked a cigarette, which I gave to Mark in the hopes of placating him, and it did for a while, at Tommy and everything went crazy again.

According to Messiaen, Karl Burns had finally had enough antagonism from Smith, and jumped out from behind his kit and began strangling the singer, in the process completely knocking over Steve Hanley's bass rig.

> He kept saying 'I'll kill you . . . you bloody cunt!' to Mark . . . A short while later after similar harassment from Mark, Tommy [Crooks] kicked Mark in the ass really hard about half a dozen times. Mark was repeating over and over how Tommy was 'a dead man'.
>
> Mark proclaimed in a whinging and ephemeral manner [to the audience] that he had been 'assaulted by a dumb-as-a-goat Scotsman and [that] we were all witnesses'.
>
> The band quit the stage after six songs leaving Mark to play 'Powder Keg' with only Julia accompanying him.
>
> Hanley looked embarrassed, but determined to get through the show. 'Powder Keg' was appropriate. After the band left the stage . . . Mark made some remarks about how he was waiting for the other three to show up . . . then he sang something about his 'Dear . . . dear New Yorkers'. He seemed halfway sorry . . . then he started singing something like 'You better listen! You better listen . . . the owner of Brownies is not going to like this and I hope he still comes across with at least 4 figures'.
>
> Which was funny . . . tragic but funny.

Another fan, David Auerbach, remembers Smith saying – ostensibly about Crooks, with whom he was apparently at loggerheads throughout the gig – 'That guy is a Scottish man, a fucking animal on drugs and a fucking idiot. I have been assaulted in public here by two or three people, you be witness to it.' [At this point Hanley is reported elsewhere to be miming playing a violin and making comical 'Woe is me' faces.]

'Bear witness, laddies,' says Smith to inexplicable cheering from the crowd, 'they're very big. I tell you what, these three, I got a taxi, some fucker pulled a gun out on me, some fucking Pakistani or someone. These three were fuckin' cowering in the fuckin' dressing room . . . as usual . . . they're nowhere to be seen. They're very hard . . . all together.'

Which almost sounds like a Fall song. In fact, the encounter is obliquely referenced in 'Dissolute Singer'. The song – on Smith's solo, spoken word album, *The Post Nearly Man*, which was released later in 1998 – carries a reference to a club owner looking for three figures at Brownies.

The band went into meltdown there and then. A second gig at Brownies the following night was cancelled following Smith's arrest and incarceration over an incident at the Quality Hotel Eastside in Manhattan's Gramercy Park involving Nagle. The singer was held in jail for two days and after release following payment of $1,000 bail, appeared in court on third-degree assault and harassment charges. He was ordered to undergo an alcohol treatment programme and anger management counselling.

Speaking to the BBC some years later, Smith described the experience with uncomplicated Salfordian logic: 'They started on me, so I started on them.'

Although this was apparently a serious bust-up even by Fall standards, Crooks says it was the sort of thing that happened all the time he was in the group. So much so, he thought such behaviour was 'normal'. In Ireland, shortly before the tour of America, Smith had 'almost got a mob set on' the band for reasons which he insists are best left unreported.

'Mark was going through a sticky patch,' Crooks says of those times, echoing Smith's own words in Malmaison hotel. But after Brownies, Burns and Crooks had been stranded in New York, their passports disappearing in the chaos. The Scotsman remembers phoning the record company to say 'Get us the hell out of here' and suggests they were even considering getting deported 'just to get out of the States'.

The night it all went apeshit proved the last time a Fall line-up would contain Messrs Crooks, Burns or Hanley. Crooks spoke briefly to Smith after The Fall leader returned his passport with a note, 'which was good of him, you know'. But his last sighting of The Fall boss was being hustled into a police car. He comments, 'I think he was 15 minutes away from [notorious penitentiary] Rikers Island.'

But all these years later, Crooks doesn't regret being in The Fall. 'It could have been amazing,' he sighs, his granite Scots tones cracking with emotion once again. 'Mark wasn't happy for whatever reason; we were all unhappy but it was like "the show must go on". Steve Hanley was the most professional person, he was totally devoted to it. It was sad for all of us.'

However, Crooks hints at what will also soon become a familiar theme – the eerie pull of Britain's strangest band. He says if Smith ever needed him, he would drop everything to play for him again. This seems a peculiar admission after what happened but Crooks seems as awed by Smith as any fan, despite being publicly ridiculed as a 'fucking animal'. Perhaps to understand the depth of this loyalty you have to have been in The Fall. As Crooks remembers, Smith is an 'extremely intelligent person, uniquely creative. Some of the things he used to do in rehearsal were inspired.' He remembers how Smith once handed him a laundry bill with the instruction 'Sing that'. The results became part of a song on *Levitate*, 'Hurricane Edward', with Crooks and Smith singing a musical short story of a Ross County farm worker whose life was devastated by a tornado.

'You don't meet people like that often, the genuine article,' sighs Crooks, who despite Smith's insistence on not recruiting people who 'liked the bloody group' was – and remains – a dedicated Fall fan. 'I didn't really bother listening to much else,' he confirms. 'The rest was daft pop music. I mean, Mark's sense of timing was incredible. I'm really sorry about what happened, but it just exploded.'

Looking back, Crooks says – almost comically – Smith taught him a lot about professionalism even though the singer could be 'prickly', before hinting at what may or may not be the source of Smith's volatile moods.

'It might be frustrating for him knowing he's one of the best and not enormously successful,' he muses. 'I don't know how many records The Fall sell. I think they're maybe a bit too sophisticated for the mass market. But there's nothing I'd like more than to see Mark have a smash hit success. I've got no hard feelings towards the guy at all.'

He also offered his take on the royalties mystery: 'I didn't get any royalties because I didn't write the songs, but I never asked for any. I was just proud to be a part of it, you know.'

After exiting The Fall, Crooks joined The Ark ('Mark without the M', as Smith had sneered to me) with Steve Hanley but it didn't work out. Crooks says he still feels guilty for having let Hanley down and asks me to pass on messages to the bassist if I find him. This will become another feature of my journey to find The Fallen: I will become the facilitator of an enormous process of healing . . . of others, if not myself.

Nowadays, Crooks is back enjoying a career as an artist and has exhibited at several major galleries, although he seems somehow unfulfilled: his greatest art, he insists, was simply being in The Fall. 'The Fall was more an art performance,' he says. 'Conceptual art at its highest level. You could put the whole group in a gallery like you were hanging them on a wall.'

A few days after we talk, Crooks sends an email thanking me for taking him back to the 'wonderful (and frightening) time' and asking me to consider him my 'friend, even though we've never met'. The following morning, another email: 'I think we both enjoyed that conversation. It's made me realise that The Fall are actually THE BEST Britain has ever produced, Beatles and Stones included.' Then another: 'If you find out that Karl Burns is alive can you email me and let me know?'

I'm on my way.

CHAPTER 3

'Sorry, boss . . . I am only a drummer.'

My life is everything Mark E Smith hates.

I live in the countryside in North Yorkshire. Smith hates the countryside, according to 'Contraflow', the third track on the 2003 album *The Real New Fall LP: Formerly 'Country on the Click'*.

I have a dog called Guinness. Smith hates dogs, having informed the world via 1988's 'Dog Is Life/Jerusalem' (from the album *I Am Kurious Oranj*) that we don't see rabbits walked down the street or cats on leads.

I am a journalist – a breed of whom he once said 'For every bloke pulling a pint, there's about 10,000 journalists writing an article about it.'

And I am a musician, having played drums for years. Naturally, I didn't mention this in Malmaison, because I know Smith's opinion of drummers and how he encourages drummers to view themselves. Witness the following exchange with Spencer Birtwistle in the BBC's *Wonderful and Frightening World* documentary:

> Smith to Birtwistle: 'You are only a drummer. I am Mark Smith.'
> Birtwistle to Smith: 'Sorry, boss . . . I am only a drummer.'

Me too.

I am only a drummer.

And a journalist.

On my third dog.

And a vegetarian.

And I live in an area where you're more likely to see a cow gazing over a hedge than a city hobgoblin and where there are absolutely no fans of The Fall.

In fact, I'm quietly confident you could knock on every single door in my obscure village and among the retired military types and pram pushers not find a single person who's even heard of Mark E Smith.

Sometimes, I wonder if I live here to escape from my obsession with The Fall. But I don't escape. You never do, if you're a Fall fan. It's even harder nowadays because much as Smith loathes the internet and distrusts the mass media, The Fall are everywhere. The Wonderful and Frightening World is now universal.

This is my morning ritual. Get up. Take a pee. Make tea. Read the papers on the internet; check for any news or gossip on my football team, crisis-hit Leeds United. Then read about The Fall. My favourite place for doing this is http://invisionfree.com/forums/thefall, the Official Website Fall Forum where like-minded Fall nutters discuss the burning issues of the day, such as the best way to photograph a set list from a gig at Huddersfield Cleopatra's Club on Friday, 12 September 1980. ('It's a beauty. The lists with Mark's writing are cherished items indeed,' notes someone calling themselves Hanley Played A Fender P.) Or what would be the ideal Fall song to be played at a Fall fan's funeral ('New Face in Hell' is understandably popular, although someone suggests 'Open the Boxoctosis #2' because of its comically appropriate lyrics about opening a 'Goddamn' box.

This morning someone's posted a video of singer Jeffrey Lewis's 'The Legend of The Fall', a sung 'illustrated history', with accompanying artwork, in which the American performer expounds on how Smith

    didn't get on with the punk scene at all
    In fact he didn't get on with most members of The Fall
    So began the underground legend of a strange and driven man
    Who worked hard writing touring and recording then would fire most
    of his band
    Steve played bass for 20 years with the band whose sound he helped
    create but even he left when Mark went to jail for punching his band-
    mates in '98.

It's hilarious and very knowing, especially when he talks of Fall fans who 'get immersed in the whole Fall universe and get obsessed with everything they've done'. Which is the reason why I'm on the Fall forum today. Over the years I've noticed there are very few people who can take or leave The Fall. People don't say, 'Oh, The Fall, they're okay'. They either loathe or completely fail to understand The Fall's scratchy, obtuse but melodic racket and Smith's idiosyncratic lyrics – or they like the stuff, grow to love it and then invariably become obsessed with it and everything else in The Wonderful and Frightening World.

And I wonder . . . why?

So, today the question I'm asking the Fall forum is: why are there no Fall 'fans', only Fall obsessives? Predictably, most responses contend it's 'the music' – that The Fall are 'the best and most challenging band for most of the last 30 years'. Which, of course, they are. But there must be something else, something that not only demands obsession but can make Fall followers out of everyone from Barnsley miners to David Bowie. Maybe we were all dropped on our heads as children, or had terrifying formative experiences with a man with a half-deranged Salford accent.

David Hughes aka 'Divvey' hits on the sort of thing I'm looking for when he reveals he is 'completely well balanced, can see both sides of an argument, am moderate in my behaviour. I am not into drugs, drink responsibly for the most part, have a good relationship with my parents . . . And I like The Beatles almost as much as The Fall.' Then, crucially, he adds: 'But my colleagues don't get me.'

Another Fall fanatic, My Balloon, thinks there are two types of Fall fans: 'those that just like the music and then those that relate more to the outsider aspect'. MikeyBoy refers to his Falldom as being 'my dirty little secret. I never tell my girlfriends about them. I'm afraid that they'll think that I'm not all there mentally.' Meanwhile, someone called Stevoid tells of 'Something in Smith's voice . . .'

However, most Fall nutters are uncomfortable with the question, as if pondering something like this would betray the stiff-upper-lip, emotionless posture Smith specialises in and which you're implicitly expected to adopt if you're a Fall fan.

Swiss Gnomes comments, 'I don't usually go that deep', while Tobydynamik confesses his reasons for being a Fall fan are 'too personal' for public airing.

And I think that's the point. Being a Fall fan is deeply personal. Sometimes, I even feel my entire life has been a succession of avenues and events that have led me, like a lamb to the slaughter or a Cliff Richard fan to Jesus, to The Mighty Fall.

Like Smith, I grew up in the suburbs – of Leeds, rather than Salford.

Like Smith, I had a largely absent father, although unlike Jack Smith – who would boot young Mark out of the house – my dad was absent because I only knew him for the first six years of my life.

He was an income-tax collector who had been a hairdresser and a chiropodist, so at a tender age I had nice toenails and a nice, perfectly combed hairstyle before it all went horribly wrong with punk.

But Dad was obsessed with the English language and I sometimes wonder if my Falldom started there. He made sure I could spell before I was even old enough for school. Every morning when he went to work, he'd leave me a new word on a blackboard alongside some kind of picture or cartoon of the type I'd later pore over on Fall albums. Tax collecting was just Dad's job: his real love was music.

He played piano in the local working men's club – exactly the sort of hard-bitten working-class enclave that hosted the early Fall gigs amidst thick fag smoke and very smelly bitter. *Grotesque*, my favourite Fall album, includes a track that is basically a tape of someone singing in a WMC as captured for posterity on a cassette recorder under the table. As well as playing piano and occasionally compering in exactly that type of club, my dad was the venue's bingo caller. Can it really be coincidence that The Fall's very first single, 'Bingo-Master's Break-Out!', is about a bingo master?

Dad took me to the WMC a lot, where I'd encounter the smells now familiar at Fall gigs and larger than life musicians like the jazzy drummer Jeff, a cabaret type who I've since thought was probably a lot like lost late 1970s jazzy Fall drummer Mike Leigh. Jazzy Jeff had a shiny red sparkly kit and gave me a pair of sticks which I stared at for years before actually getting around to using them to play a drum kit.

Only the drummer, but maybe my own interest in music started there. I often think if Dad had known this would lead me to attempt to track down 40-odd former members of The Fall, he'd have taken me to football. Still, sometimes the musicians swapped stories and I learned Dad had been a gunner in World War Two and played piano in an army theatre group called the Bangs 'n' Beans, who literally played on as the bombs fell around them in The Blitz – much in the same manner Fall musicians are required to perform in the face of psychological or physical torture from Mark E Smith and his ideology of 'creative' tension.

One day, Dad sat me down at the WMC piano and instructed me to play, even though I'd never touched the instrument in my life. As I plonked away hopelessly he told me I'd just performed 'Don't Cry, Daddy' by Elvis Presley (a Smith favourite). It's baffled me ever since: was this a similar example of the psychological trickery Smith uses to coax songs from musicians in The Fall? Or was Dad just kidding me to make me feel better? Or was his choice of that song somehow foreboding? He passed away a few weeks later and there was a hole in my life that could only be filled by 26 – or is it 27? – albums by The Fall.

Other events in that period seem to point me to The Fall. I was a huge fan of Gary Glitter, and The Glitter Band once used a two-drummer line-up like The Fall. Carol took my virginity and a couple of weeks later handed me *Grotesque*, and we'd listen in my bedroom to songs called things like 'C 'n' C-S Mithering' instead of doing what teenagers are supposed to. I often wonder why she dumped me.

One of my first Leeds United matches was against Smith's beloved Manchester City, and ended in a baton charge and a massive Fall-like punch-up. I've often thought following a football team – especially the troubled Leeds United – is like following The Fall. Periods of greatness – the Don Revie era – are followed by declines and returns to form. There's a certain amount of suffering involved in being a Fall fan. You put up with bad gigs and the occasional so-so album because you know they will return to greatness.

Then again, like the dark theatre of watching painful tackles in the pouring rain, sometimes even The Fall's lesser moments can be perversely pleasurable. As Peel said, 'Sometimes it's not always what you want. But they're The Fall, that's all you need.'

But The Fall don't figure everywhere in my life. I listen to and like a lot of other music – although always return, like a dog with its tail between its legs, to The Mighty Fall. I met the love of my life, Suzanne, at a Stone Roses gig, not a Fall gig . . . but I admit the relationship was sealed when she moved in – to my dead parents' old council semi, in 1989 – with a record box containing *Live at The Witch Trials*.

While it's an exaggeration to say our life revolves around The Fall, we do go to a lot of Fall gigs and occasionally over breakfast discuss what may have happened to Craig Scanlon or Karl Burns.

And I wonder what unites us. All of us. Carol, Suzanne, me and all the other Fall fans around the world who wonder what happened to Craig Scanlon. Carol, stubborn, quizzical, even paranoid as a girl, had her own adolescent issues (and a strict, not particularly communicative, disciplinarian father). Suzanne also lost her father at an early age (she was 17) and has been shifted about (from Germany to London to Portsmouth to Leeds to our current country ghost town). She is not quite cynical but probing. Disaffected. With an absence of a knowledgeable, hectoring father figure in Sta-Prest trousers. You can find similar travails in the lives of Bowie (family history of mental illness) and Barnsley miners (their spirits and bodies broken in the miners' strike). It's as if we all have a crack in our psyches or a scar in our experiences that makes us susceptible to The Fall. My pet theory on Fall fans is that if such a crack exists, Smith's music will eventually track you down and indoctrinate you into The Wonderful and Frightening World. The crack in my life maybe grew wider when Mum died three years into my apprenticeship in Falldom. But maybe we're all in some way looking for leadership and guidance, then along comes Mark E Smith.

I wonder if it's the same for his musicians.

CHAPTER 4

'After a while in The Fall you're no longer normal.'

Aweek after speaking to Tommy Crooks I'm in a Manchester city centre pub, to meet the Hanley brothers, Steve and Paul. Steve is the stocky bassist Smith admitted 'defined' The Fall until his hurried exit after the same New York rumpus that did for Crooks, and was in the Fall line-up I first encountered in 1981. Over the years, I must have watched the elder Hanley dozens of times and never ceased to be amazed by the sheer ferocity of his work. Mostly, it didn't look like he was playing an instrument so much as grappling with a wild animal that needed urgent taming.

And yet, through willpower and physical strength, he had the beast under control, lashing out basslines equal in intensity and pithiness to Smith's ranted words. My favourite gig involving Hanley was at the Fforde Grene in Leeds on 29 July 1983. The big pub was typical of venues The Fall played at the time – rough and unwelcoming, on the outskirts of the city – so you had to make a real effort (in my case, take two buses) to get there. In those days The Fall's records were getting closer and closer to the charts, but following them still felt like being part of a huge cult. In the sweltering Fforde Grene, with the group lashing out their new songs of the day – such as insistent, bass-driven 1983 single 'The Man Whose Head Expanded', about a man who is convinced a soap-opera writer is following him to get ideas and will then kill him – it felt like being a part of a secret society, with everyone in some special, possibly dark secret. That night above all others I was peculiarly drawn to Hanley, who wore first a donkey jacket and then a sweat-soaked blue shirt. He looked focused but somehow pained and even repelled by his hard graft. If his big hands had held a spade and not a bass guitar, he would have looked for all the world like he was burying a body.

Steve Hanley's melodic bass appears on virtually every classic Fall album of the 1970s to 1990s – from 1979's dark, vengeful *Dragnet* through to 1993's *The Infotainment Scan*, a playful, dancefloor affair where Hanley's bass-powered songs like 'A Past Gone Mad', in which Smith asks the listener to 'slit my throat with a garden vegetable' if he ever ends up 'like U2'. Generally, if you ask any Fall fan what his or her favourite album was, Hanley will be playing on it. Then, he was gone.

Also onstage at the Riley-Smith Hall in 1981 was Paul Hanley, who doesn't quite occupy the same position in Fall mythology as the vanishing Karl Burns but is still universally cherished in The Wonderful and Frightening World. Drummer between 1980 and 1985 (and thus on *Grotesque*), his playing was more minimal and more repetitive than Karl Burns, and Fall fanatics are still prone to misty-eyed reminiscing about the time Paul Hanley and Karl Burns played together – as they did at the Fforde Grene – in a fearsome two-drummer line-up.

The pub is half empty, and I contemplate the prospect of being stood up by my heroes. Suddenly, I see a ghost in an adjoining room. The figure of Steve Hanley seems to appear then disappear, like a mirage. I venture across to the doorway and there they are.

Steve Hanley looks older than I remember – as he would, since hardly anyone has seen him in a decade. Then again, even in 1981 he looked prematurely aged, as if literally being withered by the ardours of playing in Britain's most demanding group.

As he sits down, I can't help notice a slight tremor in his fingers as a result of spending 19 years grappling with the beast.

His brother Paul looks much younger, thicker-set and still with his dark hair, but he got out of The Fall after five years whereas Steve served the sort of sentence you don't even get for armed robbery. However, meeting them is as enjoyable as I could have possibly imagined, as their conversation flits from horror to humour and back again just as ably as they once anchored the Fall sound.

'It's a bit like being at school,' ponders Steve Hanley, cradling the first pint. 'It's only when you leave and talk to other people, do you realise what yours was like.'

They're both grinning but the laughter seems ever so slightly shaky. They don't look like rock stars so much as manual workers, but in conversation are more like retired soldiers, recalling tales from the wars. 'It was a house of horrors!' Paul says, and both of them erupt.

The trendily made-over pub surroundings seem a world away from dingy old 1979, when Steve Hanley joined The Fall. Britain was a grim, industrialised place, exhausted by the musical and social upheavals of the 1970s and crying out for change, only to be dragged into the 1980s and turmoil of another kind by the victorious Margaret Thatcher. Conflict was in the air: the Shah of Iran had just been overthrown by revolution and Saddam Hussein became President of Iraq. However, the position of Fall bassist was about to become unusually stable as Hanley began the first of his 19-year term – he'd been in St. Gregory's Grammar school bands with guitarists Marc Riley and Craig Scanlon, and just hung around with the group until one day he was in.

Ironically, given the fact he'd still be there almost two decades later, in that week – in April 1979 – Gloria Gaynor's 'I Will Survive' was Number One. He didn't think he'd last a week. At his first gig, the PA packed up and Smith walked off leaving the group playing instrumentals. The bassist smiles: 'The shape of things to come.' However, he soon realised The Fall was not like any other group. Record companies would be kept at arm's length and denied influence over the music. They simply 'got what they were given'. Steve notes that if bands today sold the amount of records The Fall did in the late 1980s and 1990s they'd be doing 'very well indeed'. However, just like today, every time they seemed on the verge of a breakthrough to the ultra-mainstream, something – or someone – would mess it up.

'I can never work that out,' sighs Paul, only to be contradicted by his brother.

'I can. It's Mark!' he explodes. 'We were either really loved or really hated. Which is exactly how he liked it.'

Steve suggests that what Smith called 'detachment' was there right from the start. He says he never knew which Smith he'd get. One minute, the singer would be tearing him to pieces, the next quietly asking if he fancied a pint. Which may be part of the Fall psychology, but Hanley suspects something more.

'There's a lot of pressure, being Mark. He's not an angry person all the time,' he says. 'In the music industry, people get what they want by being unreasonable. The clever bands have someone to be unreasonable for them. To his credit Mark's never done that; if something nasty needs to be said he'll say it, that's why he's never really had many friends. He's always been the one carrying that burden.'

The pair had numerous late-night conversations but one subject never discussed was the direction of the band: it was as if it had its own life, something relentless, bigger than the members.

Like Tommy Crooks, the Hanley brothers remember huge creative freedom and a lot of the time would come up with all the music for Smith to merely sing over the top. 'There was never any question of him saying, "I write all the songs",' says Steve. One of the singer's methods has always been to work continually on new material, the life-force of the group. 'The thing about The Fall is they're never jaded with the songs,' says Steve, explaining that songs would come and go almost as rapidly as musicians. But the trump card was threatening the sack. Paul remembers one of Smith's favourite jokes, taking new members abroad so he could send them home.

'Tension is created, manufactured . . . Mark winds people up. It keeps it interesting for him, but he wants to get a reaction from musicians to get a performance. On a 20-date tour he'd rather have 10 shit gigs and 10 great gigs than 20 that are middling. That's what he hates most. Sometimes he'll walk off, and the audience know that, but are willing to take that chance.'

His brother nods sagely, noting that Smith 'doesn't do average'.

'You'd come off thinking it was great and Mark and Kay [Carroll, Smith's girlfriend, who was The Fall's only long-term manager from 1977 to 1983] would be going, "You were fucking terrible. You're playing like a fookin' pub band!"'

'Chairs would fly,' laughs Steve, describing gig post-mortems that could go on for hours and then degenerate into 'guerilla warfare'. He recalls how John Peel had once said on the BBC he'd 'never seen such an air of malevolence'. Everyone assumed Peel was referring to the gig – in fact, he meant the dressing room. Paul Hanley remembers how the musicians would stand with backs to the wall as Smith and Carroll reached the kind of fever-pitch fury normally associated with Manchester United's manager Sir Alex Ferguson, whose famous 'hairdryer' bawl-outs have reduced many young players to jelly.

'A couple of my mates came into the dressing room once and it was all going off,' remembers Paul. 'They were like, "Jesus!"'

Carroll's role in The Fall has been almost forgotten in the mists of time and punch-ups, but in the early years she was arguably as important as Mark Smith. As manager, mouthpiece, ideologist, occasional kazoo player and backing vocalist (meaning she is on my list of Fallen to track down), Steve suggests he was 'terrified' of Carroll and – when he was 16 – she was even scarier than the singer.

'She was in her thirties and had seen everything,' he says. 'I'd never met anybody like her. I mean, she was very nice, but she was intimidating. Physically aggressive, in your face. She was The Fall then, more than Mark was. A lot of the things that people associate with The Fall all came from Kay.'

Steve remembers Carroll's favourite phrase was 'No sell-out'.

However, after growing arguments, Carroll abandoned The Fall outside an American bar in 1983, and Hanley argues that The Fall never again had strong management. Instead, the burden on Smith just became heavier. There had been a 'string of people who Mark tells what to do' but this had led to mismanagement and that, for him, was the root of the New York fall-out.

As he tells it, the group were suddenly in financial trouble after receiving an enormous tax bill. Smith was depressed and worried about money, as he told me, but Steve Hanley says it went much further – both he and the boss were in danger of losing their houses. The paradox still haunts him – a band who were hailed as a national institution facing letter-boxes clogged with bills.

'Whether you're in it for the money or not, you need to live,' Steve ponders, adding, softly, 'It shouldn't have got to that.'

After the onstage meltdown, Steve abandoned Smith in New York and walked out on The Fall, something he'd vowed never to do. He wanted to be there playing at the end – if there ever is an end to The Mighty Fall – like the band on the *Titanic*. He appreciates it 'wasn't nice' to leave Smith, but he'd simply had enough. In his 19 years in The Fall, the world outside had changed beyond recognition. Thatcher made way for John Major and then Tony Blair. The bassist made his exit with hip-hop, in the form of Jason Nevins vs Run DMC's 'It's Like That', at Number 1. Meanwhile, through it all and beyond, The Fall trundled on and on, as Peel had said, 'always different, always the same'.

Paul Hanley had left twice, in 1983 and finally in 1985, the year The Fall released the classic, dark, spiky *This Nation's Saving Grace*, as the parallel mainstream universe softly rocked to Jennifer Rush. But there was no 'Power of Love' within The Fall. Paul Hanley quit after a row in which Smith blamed him for the band's gear getting stolen. He sips his pint, breathes in and exhales deeply: 'I was 20 and thought I could go off and form my own band and we'd be bigger than The Fall!'

Over two decades later, he still regrets it: 'I should have stayed.'

Steve thinks he left too late; Paul, too soon. The expected musical career never really happened. For the last 21 years, he's been working as a computer operative. But he insists being in The Fall 'changed me completely'.

'It's the only thing I've ever been good at. I mean, I'm all right at my job, but I was really good at playing drums. The bloke next to me can do my job better than I can, but he couldn't play drums in The Fall.'

Paul Hanley is not the only one carrying scars. Steve says 'you never get over' being in The Fall and reveals that when he left it took him two years – and acupuncture – just to 'calm down'.

He's now working as a school 'site manager'.

'I'm a caretaker, basically,' he explains, adding that his name hangs on a sign outside the school, where it must be the ultimate collectors' item for rabid Fall fans. It seems a cruel fate and it's a mystery why one of British music's greatest bassists is not musically in demand. For a second, I'm haunted by the thought of the ultimate Fall musician being taunted in the school playground by pesky kids singing Fall lyrics: 'Eat yerself fitter!' 'Mister, are you Totally Wired?'

But then, the more I think about it, he probably deserves a quiet life. And where can you possibly go musically after playing in the Mighty Fall?

I ask the same question I asked Tommy Crooks. Would either of them go back?

'I would,' says Paul in an instant.

Steve wouldn't. Too much has gone on.

His younger brother reconsiders, and he's smiling. 'I would if he would!'

In fact, they both still play together occasionally – as the rhythm section of The Lovers, a band fronted by ex-Inspiral Carpets singer Tom Hingley. One night onstage, Hingley made the mistake of grabbing Hanley's bass. 'I said, "Gerroff, I had 20 years of putting up with that in The Fall!"' Hingley hasn't touched the instrument again.

Steve admits he misses the Fall lifestyle, perhaps he even misses Smith.

'He can be very funny,' he says. 'Hysterically funny.' However, Steve was hurt by Smith's assertion in a BBC documentary that the 1998 Fall line-up were past it: he'd been 'carrying three old fellas who were shite'.

'A disgraceful thing to say,' says Steve, and while Smith 'wasn't bothered' about losing Crooks or even Burns, he reveals that the singer had tried to get the legendary bassist back.

'He just has that attitude that he can get someone else in, like he said, "If it's me and your granny on bongos, it's The Fall!"' he considers. 'But he would never have sacked me. If I was such a twat for leaving him in New York he wouldn't have tried to ring me.'

The singer left a message on his answerphone. But it wasn't returned. Instead, Steve Hanley set sail in The Ark with Burns and Crooks, but, he insists, contrary to what Smith told me, none of them had planned on leaving The Fall.

'The only thing we talked about was maybe doing something while he was busy,' elucidates Steve. 'I wouldn't have swapped being in The Fall for anything. I certainly wasn't looking to join anyone else.'

Neither of the Hanley brothers has run into Smith since, but both suspect, despite everything, they'd have a pint together and it would be just like old times. That strange loyalty again.

Steve considers sagely, 'You have to separate the great stuff we did from what happened at the end.'

Shortly after abandoning The Fall, Steve found himself watching the latest line-up when they played in Manchester with the Buzzcocks. He's laughing: 'I still didn't recognise any of the songs!' Some time later, his son came home one night to announce excitedly that his own band had landed a support slot with The Fall. Thus, one of The Fall's greatest ever musicians found himself watching his own son support his former band. 'I thought Mark would give my lad a hard time,' he admits. Smith was as good as gold. 'The drummer gave him a hard time!'

SMASH. We're suddenly interrupted by the noise of flying glasses as the pub's glass collector sends the table crashing. Everyone jumps. Everyone except Steve Hanley. The veteran of Fall dressing rooms doesn't even flinch.

I feel I could talk for hours to the Hanleys but both have domestic duties which call them away from The Wonderful and Frightening World. Before we say our farewells – and I kick off Fall Reunited by giving him a phone number for Tommy Crooks – Steve tells me his theory about The Fall.

'The Fall work best when it's Mark and four or five normal people who he can bounce his ideas off,' he muses. 'The trouble is that after a while in The Fall you're no longer normal.'

This, he thinks, is the real reason Smith changes the line-up and why some people disappear. Steve reveals he spotted Mike Leigh – The Fall's cabaret, jazzy drummer from 1979 to 1980 – in PC World and apparently he's now in insurance. As for Karl Burns, he was definitely 'not normal', certainly when he was in The Fall. But where is he? He seems to have completely vanished.

'I found him in my back garden once,' Steve reveals. 'Another time he was in the back of my car. But you'd pay to watch him play drums on his own.'

I would. But I have to find him first.

CHAPTER 5

'I'm losing my hair through stress!'

Karl Burns is proving elusive, but at least word is getting round. Every day or so I'm getting an email or message on my answerphone from a member of The Fallen who say they may be willing to talk. But today's is the most surprising one so far – from Ben Pritchard, guitarist in the current line-up.

I hadn't expected this at all, not least because Smith – even while he may have 'mellowed' – is fiercely controlling of the group's media presence and even at this stage I can't imagine him condoning one of his musicians talking to me.

But in an initial phone call Pritchard says it's okay – he won't be doused in petroleum or suspended from a bridge over the M62 by his trousers. 'There won't be a problem,' he insists, and it crosses my mind he may in fact be a double agent sent by Smith to find out who's been talking. But on the phone line there is laughter. 'You're tracking down everyone who's ever played in The Fall?' he splutters. 'Are you crazy?!'

Maybe I am. Pritchard doesn't know the half of it. I've only just started trying to locate The Fallen and already my eyes are going square from gazing at the internet, my retinas burning from hours poring over album covers in search of clues for musicians who left in 1979. Then there are the telephone fiascos, calling phone numbers so old the codes have changed several times. But then again, if anyone will understand the nature of my mission it'll be Pritchard, who must be familiar with obsession, perfectionism, dementia and things becoming weird . . .

He is, after all, in The Fall.

What I know about him is this: in his late twenties, the guitarist played on 'Dr Buck's Letter' (on 2000's *The Unutterable*) before he was in The Fall. However, he officially joined in February 2001, appearing on November 2001's *Are You Are Missing Winner*, an album of berserk rockabilly rock which neatly divided critics into those who thought it carried the spirit of Gene Vincent and those who thought it a sprawling mess. Myself, I hated it at first and grew to love it – sometimes Smith's abnormal vision isn't immediately appreciated by people who are remotely normal. Anyway, Pritchard's appearance seems to have coincided with a re-energised Fall after the drama and debris of New York. 2003's *The Real New Fall LP: Formerly 'Country on the Click'* – it was so titled because a leak on the internet meant a hurried remix – was a marked return to form and 2005's *Fall Heads Roll* – which earned a five-star eulogy in the *Guardian* – was better still. Fall fans don't put him in the top drawer of Fall guitarists occupied by Brix Smith and Craig Scanlon, but he is loved rather than religiously worshipped. Fall fan sites regularly carry tributes to the way Pritchard stares longingly at the ceiling during gigs, usually a precursor to receiving a schoolmasterly prod or shove from Smith. Moreover, as we talk he's already survived four years, making him a relative Fall veteran.

'I know,' he sighs. 'I should get a gold watch . . . What's my secret of surviving? Long, long story. Look, can't do an interview now, I'm playing football in a few minutes.'

Football?

You really don't expect Fall members to play football. Given the carefully sculpted mythology of the group, I've always thought Fall members would spend their spare time slumped in working men's clubs, reading about the Industrial Revolution or the Third Reich (a Smith favourite) while staring at pints and grumbling disconsolately about the ways of the world. Watching football is one thing – Smith regularly attends Manchester City's Eastlands stadium himself – but playing it is another. Playing football seems too healthy. Too mainstream. Too normal.

'It's the only way I get to relieve any stress,' explains Pritchard. Which does makes sense.

We arrange to speak at 2 p.m. the following day.

'It's not a normal group,' he begins, bang on time, but still sounding slightly tense despite the kickabouts. He can't compare being in The Fall to being in another group because he hasn't been in another group, but suspects few operate like The Fall. He offers two familiar analogies: one, being in The Fall is like a 'psychological experiment'; two, it's 'boot camp: you're thrown in at the deep end and you either sink or swim'.

What this means, he clarifies, is a new Fall member goes through a rite of passage – the sort of initiation you get in cults like the Hells Angels or the army. However, in The Fall, you never know when your trial by fire will arrive.

Pritchard had entered his fourth year before Judgment Day came calling. Unbeknown to me, Smith had already obliquely referred to it in the suggestion that Pritchard had 'begun a resignation letter, but by the time he'd finished it he was back in the group'.

In fact, Pritchard insisted he hadn't resigned at all. According to him, he was fired.

The Fall were three-quarters of the way through a 2004 American tour which, as usual, became stressful. Not least because Smith had broken his leg – according to a Fall spokesperson, by careering down a slope into a concrete post while attending a rockabilly festival in Great Yarmouth – the accident that led him to hospital in Cheetham Hill. With the boss plastered – but not in the usual way – the nine-legged Fall made it out to the States in what Pritchard describes as a 'horrible, hostile atmosphere'. Pritchard says that this coincided with the reappearance of Ed Blaney, the mysterious, occasional 'broker'-cum-manager who also played guitar (placing him at Number 36 on my list of wanted Fallers), but was employed by

Smith as a sort of extreme sergeant major, to drill the troops into line. Pritchard says that when Blaney got to work, things almost immediately went pear-shaped.

'Every time he got involved something went wrong,' says Pritchard. 'I mean, I'd love to be able to say Ed was a nice guy but he wasn't. He used to threaten us.'

Threaten you?

'His mentality was that he was Mark's manager, not The Fall's. He would leave us all for dead as long as he could take care of Mark. So, about a week after he joined the tour, everything fell apart.'

Pritchard suggests that Blaney had fuelled Smith's suspicions that their latest tour manager was stealing from the band. Not only that, but the line-up themselves were about to walk away. It seems slightly unreal that an artist of Smith's stature could be coaxed into paranoid theories involving the petty cash . . . but then again, this is The Fall.

The musicians – Pritchard, bassist Steve Trafford and drummer Dave Milner – found themselves abandoned in Houston, in George Bush's state of Texas. They had no money. They did have non-refundable tickets to Manchester but those weren't valid for another two weeks. An alarming prospect for most musicians but, according to both Pritchard and Tommy Crooks, an occupational hazard of playing in The Fall.

'We had to go home with our tails between our legs,' he says. 'The real twist is that we were carrying his [Smith's] wheelchair with us. He'd dumped us and expected us to take it home!'

Pritchard reveals that when he finally arrived home from the USA he received a 1 a.m. phone call from Smith terminating his services. However, dutifully loyal, the guitarist refuses to blame his boss, pointing the finger squarely at Ed Blaney – 'Ed thinks he knows Mark and he tries to behave the way he thinks Mark would behave.'

Pritchard cites other, even more bizarre cases involving Blaney's bad behaviour – where the band had had to pull the 'broker' away from promoters he was attacking and even occasions where The Fall's 'manager' was fighting their own crowd.

How on earth is this allowed to happen? Where, in all this, for instance, is 'site manager' Mark E Smith?

I put this to Pritchard, who says Smith has a period every so often where he goes a little 'nuts'.

'He locks himself away and we don't see him for a couple of months. But when we got back from the States last year there was something wrong. I said, "Mark, what have I actually done?" I couldn't get a straight answer. He was a bit inebriated as well. He just said, "I think we should go our separate ways".' Pritchard says Smith kept calling him 'Judas' – a word which he says bears the imprint of Ed Blaney.

Pritchard seems more than a little paranoid about Ed Blaney, but he swears most of the paranoia in The Fall is Smith's: 'If people plant a seed, the tiniest thing can turn into this huge paranoid explosion.' I worry again that Pritchard's boss wouldn't like his guitarist spilling these beans and remember something Smith said to me in Malmaison – 'I'd trust you [a journalist!] more than a guitarist!' In fact, Pritchard says, after so long in the business, Smith has been ripped off so many times he finds it difficult to trust anyone. Despite people 'screaming' to work with The Fall, Smith takes a lot of responsibility on himself and, as the Hanleys also suggested, this leads to 'greater tension'.

However, perhaps realising he'd lost a(nother) valuable member, Smith acted quickly to bring Ben Pritchard back. I was hearing two different stories of the same exit from Pritchard and the boss. Why would Pritchard lie? But similarly why would Smith insist he'd resigned? To save face?

Whatever the truth of it, since returning – within three days, that much was true – Pritchard noticed he was now acquiring 'bits and bobs' of responsibilities. Smith, almost uniquely, was lowering his guard. On the other hand, he insists he doesn't want to make the mistake made by many in The Fall where they 'get a bit of attention and think Mark's their best mate. Then they can't believe it when they get fired. I appreciate that I could get fired at any moment. In no way, shape or form do I believe me and Mark are best pals,' he says of the man who, after all, dumped him at a foreign airport. 'He is my boss and I work for him.'

Is it really that simple?

Like Tommy Crooks, Ben Pritchard joined The Fall almost by an accident. He grew up in Prestwich and often spied the singer in various locals, although for a while he thought he was just a weird bloke who drank too much rather than a living legend of British music. Fatefully, Pritchard also lived near another friend of Smith's, Steve Evets, who, inevitably, has also been in The Fall. Once, when Smith was, yet again, a member short, Evets suggested young Pritchard. No matter that Pritchard wasn't a good guitarist; he owned a guitar and that would do.

'When I joined the band, I thought, "Wow, isn't it great, I'm in The Fall",' he enthuses, but reality soon set in. Almost immediately upon joining, various people around The Fall said he played too many chords. Thus, Pritchard was subjected to the most mythical and secret part of Smith's psychology – the complex 'moulding process' (which Smith has jokingly called 'brainwashing') involved in turning an unsuitable musician into a member of The Fall.

'I was a terrible guitarist when I joined,' he admits, but suggests this might have been precisely why Smith wanted him in the group. 'The challenge is to take someone wrong for the group and make them right.' Music doesn't come into it. Smith never says, 'Play this.' In fact, the quality required in The Fall is a 'frame of mind' – and it's arrived at via boot camp.

Onstage in The Fall, Pritchard soon became used to flying elbows from the boss, being constantly jostled onstage and on a few occasions drinks being poured over his head. Ninety per cent of musicians would probably cut and run, but Pritchard understands this experience as pivotal to the Fall creative process. Survive the Fall assault course and the reward is Smith's respect. It seems a bit like the relationship between angry sergeant majors and newly recruited army cadets.

'I'm losing my hair through stress,' admits Pritchard. 'It's good to talk about this. I don't really get to talk about this with anyone else, because no one understands . . .'

And there it is: the true reason for the phone call. This isn't an interview. This is therapy.

Pritchard clears his throat and we're suddenly talking about the group's most recent dates. Because so many people adored *Fall Heads Roll*, the band were booked into bigger venues than they had occupied for years. And all were selling out, which Pritchard suggests was an 'added pressure we could have done without. Mark made it very difficult for us all, because he was under a lot of stress . . . He doesn't like being told that he's got a good group. And he *really* doesn't like his group being told that they're good!'

Pritchard's analysis was curiously similar to Steve Hanley's, from the days when Kay Carroll would accuse The Fall of 'playing like a fookin' pub band'. The ideal is the musicians will play well but not realise it themselves. The fanatical but undeniable logic seems to be if the group get to know they're playing well, they'll stop. 'So he makes a point of putting us right back in our place,' sighs Pritchard, allowing himself a brief giggle and revealing that Smith did indeed accuse them of 'sounding like a fookin' pub band!'

'I know he doesn't mean it,' he claims. 'We understand why he's doing it, but gradually it did bring everyone down.'

Pritchard reveals situations on tour he describes as 'moments'. 'Moments' can happen anywhere – onstage, in hotel rooms, especially in dressing rooms, the principal theatres of Fall warfare depicted by the Hanleys. 'I don't want to go into details, because I don't really want to think about it.'

Shortly after arriving home, Pritchard noticed his already rapidly disappearing hair was now falling out in even greater clumps. As The Fall's most senior member he found himself in the particularly uncomfortable role of Fall guy.

'He knows he can shout and bawl at me, and the rest,' he admits, 'and he knows through tried and tested methods that I will bear it. I won't let him down because he shouts at me and he knows that . . . and he knows he can use me as a whipping boy. But there was a lot more of that on this tour.' He pauses, remembering some 'really low moments', but then he brightens, pointing out that, understandably, when you have those low moments the good moments mean more.

A normal person might wonder why musicians put up with any of this and, indeed, why they don't get a less stressful job bashing out covers on cruise ships or even playing for a relatively less demanding employer – someone like notorious diva Mariah Carey, say. But a normal person wouldn't join The Fall, just like a normal person wouldn't try to climb a mountain or risk death to break the land speed record. There must be an incredible sense of pride being in such a legendary and bizarre band. But maybe even the most determined Fall explorers have their limits.

Pritchard says the band came unusually close to imploding at a recent gig in Stoke. As demand for the tour outstripped supply, the promoters started booking gigs on what were supposed to be the band's rare days off. What had been a gruelling schedule became murderous.

'There were moments on this tour when everybody, including Mark, was at the end of the line,' he says. 'There were days when we were battling against the elements, when Mark was being impossible. There were a few gigs where we should not have carried on. Mark specifically requested that some gigs got cancelled, but Stoke was the first one where he was told it was already sold out and he had to play.

'Mark does not like to be put into a corner like that and that show was particularly nasty. He's got no one else to take it out on but us. He does this but he always ends up apologising for it. We understand. We love the guy to death and sometimes we hate him.

'Sometimes I think he expects us to let him down,' he ponders quietly. 'You almost want to bang his head against the wall and say, "Look, we're here to help you. We're not your enemy." We want to do a good job for him as much as ourselves . . .'

Pritchard's relationship with Smith is starting to sound hugely complex. The more we talk, the more I suspect the guitarist – and, perhaps, others I've yet to find – sees Smith as a disciplinarian father figure.

And maybe there was something in Smith's unusually frank admission in Malmaison that while he had never had and would never have children, there was, very occasionally, a paternal undercurrent to his relationship with his 'lads'.

Despite everything, Pritchard's admiration for Smith and The Fall ideals seems boundless, almost religious. He talks of how Smith could have done massive money-making tours of the United States but has never had an interest in 'selling out'; how other groups get treated like 'royalty' but you'd never find a 'pompous arsehole' in The Fall because 'no one could go in and . . .'

. . . come out the same person as they were before?

He side-steps the question, pointing out his pride in the way The Fall tour – together, in a van like a 'cell'. None of the massive tour buses or luxuries that spoils other bands. He sounds a bit like Smith.

And yet, for every instance of Smith acting like the cruel father, there are touches of benevolence. Surprisingly, in light of what he's told me, Pritchard suggests Smith has often gone out of his way to make the boy feel looked after: 'I was young when I joined, very stupid, very naive. He has taken time out to make sure I'm all right. As a result I do see him quite a lot when we're not working. The rest of the band' – who Smith apparently dubs 'the South Manchester cunts' – 'he might take out for a pint in a blue moon. If he needs taking anywhere, I'll drive him. I'll do anything for him. I do care about the guy a hell of a lot.

'He cares about me as well. He wouldn't admit it, because he'd think it was soft. But I do have quite a good relationship and that is maybe why I've been here so long,' he insists. 'I know it's contradicting what I said earlier on about mates. I'm not his best mate, I'm not saying we're best friends but . . . I think out of everyone he'd least mind you talking to me. I'm not here to slag him off. He knows what he wants me to say and he knows what he wouldn't want me to say. He doesn't like to give his secrets away, Mark. People say, "How do you do it, what's your trick?" He'll never ever tell anyone. Deep, dark secrets. The reason he's doing it . . .'

I'm curious. Has Pritchard become privy to Smith's fabled and jealously guarded 'secrets'?

A pregnant pause.

'Er . . . Not so much his secrets, no . . . but I know the man very personally. I do get to see . . .' He doesn't finish the sentence. Instead, and in place of any kind of further outpouring, the drawbridge is silently but hurriedly pulled up as Pritchard remembers his responsibilities, and where he stands.

'By no stretch of the imagination do I feel my job is safe,' he affirms. 'If there are eggshells around, I'm walking on them. If I get fired tomorrow, there'll be 100 guitarists waiting to take my position.'

After four years – and counting – in The Fall and at least something of a relationship with Smith, Pritchard was still 'battling' for his job. Which is maybe how it must be in The Fall.

'They must get very bored, these other groups,' he declares, before giving me a few phone numbers for Fallers he's seen off in his time. 'You know, it's great getting in the van, unloading the gear, doing a sound check. These bands . . . they don't even do a sound check half the time . . . then it's back to the hotel straight after the gig. What a boring life. It's a lap of luxury they haven't really earned.'

Approaching his fifth year in The Fall, Ben Pritchard has a goal in life.

'One day, when all this is over, I want to be able to look back and think I did a good job,' he declares. 'We can all walk away from it feeling very proud. When that will be, I don't know. It depends how long we fit in with Mark's vision of the group. But one thing I can say is that we'll be here as long as Mark wants us. There is no way this line-up now will ever quit.'

This comment will return to haunt us both, but on that note we say goodbye. I try to remind myself I've just been talking to a pop musician and not a soldier returning from Fallujah or some member of a religious cult. But I can't help wondering what else is going to lie out there. And how on earth has a British pop group not just come to operate like this, but in doing so become an institution?

I need to go back. Right back to the beginning.

CHAPTER 6

'We were best friends who fell out.'

What *was* it like in 1977?

Whenever I read about it now, it seems to have been all about the collapse of the post-war political consensus, the beginning of the end for Jim Callaghan's Labour government and the beginnings of a shift to the right which would lead to the election of Margaret Thatcher. Jimmy Carter succeeded Gerald Ford to become the thirty-ninth president of the USA. South African campaigner Steve Biko died in police custody, which meant he could at least avoid Fleetwood Mac's omnipresent, multi-million selling *Rumours*. I remember running into my mum's bedroom one night because I'd just heard on the radio Elvis Presley had died. Many British households spread the sad news via BT's new plastic Trimphone.

On 7 June 1977, the Queen had her Silver Jubilee and a load of us kids on my estate got together to throw a celebratory party in the community centre up the road, where the sound of breaking glass at the end of some raucous punk record or other caused my pal Michael Clarke's mum to think the building was being broken into. But very shortly after that, the music playing in many of our heads was an alternative national anthem released the week before: 'God Save The Queen' by the Sex Pistols, which should have shot to Number 1 but was banned and demoted to Number 2 in favour of Rod Stewart's 'I Don't Want To Talk About It', which was deemed much less offensive.

These, then, are my memories of 1977. For most of it, I'm at the Royal Wolverhampton School in the West Midlands, having been sent there because Mum was ill, Dad had died and a charity paid for me to get a 'decent education'. So there I am, struggling to fit in with my Yorkshire accent and at the mercy of teachers who are often called upon to administer a caning. I turn 14 in August – a proper teenager by now – but I'm already aware something else is in the air.

The first I hear of the Pistols is some time earlier the same year – it may even have been the year before – when a London-based pupil called Mark Chivers came back from holidays excitedly announcing he'd seen this band who did cartwheels and threw up onstage. Shortly after, Chivsy announced we should all call him Mark Mutilation. It wasn't a name we'd easily forget and if we did, he'd stencilled it on the back of a ripped-to-pieces tracksuit he sported along with a new haircut modelled on a hedgehog.

Before long, the section of the music class where we're allowed to play our own records will reverberate not to the previous term's atrocities like 'Crisis? What Crisis?' by Supertramp (which Chivsy was into at the time) but 'In the City' by The Jam and the Pistols' 'Anarchy in the UK'. When this record in particular hits the turntable, about a quarter of the class rejoice in glee and the rest react as if somebody has farted.

Which is pretty much how I remember punk. Historians and the Pistols' chart success tell us it swept the nation, but I've often wondered how many of those singles were bought by wives, families and friends of EMI executives anxious to protect their investment.

Around the country, the really big phenomenon that summer is *Saturday Night Fever*, the disco film starring John Travolta, which provokes small children and adults old enough to know better to experiment with dance moves and chest-hair wigs. Punks are supposed to exist in massive numbers but, like rats, you glimpse one rarely, when they are generally accompanied by a chorus from passing old ladies moaning, 'Have you seen their hair?'

Nationwide, the impact of punk probably mirrors that in our school; a minority interest, but those who are interested put it above everything else. I spend a Saturday afternoon taking lessons from Chivers on how to pogo. The idea is to leap up in the air and pretend to head an imaginary ball. I've often wondered how many footballers over the years developed an aptitude for football while dancing to The Stranglers.

Another day, three of us spend a physics lesson covering our school uniform with ink, then head off to see The Jam, only to find their audience full of cardigan-wearing hippies. And that's how I remember summer 1977: not a seismic cultural revolution but a mere ripple on the pool of things to come. If punk was reaching the provinces, the Midlands – and to an extent my hometown, Leeds – were left out. The winds of change were discernible – hippies smelled of patchouli oil, punks reeked of new leather and Cossack hairspray, which gave a desirable 'extra firm hold' – but the new music seemed to make more of an impact in Manchester than anywhere else outside London. But at this point, I've never heard The Fall. Then again, before May 1977, nor had anybody else.

Almost three decades later, I'm winding my Punto through the hills and dales of the Peak District, headed for Buxton, Derbyshire, to meet Tony Friel, who three years ago played in the Woodbank Street Band. It's thanks to their website I find him.

Now in lecturing and electronic engineering, he lives in a house so tiny, if you blink while driving past you miss it, which may be how he sees his role in The Fall. It was certainly significant – Friel founded the group in 1976 – but he only lasted a few months and I'm here to find out why.

I pull up outside the cottage to find no Fall fans outside, nor is there a blue plaque proclaiming that 'The bloke living here formed one of the most notorious and legendary British pop groups of the last 30 years'. And if there were, Friel would probably take it down. He has hardly ever talked about The Fall and seems to have purposely relegated himself to a mere footnote in history – The Fall's very own Pete Best. However, despite being born in 1957 like Smith, the man opening the door is nowhere near as ravaged – he is vegan and looks like a gym teacher – but then again he hasn't spent his whole life in The Fall. Still, he owns a bass guitar – which looks expensive in a corner – and his living room overlooks the most breathtaking scenery – his very own Wonderful (and not particularly Frightening) World.

Friel pours herbal tea – anathema to Smith – and takes me back to the start, when he was a 15-year-old who 'bumped into' Mark Smith's sister Barbara in the same way Smith encountered Tommy Crooks. Friel dated Barbara and first met Smith in Sedgley Park, Prestwich, when the future singer was on the sofa with his girlfriend Una, with Friel and Barbara cowering behind them on the floor. Friel remembers Smith didn't take too kindly to a leather-jacketed miscreant dating his sister, but after initial 'tension' the pair became firm friends. Popular perception has it that Smith grew up in a shoe, but Friel says, while the Smiths weren't wealthy, they were 'fairly well-to-do', had a 'very nice' detached house and Smith benefited from a grammar school education at Stand Grammar School – which unfortunately for Fall sightseers has since been knocked down.

Smith has often told how his strict father would banish him from the house, so he'd take refuge in the local library and the worlds of books and music. Not that he discovered the sounds that shaped The Fall. Friel remembers he liked Jethro Tull while Smith was more into Genesis. 'It was pretty abysmal,' he recalls, but the mid 1970s were.

In Malmaison, Smith told me how he had to really seek music out, and the bands he discovered have obviously made a lasting impact. He told me how he'd recently taken the whole Fall to see The Troggs, who were 'fucking amazing' despite being in a village hall full of old grannies and singer Reg Presley talking for ages between numbers.

'These stories are going on for half an hour and The Troggs are snoring,' he said. 'It was funny, but that sort of music was the only thing around when I was at school.

'There was fuck all to buy,' he remembered, explaining that the onset of CD has meant 'all the shit I was avoiding when I was 16 is now on every jukebox. The Eagles and stuff like that.'

Another band he really liked then were 1960s keyboard heads The Seeds – but the future Fall were soon fired up by reggae and the energy of punk. Although Smith has since dismissed the class of '77 as 'bad heavy metal', Friel insists the energy of the period certainly rubbed off.

The first Fall bassist remembers 'taking lots of amphetamine' and going to heavy metal clubs, a forgotten subculture of the 1970s scene. They played 'bad' music but were better than the equally long-lost skinhead clubs, where attendance usually meant risking a kicking. The way Friel describes a typical night out then doesn't sound that different to a Fall gig now – 'We used to get drunk, take speed and take the piss out of people. It wasn't tremendously malicious. We bonded as a group because we weren't like other kids. We were outsiders.'

The Fall could literally have been The Outsiders; it was the name Friel favoured after literature-mad Smith introduced him to the Camus novel. However, after a 'discussion' they settled on The Fall – also a Camus title – and The Outsiders was relegated to become a never-recorded song.

The early Fall's stroke of genius was to ally the energy of punk and Smith's literary leanings with the repetitive nature of another Smith interest – German Krautrock bands like Faust and Can – which bequeathed the Fall ideology (as documented in 'Repetition'), one of repetition in the music which must be adhered to at all costs.

Otherwise, their beginnings were not quite the stuff of legend. Adding another pal, Martin Bramah, on guitar, Friel invested in a £50 bass guitar and Smith's nurse girlfriend Una (Baines) bashed biscuit tins for drums. In the early days, Smith also played guitar and, intriguingly, Friel swears the 'non-musician' came up with tunes so strong he remembers them today. But Smith wanted to concentrate on his words and by the time The Fall debuted at Manchester's North West Arts Centre on 23 May 1977, Smith had dropped the instrument.

Dick Witts – another friend of Friel's who briefly managed the fledgling Fall – remembers the venue as being 'like a fashionable restaurant in the late 1970s, with everything white. It was done out like a small white cave.

We just took the tables and chairs out. Mark and Martin, who were taller than the others, had to bend down because of the low ceiling. It wasn't really public, the audience was just a group of other musicians sitting around listening.'

'Mark just got up and did it,' says Friel. 'I don't think he thought he could be a proper singer, so he developed a thing which was almost reggae, semi-talking.'

Friel remembers the 1977 Smith as a 'funny, witty bloke' who introduced him to authors like Philip K Dick and H P Lovecraft before dropping out of college. Smith got a job as a clerk and, as a result, Friel believes, he saw the first written evidence of what would become Smith's trademark finger-pointing style.

'He didn't do any work,' he grins, 'but he used to write me these letters, full of asides about his co-workers. I've still got them.'

But otherwise, Friel remembers the members of the group as being 'all tremendously nice, actually', which doesn't sound very Fall. In fact, ructions began almost immediately and Tony Friel managed to avoid the dubious honour of being the first to leave The Fall. That unfortunate accolade goes to a drummer – whose name no one can remember, he is usually called 'Dave' or 'Steve' – who was an insurance salesman and briefly in The Fall when Una Baines switched from biscuit tins to keyboards.

'I think he was called Steve. He was a nice guy, but pretty naff,' insists Friel, explaining that the hapless sticksman penned a song called 'Landslide Victory' anticipating Thatcher and therefore, however prescient, simply had to go.

In the manner of various Fall line-up shuffles ever since, Friel already had an eye on a replacement – Karl Burns – who he'd seen play and knew would fit in with a rock band. Thus, 'in the nicest possible way, which wasn't probably very nice, really', 'Steve' – or 'Dave' – was given his P45.

The Fall were just weeks old and already there was a member of The Fallen.

The next head to roll was Friel's. As he tells it, he wasn't keen on a 7-inch deal the band were about to do with Step Forward Records. But the main reason was Smith had started going out with Kay Carroll, who worked at the local psychiatric hospital and who Friel didn't take to at all, especially when Smith announced she was their new manager. 'I thought she muscled in,' says Friel, 'although Mark asked me to stay.' Nevertheless, after an ultimatum – 'It was her or me' – Friel discovered he was the one taking the bullet, in December 1977.

Although his former pals became legends in music, he swears he has no regrets other than falling out with his best mate, Smith. He suggests he'd 'play for Mark' again. After exiting The Fall, Friel formed a band called The Passage with Dick Witts but fell out with him too.

'I was drinking too much, taking too many drugs and being too snotty,' he admits. 'I was a bit of an arsehole. I wasn't sacked but I should have been. I left, but looking back I was fed up with it. I wanted to get back to doing something with some guts.'

Then he made a record with Karl Burns, but managed to extricate himself completely from Fall circles by falling out with Una Baines, for reasons he refuses to divulge.

Lately, he's got the music bug again and is playing in a 1960s covers band, The Scavengers, whose set includes songs by The Move, a band also recently covered by The Fall.

Always different, always the same.

And yet, it doesn't quite add up. Friel's tales of drugs and fallouts with everybody don't square with the 'nice' Fall he depicts or indeed the gentle chap before me now. I can't help suspecting either his memory is fading or he's giving me a rather sanitised version of what happened. Either way, I seem to have jolted something, perhaps a sense of what might have been if he'd not attempted to face off Carroll.

As I'm leaving the house, he shouts after me, 'If you find Karl, let me know.' A few days later, the letters from Smith appear on Friel's personal website but almost immediately vanish.

CHAPTER 7

'I knew Mark got me in to fuck off Friel.'

I track down Kay Carroll – now married and surnamed Bateman – to Portland, Oregon, where she's working as a doctor's assistant. Even with several thousand miles' distance, I get an immediate sense of the character who so 'terrified' the Hanleys when she emails to ask if I'm 'a stalker'. Credentials suitably established, she breaks several decades of near silence to mail me an hour of taped Mancunian vitriol.

'I knew that Mark got me in to fuck off Friel, and it worked,' she says. Within that one line, it's easy to see why Carroll and Smith connected – as girlfriend, then manager. They thought and even spoke alike. Perish the thought, but Carroll's sneering Salford burr sounds curiously similar to Mark E Smith's.

She makes me laugh when she compares her work in nursing to The Fall – 'head injuries, retarded people, nothing changes, David!' – and calls me by the name used only by my mother. As she rants wonderfully on, it tran- spires she's answering my emailed questions while driving and, later, while cooking the dinner. 'Which doesn't really fit in with the image of Mother Carroll from Hell,' she shrieks. It doesn't, really. Maybe, like Smith, she's mellowed.

She begins by explaining how she met Tony Friel, which didn't involve herbal tea or vegan suppers. They were both tripping on LSD: Friel and Martin Bramah were talking in a corner, and she thought they were talking 'nonsense'.

'I just fired from the hip,' she spits. Although Carroll occasionally sang backing vocals, her chief role was as Smith's strategist and attack dog, to be employed against anyone who stood in the way, whether journalists, record labels or musicians.

Carroll is still scathing about Friel, who she labels a 'poser': 'Here was this guy who couldn't play bass very well and he had a fretless bass.' I can't help but smile when I recall Friel's brand new bass guitar. However, more seriously, she suggests that although there was a personality clash, the real reason Friel was outed was musical. Friel was a 'serious musician', Smith a 'poet'. The twain could never meet and from that moment – with Carroll doing the dirty work because Smith 'didn't want to lose face', Smith wrested control of the early Fall.

Carroll confirms Smith's suggestion that he has no respect for musicians but adds that he 'likes his power'. Thus, from the very start, the entire dynamic of The Fall was about tension, musical and otherwise.

Carroll says although she didn't always agree with our leader, she understood why certain members had to go. Like Smith, she came to recognise very early on that turnover in the group could be beneficial. Every time a member would depart, she'd think the band was all over, but a new member would come in and the band would move up a gear. There were 13 line-ups during her tenure (1977 to 1983) alone. She suggests Smith didn't start out thinking, 'Let's get rid of these musicians,' but over time realised it could work to his advantage.

Together, the Smith-Carroll team was formidable. Carroll remains in awe of Smith's mantras about complacency and routine being the enemies of music, and she thinks Smith never let anybody feel a part of The Fall, instilling 'stress and edginess' with ploys such as telling the musicians the songs they would be playing mere seconds before they went onstage.

'They'd be jogging around in the dressing room excited and he'd be still doing the set list . . . he got off on that edge,' she says, with the barest hint of a laugh. I'm reminded of a story Waterboys singer Mike Scott sometimes tells onstage about Beatles and Rolling Stones manager Allen Klein who had 150 lawsuits going at any one time, people who were suing him and whom he was suing. This bugged Scott for years – 'How can somebody live like that? How would you get any sleep?' he asked – before the penny finally dropped. 'I realised he liked it. He actually got off on that tension.'

Carroll certainly agrees with what Smith told me about some of his behaviour being tongue-in-cheek, revealing that his more humorous psychological ploys started very early. Once, in Belgium, Karl Burns had been given a load of Belgian francs to spend and given the impression it was an awful lot of money. Carroll and Smith, the terrible twosome, howled with laughter when the naive drummer returned 20 minutes later, exploding, 'This won't even buy me a fucking packet of cigarettes!'

Carroll suggests that although Smith's antics could be very funny, they were tinged with darker relish: 'Mark's the sort of person who likes pulling wings off flies.'

She tells an eyebrow-raising story suggesting Smith's manipulation and domination began in early childhood. When Carroll was 18, her brother had been at primary school in Prestwich and the eight-year-old would often come home 'totally unglued' after telling Carroll about a boy in school who'd been making his life a misery. She'd suggested confronting the boy but her brother said, 'No, he'll deny it. He's really, really sneaky.' So it was left.

Ten years later, her brother came to visit when Smith and Carroll lived together in Kingswood Road and 'Mark just went, "Noddy!"'

'My brother went white,' she continues. 'I went, "Do you guys know each other?" Afterwards he just said, "Kay, that's the bully. That's the guy who made my life miserable!"'

'It was amazing and really telling,' she says pointedly, although bullying is hardly a cardinal sin. Involvement in a similar outrage managed to get me expelled from school. It's what kids do. Admittedly, few of us carry on into adult life.

Nevertheless, the discovery that Smith was her brother's school bully didn't stop Carroll falling for his charms. All these years later, her sentiments seem to flicker between love and hate, mirroring Fall devotees who try to give up on the group but always, always return.

It's weird hearing Carroll talk. Now almost 60, her accent has been roughened by years of 'the weather, and the cigarettes'. But she sounds sad and genuinely surprised to hear the Hanley brothers found her terrifying. In fact, if Carroll is firm on one thing, it's that there was camaraderie in The Fall. 'Camps' certainly existed within the band, but the musicians had Smith 'on a pedestal' even before they joined the band, which might explain why they put up with stress. But however intense things would get, it was always The Fall against the world. Even now, Smith routinely begins Fall gigs by stating, 'We are The Fall' – whoever is actually in the group at the time.

Carroll is proud of being associated with The Fall. She also insists she 'loved' the musicians and has her own spin on the group's continuing appeal: 'The Fall are interesting because it's not about music. What was created was atmosphere and tension. You'd go to a gig and it was like the audience had all been in a plane crash and ended up in a field. They had nothing in common whatsoever. Some people loved the music, others the "Fuck you, arsehole" attitude, others the intelligence. The Fall were and are an enigma.'

Her comments about people in a field strike a chord with me. When I used to see bands other than The Fall, I'd wear whatever fashions were appropriate – long raincoats and (later) camouflage gear for Echo & The Bunnymen, a leather jacket and embarrassing bondage trousers for anything vaguely punk. And yet, when it came to The Fall, all of us would dress as nondescriptly as possible, like labourers. The Riley-Smith Hall audience even included builders in their hard hats. It was as if to display any interest in fashion or show any form of kinship with a recognised youth culture would somehow fall below the standards expected while following The Fall.

Carroll was yet another who seemed to be drawn weirdly into Smith's orbit. In 1977, she was working at Prestwich Psychiatric Hospital, alongside Una Baines.

'I tried to score drugs off her, to tell you the truth,' Carroll explains while mashing her potatoes. 'She was incredibly political and tenacious, and I liked her a lot. If it hadn't been for Una I don't think The Fall would have happened. Una told me this story that when they were at Mark's parents' house they had a tape, and Mark started talking prose over it. Yeah. Mark was a rapper, really, before they invented it.'

For Carroll, Baines – perhaps one of the more overlooked characters in the whole Fall story and certainly one of many since disowned by Smith – was 'pivotal' at this early stage. Perhaps if it had not been for her Smith might never even have become a singer.

'It was Una who got him to do it into this tape machine,' Carroll insists. 'He's always had great women in his life – including me – who fought for him and gave him confidence.'

However, Carroll says that when she became involved, the Smith-Baines relationship was already 'on the down curve'. Carroll insists both singer and keyboard player would confide their troubles about each other. 'So, I could see the demise coming and it got really freaky.' Carroll suggests that Baines was paranoid, but blames Smith, saying that later 'He almost drove me insane telling me it was in my head. So Una and Mark split up.' She remembers one night when Baines came back to the Fall house in Kingswood Road accompanied by a man and, whatever the significance of this, 'Mark was like a bull in a china shop'.

Her voice sounds rawer now. Nearly 30 years later, these are powerful emotions. According to Carroll, her relationship with Smith began innocently in Kingswood Road. Smith was so anxious about Baines coming back with other men Carroll had offered her bed, but as a friend.

'It was done with that naivety,' Caroll emphasises, but 'something happened'. Carroll believes it worked out for the best. 'Una always said that she hoped me and Mark would get together.'

The progression from friendship to bed to co-conspirator to manager-backing vocalist was speedy. When Carroll took the reins, she'd started to get to know Buzzcocks manager Richard Boon and had learnt from his mistakes.

'We were all trying to walk this goddamn line where we wouldn't give up any creative control,' she says of the early Manchester punk and post-punk scene. According to Carroll, Smith was the only Fall musician who realised how important this control could be. Thus, from a very early stage, the idea that Mark was The Fall and The Fall was Mark began to permeate from the music into the business.

Carroll suggests the band had innumerable offers from record companies and could have 'sold out', but neither she nor Smith would bite: 'The guys [musicians] were pissed at me but I tried to get a deal where we wouldn't have to compromise,' she says. 'They weren't going to mess his art up. Those guys wrote his licks and they weren't given enough respect by Mark, but at the same time they wouldn't have got anywhere without him.'

Perhaps history hasn't given enough credit to Carroll. An arch-manipulator and provocateur, she suggests The Fall's entire 'no sell-out/outsiders' stance was her creation . . . her 'musical instrument'.

'I brought an ideology to The Fall and Mark carried it on,' she says while driving. The rumble of the American freeway seems light years away from the hardline politics of dealing with the British record industry in the 1970s. From the outside, it's always looked as if The Fall often changed labels because Smith was difficult to deal with, but Carroll insists it was all a grand design. One-off deals with labels meant heightened creativity and more control.

She tells a story about approaching Richard Branson's Virgin label with the first EP 'Bingo-Master's Break-Out!'. According to Carroll, Richard Branson's label offered £26,000 – a lot of money for a new band in 1977 – but on the condition The Fall went back into the studio to remix Friel's bass. Carroll was appalled.

'I thought, "Are we selling a car?"' She grabbed the tape of the band's music and returned home to a disappointed Fall. 'Mark knew what happened but I never told Tony and that's why it's so ironic that Tony resented me,' she says.

Maybe if Friel had known, he'd have stayed and adapted, and the entire history of The Fall would have been quite different . . . or maybe not. So, Friel played on the first ever Fall single, but was out of the group by the time it was released. The Step Forward Records deal dismissed by Friel certainly suited Smith. If it didn't work, The Fall could up and leave, and The Fall retained the publishing rights, which was unheard of at the time.

Carroll notes that over the years Smith has been very careful to retain ownership of songs. Underpinning this was a notion – which seems to fire Smith to this day – that signing to a record company for any length of time meant a band would become 'soft'.

The other big dynamic driving The Fall in those days – and almost certainly to this day – was drugs. According to Carroll, the manager and singer took amphetamine 'the whole time' they were in The Fall together: six years in total.

'It definitely has an edge,' she says. 'You do get paranoid.' Carroll describes an atmosphere around the early Fall completely different to the innocence portrayed by Friel. There was tension; there was weirdness. Things got 'really crazy'.

The first notable casualty of this drug use was Baines, who had taken up with Jonnie Brown – a Rotherham student who was, for all of three weeks in January 1978, Friel's replacement. Baines was using acid. Brown was on heroin, a drug Smith has always given short shrift. The combination of Baines and Brown and two very different narcotics was as volatile as nitro-glycerine. Carroll insists she 'had no idea' that Brown was using heroin but admits if she had, it probably wouldn't have made any difference.

'I was putting everything up my nose so who am I to judge? Funnily enough, I think he came in to take Una away. Jonnie was one of the sweetest people, I certainly had concerns about him and Una. They were just out of their heads, doing cough medicine and whatever. They were two drug-embracing human beings enabling each other.'

Baines apparently had some form of breakdown, but Carroll refuses to blame Brown: 'He became the scapegoat, but ironically for a time he was the sanity in the madness. He got a raw deal like all the ex-members.'

'They were strange times,' she comments, before admitting she could have easily gone the same way as Baines.

Gradually, her relationship with Smith encountered problems. They were 'very driven', the manager loved the singer and the whole thing was fuelled by amphetamine. Later, Carroll says she started finding 'love letters' in the flat to the increasingly high-profile vocalist, who by now was being photographed by *NME*.

'I could fill up another tape with instances,' she sighs. She became convinced that Smith was cheating on her but the singer would say she was paranoid, due to the drugs she was taking. Sometimes, she says, she'd come back from meetings in London and catch him in bed with women. But, contrarily, she insists Smith wouldn't let her go.

Like Smith, possibly, Carroll has a more vulnerable side. It seems strange listening to this stuff – it's personal detail I didn't expect to hear. But Carroll is clearly benefiting. Like Pritchard, she suggests this is 'therapy, David!'

By the end, the manager and the singer were having 'major fights'. Carroll remembers 'punching out' a couple of girls, until finally she could take no more. After co-sculpting The Fall, she eventually walked out on them after a row outside an American bar in 1983.

What made the partnership ultimately destroyed it.

'Mark is powerful,' she ponders. 'Sometimes you have to meet people in your life to work your karma off. I'd done horrible things before I left The Fall and maybe it was my karma. He did get the better of me but in the end I got the last laugh because he's still not paid for the amount of damage he's done. Or maybe he has.'

Even with 25 years' distance, Carroll keeps in touch with Fall gossip and suspects Smith is 'very lonely'. Her voice lifts as she says she prefers to remember the good times, and there were many, like recording 1979's classic 'Totally Wired' single in a studio in Rochdale. She says the version the Fall world loves only came about because she rejected the first draft – 'I went apeshit. It had no balls' – and convinced the band to let her remix it herself.

Then there was the time Smith was attacked onstage at London's Lyceum – ironically during 'A Figure Walks', his prophetic discourse about stalking – presumably remembered as a 'good time' by Carroll because the memory appeals to her sense of humour and unquenched thirst for vengeance.

Carroll remained in America, where she last saw Smith in 1986. The Fall were playing in New York and she spied Smith wearing a leather coat. 'Who do you think you are, Marc Bolan?' she asked, and was inevitably turfed out of the dressing room just as she had once turfed others out.

She remembers the moment The Fall came onstage. The New York Mets had just won the title. 'Everyone was cheering and bowing, and Mark thought it was for him,' she howls. 'That was a really funny moment.' She laughs some more as she remembers an interview with David Bowie in which he'd said he thought The Fall were really interesting but he 'didn't like them as much after 1983'.

'When I left!' she shrieks. 'I can't tell you how great that made my heart feel.'

When she ran out on them, Smith told the media she had contracted 'a physical illness' – before he knew she had contracted cancer. (She's all right now.)

Carroll has regrets – 'That I didn't hit him more!' – but confesses, 'God love him, even though he is an arsehole.'

According to Carroll, The Fall were and remain virtually unmanageable, but she was the one person who almost pulled it off. She frets that with all the fallouts and punch-ups Smith is turning into a parody. However, she suggests The Fall's crazy turnover of personnel appeals to 'that side of us we all have where we have to peek at an accident that just might happen . . . I'm not sure if Mark knows that one or not but it wouldn't surprise me if he did.'

Before she wishes me a taped 'good luck', Carroll wonders aloud if I'll ever crack the 'enigma' but leaves me with a startling confession: 'Some weeks I wouldn't go near it, some weeks I wish I'd never left, others I'd go back in a heartbeat,' she says, echoing the Hanleys, Tony Friel and Tommy Crooks.

After communicating with Carroll, I'm again asking myself something I've often wondered. What created Mark E Smith?

'You want a goalie who gets bloody shot at!'

There haven't been a lot of people in music who operate like Smith, but there are a few.

The obvious comparison is with James Brown, whose hits with tracks like 'Sex Machine' earned him the title Godfather of Soul. But for musicians who played with him, the late legend was more ringmaster than Godfather. Musicians were subjected to rigorous discipline covering everything from the exact minute members of his band would attend rehearsals down to what they wore onstage. Maceo Parker, a saxophonist in Brown's famous All Stars band, once told how Brown placed equal importance on wearing the correct bow-tie and patent-leather shoes greased in exactly the right manner as hitting the correct notes. Woe betide anyone who failed to meet these exacting standards: they'd be fined, admittedly not for hitting the tom tom, or despatched from the band. Once out of the Brown enclave, musicians were expected to leave behind their shiny shoes and bow-ties – which must have been a wrench – and return to normal life.

I hear about another similar taskmaster when my editor sends me along to get a drumming lesson and an interview from African percussion legend Tony Allen. These days, the youthful 70-something plays with Damon Albarn and Clash bassist Paul Simonon in The Good, The Bad & The Queen. But his greatest contribution to modern music was to invent the influential 'afrobeat' – which inspired Brown's funk – alongside Nigerian legend Fela Kuti. Once Allen has finished scrutinising my drumming – he doesn't fine me for hitting the tom tom, but teaches me a whole new way of playing hi-hat – we start talking about Fela Kuti.

'Very strict, very disciplinarian,' he tells of Kuti, who fronted enormous ensembles requiring absolute perfection. If a musician ever missed a note or played something ever so slightly wrong, Kuti would stop the music to humiliate the hapless offender on the stage.

These days, as well as playing with Albarn, Allen fronts his own bands and I wonder aloud if Kuti's discipline rubbed off.

'No, I'd never stop the music,' he insists softly, before chuckling, 'I'd just stop that one musician!'

However, these are purely disciplinarian approaches. What fascinates me about Smith's approach to musicians is that his techniques seem to enter into the realms of the almost supernatural, or psychological warfare. He's certainly not the first rock singer to attempt a mental or almost occult approach. Perhaps the most notorious is Don Van Vliet, aka the legendary

Captain Beefheart, notably a Smith favourite. For the recording of classic 1969 album *Trout Mask Replica*, Beefheart effectively imprisoned his band in a house and made them rehearse for up to 14 hours a day. Drummer John French described their living conditions – playing for months on end, often without food, which has obvious echoes of The Fall – as 'cult-like'. In a macabre twist, which Smith would surely love, Beefheart restricted the band from leaving the house by making them wear women's smocks at a time when cross-dressing was a federal offence. To leave the house risked arrest as well as ridicule.

Meanwhile, in a feat worthy of The Mighty Fall, Beefheart nipped off to the pub, safe in the knowledge that by the time he came back, the musicians would be so bound up in creative tension they'd deliver a classic album. It worked and it's clearly significant Smith is a big enough Beefheart fan to be able to quote freely in Malmaison, 'If you can't hear the drums, the music's not there.'

Beefheart – who eventually retired to the desert, where he may or may not bump into Karl Burns – had quite a lot of strange ideologies and practices. On the internet there's a notorious list of 'Ten Commandments For Guitarists', in which Beefheart apparently laid out his own surreal instructions for would-be Magic Band guitar-pluckers.

These included such gems as 'Listen to the birds' – because 'that's where all the music comes from'. Guitarists were told their instrument was not a guitar but 'a divining rod'. They were told to 'Practise under a bush' – 'Eat a multi-grained bread and play your guitar to a bush. If the bush doesn't shake, eat another piece of bread.' Other commandments included: 'Walk with the Devil' (on the grounds that 'an electric guitar attracts Beelzebub'); 'Do not think' (on the grounds that this removes feeling); and – my personal favourite – 'Do not wipe sweat from the guitar' (on the grounds that great music had to have 'that stink').

Gary Lucas, a Magic Band guitarist, suspects the Commandments are a hoax, but are consistent with instructions he was given while in Beefheart's employ. He reveals that Beefheart told one drummer to copy the sound of him throwing a metal ashtray against a wall. He had a theory called the Exploding Note Theory, that notes should have no relation to the previous note and be like 'bombs exploding in the air'. Perhaps, next to some of the Captain's mad pronouncements, Smith's favoured commands are pretty tame. Equally, very few of Beefheart's or Brown's musicians lasted as long as 19 years, as did Steve Hanley, or emerged from the experience needing treatment.

Other stars have issued bizarre musical ideologies – rocker Jerry Lee Lewis has said that to get the sweetest tone from a piano, you must set it on fire. However, these artists issue their mad commands to seasoned musicians, not uncultured guitarists stumbled over in the pub. Which gives Smith's ability to craft great music with The Fall a whole different dimension.

The more I find out about him, the more he brings to mind a great football manager than a director of musicians. In Malmaison, he was able to offer strategies for winning football matches just as he was for music. At one point, he even told me exactly what is wrong with the England football team, describing it as a music 'supergroup': 'It's like picking the best guitarist in Britain, the best drummer and the best singer, it's ridiculous and it's never going to work.

'I know that,' he said. 'See, [Sir Alf] Ramsay [manager who led England to the 1966 World Cup], people never liked him for it, but he'd always have the full-backs from the Second Division. Gordon Banks' Stoke City were bottom of the First Division. They'd conceded more goals that World Cup season than anybody else, but it works.

'You want a goalie who gets bloody shot at every week. You don't want the Arsenal goalie or whatever in any national team, because he's never got anything to do! He might pull off the occasional beautiful save, but he's never going to be any good against a gang of Poles who are going to get shot if they don't score.'

When I look for people who succeed with similar methods to Smith, I turn to football as much as music. In the early 1980s, as manager of Aberdeen, Sir Alex Ferguson inspired an unfashionable group of un-fancied players to win the 1983 UEFA Cup Winners' Cup. Ferguson's ideology – which bears a similarity to Smith's view of musicians – is that no player should be bigger than the club.

He also seems to display an uncanny knack of knowing just when to jettison a player – you could compare Ferguson's dispensing with David Beckham to

Smith's ability to dispense with star players like Martin Bramah – in order to reshape the team. Not that Smith – as a City fan – would relish being mentioned in the same breath as a manager of United. However, while Ferguson's youth policy nurtured the likes of Paul Scholes and Ryan Giggs (the Ben Pritchards of Man United), lately he's had to rely more and more on big money signings – football's equivalent of flashy lead guitarists and thus alien to Smith.

But the footballing comparison I turn to more than anyone is with 1970s Nottingham Forest and Derby County manager Brian Clough.

Like the Prestwich-Salford Fall, Forest and Derby were from unfashionable backwaters. By virtue of shrewd management and psychological tactics, they were inspired to win league titles and, in Forest's case, the European Cup, twice. Clough could spend money – he signed Trevor Francis from Birmingham City to Forest for a record British fee. But his teams were mostly constructed from unknown players and low-key signings, which the former player 'moulded' into a winning team.

His exact methods were secret at the time although they have dripped into the public domain courtesy of former players. The principal method seems to have been to develop an elaborate, extreme example of the 'carrot and stick'.

Like The Fall, Clough's players never knew which was coming next – one day he'd be buying them all steak and chips, the next humiliating them in public. A typical story is the one about a former centre-forward who scored a hat-trick in the first 45 minutes and came off expecting to be congratulated by the boss. Instead, Clough punched him in the stomach – for missing the easy chance that should have given him a fourth.

As Clough's fondness for the bottle developed alongside his success, his behaviour became more extreme, typified by an incident in which he swung at one of his own fans – for invading his territory, the pitch – and almost immediately relented to give him a kiss. Nevertheless, his players – many of them now successful in management themselves – usually have an unstinting respect and even love for the demanding but successful instructor they still call 'the gaffer'.

Like Smith, who views the music business with thinly veiled disdain, 'Ol' Big Head' was so outspoken he offended the football top brass so much they refused to make him England manager when he was the obvious – if not the only – candidate.

The other aspect of Clough's reign, which echoes Smith's, is that he worked best when he had someone else alongside him. Where Smith had Kay Carroll – and later, Brix, Julia and now Elena – Clough had his assistant manager, Peter Taylor. His faithful sidekick was entrusted with various tasks including recruitment and operated as Clough's 'eyes and ears', often reporting back to him with tales from the training room and boardroom just as Carroll was trusted to handle the business and keep the musicians on their toes. Similarly, when Clough managed alone – notably at Leeds – he was unsuccessful, although there were various other factors. Facing player battles at Leeds and feeling isolated between the twin rocks of dressing room and boardroom, Clough ended up pleading with Taylor to return to his side – obvious echoes of the way Steve Hanley told me Smith asked him back.

As someone who is very well read and versed in football, it seems inconceivable Smith hasn't read about Clough and perhaps taken the odd tip here and there. Other historical figures have the aura of Smith about them. If what Friel and Carroll say is true, there's a Machiavellian streak to Smith's plotting and musically he seems to follow the political philosopher's doctrine that 'the end justifies the means'.

Yet, Carroll's tales about how Smith dealt with her brother 'Noddy' and Tony Friel bring yet another literary figure to mind, in a poem by T S Eliot.

Macavity, Macavity, there's no one like Macavity,
There never was a Cat of such deceitfulness and suavity.
He always has an alibi, and one or two to spare:
And whatever time the deed took place – MACAVITY WASN'T THERE!

Which could also explain Smith's loathing of canines.

However, comparing Smith to anyone else is ultimately frustrating. Like Macavity, The Mystery Cat, the more you try to pin Smith down, the more he slips away.

CHAPTER 8

'I took a lot of drugs and was a bit of a nutcase!'

In The Wonderful and Frightening World, you can go from horror to humour and back again at any given moment.

I'm heading for a café in Manchester's leafy Chorlton, where I've arranged to meet Una Baines. As I'm crossing the road towards the tiny establishment I suddenly realise what a mad assignment this is. Baines hasn't been sighted – or photographed – for years. All I have to go on is a fading photo from 1978 in which she sports a hairstyle like the auburn one in Abba and has weird staring eyes that seem to be gazing in opposite directions.

I tiptoe in through the white wooden door and instantly recognise a woman – but it's not Una Baines, it's a friend from Leeds I haven't seen in years. When I tell her what I'm doing here, she laughs and shrieks, 'I know junkies!'

You what?

'I know John Quays.'

Ah, I get it. John Quays is a character in the 1977 Fall song 'No Xmas for John Quays'. It's always been assumed 'John Quays' was a pun on 'junkies' allowing Smith to make scornful and, perhaps, a tiny bit hypocritical judgments on those who use hard drugs, relating the story of a junkie who thinks he is more interesting than the world. The John Quays character is certainly a play on words. However, my friend insists there is a real John Quays – he was one of the hazy, crazy, druggy entourage that used to hang around The Fall. Apparently, she knows him well because he lives just round the corner. I'm starting to feel I can hardly go out of the house without stumbling down another avenue of The Wonderful and Frightening World.

Suddenly, my friend's attention is grabbed by a middle-aged yet still youthful-looking woman staring quizzically in our direction. She wears a plastic coat and her once brown hair is now dyed blonde, giving her the slightly ethereal air of a 1960s heroine but with a Manchester accent and slightly uneven teeth. The moment I sit down with her, the Velvet Underground's first album featuring Nico wafts out from a speaker.

'I used to spend hours listening to this,' says Una Baines, delicately pouring tea. Her eyes are just like those in the fading photo – childlike but wild – although thankfully looking in the same direction these days. In a way she's like The Fall, imperceptibly off-kilter but with the sort of self-effacing sense of humour you'd find in songs like 'Carry Bag Man', or even an episode of *Coronation Street*.

'Oh, my God,' she yells, as I tell her about that photo. 'I looked like a Nazi storm trooper!' When I tell her I'm tracking down everyone who's ever played in The Fall, she howls in disbelief. 'How many years is that going to take you?'

However, when I make a joke about how I might end up looking in mental institutions, the laughter stops dead and she places a hand over the microphone. For the next hour, Baines will matter-of-factly explain that some things about her past can't be printed for the sake of her family. Occasionally, she forgets to cover the microphone and so simply whispers, 'You won't print that, will you?'

Baines met Smith in 1976 at a summer fair in Heaton Park – the leafy greenery still bordering Prestwich – and as they became boyfriend and girlfriend she ended up in the fledgling Fall with Tony Friel and Martin Bramah. She'd grown up with two brothers so it just felt like another 'gang of lads'.

Back then, she says, they were all creative people who were trying to expand their boundaries: 'musically, politically, personally and narcotically'. She paints a picture of a lost, forgotten Britain, where *NME* still had a 'Titpic' (pin-up) and young women in office jobs were forbidden from wearing trousers.

'That's why I wore those ridiculous boots in those photos,' she laughs, 'and skirts down to there . . . it seems a universe away.' Baines describes herself in those days as very young and paranoid: 'I took a lot of drugs and was a bit of a nutcase.'

Maybe, but she was also a radical feminist at a time when to be so risked derision. Baines remembers being labelled a 'man-hater' and being showered with abuse on demonstrations. However, she rejects Kay Carroll's suggestion that they were surrogate sisters, saying she 'didn't really click' with the older woman.

'I used to think, when I'm 29 will I think like that?' Baines plays down Carroll's well documented feminism and insists, herself aside, the biggest feminist in The Fall was actually Mark E Smith.

Although The Fall have had many female musicians (not all of them his wives), Smith is often thought of as a typical, working-class male traditionalist, but Baines says in those days he was the opposite. Together, they'd check out women's groups and opinions across the political left – including the International Marxist Group. However, Baines says they quickly realised it was 'bollocks', especially when someone had a go at her for liking American female punk icon Patti Smith.

'That's when I started to question everything,' she says. 'I had a problem with people who believed in armed revolution. What's the point in more conflict? Up the workers? Why, are they going to behave any better?'

Interestingly, Baines suggests their interest in politics may have triggered The Fall's now fundamental scepticism: 'I think Mark's politics now are neither left nor right. He's very sceptical of anything that's banner-waving or sheep-like, like a club . . .' Which could possibly explain his attitude to his musicians.

In those days, The Fall were democratic and perhaps still left-of-centre. Baines insists the firing of the hapless Tory drummer 'Dave' – who may have been called 'Steve' – was by consensus.

However, within the gang Baines was an individual. A female musician was rare enough in those days, never mind one as odd as Baines. After deciding that bashing biscuit tins for a drum kit was really not a good idea, she took out a bank loan to get herself an electric piano which she calls 'the worst keyboard in the world'. She then got it into her head the bank owed her the money and she would don the boots to march into her branch screaming, 'You owe *me*!'

Apart from her curious approach to finance, Baines seems to have been the first Fall example of what Ben Pritchard called Smith's 'moulding'. The frontman encouraged her to keep her keyboards as simple as possible, which explains why they sound something like a cross between The Seeds and a cat landing on a gas ring. Strangely enough, similar – maybe squawlier – keyboards still feature in The Fall – with Smith's wife Elena playing what he described to me as 'Miiiaaoowwwww . . . space music'.

Baines plays down her own contribution by insisting it was obvious Smith would make an impact, because he was a 'great writer'. But while her boyfriend took up with Kay Carroll and began the group's ascent, his former girlfriend was falling, out of the group and into her own, very personal Wonderful and Frightening World.

As she tells it, she was always an imaginative child and spent hours in a solitary private world. She had two invisible horses – one white, one black – and a terrible fear of anything 'normal', longing for 'anything that was beyond the day-to-day'. Her mother had five children and her biggest dread was ending up 'pushing a pram at 16'.

One day she was listening to Paul McCartney on television talking about

The Beatles' LSD trips . . . and at that moment, she thought she'd been handed the keys to another more adult world. She says she started taking drugs long before The Fall, but once the group took off – aided by her keyboards on 'Bingo-Master's Break-Out!' – her consumption escalated, particularly once Smith dumped her for Carroll and Baines took up with Jonnie Brown, 'running off and living' with the art student for a 'crazy nine weeks'. In the beginning, she didn't realise the new Fall bassist was into heroin, a drug she associated with squalor and needles, not a clean-looking, handsome, intelligent arty type.

'So it was quite seductive,' she relates. 'I wanted to break down boundaries, but with hindsight taking drugs was not the way to do it. It was actually quite dangerous. It wasn't a normal state of mind.'

Eventually, Baines was stuffing so much into her body, often at the same time, she suffered an overdose of cocaine and morphine – the 'speedball' cocktail instrumental in many rock deaths. She says she lost weeks out of her life.

'There's days, weeks that don't make sense,' she whispers, although this period is censored by lack of memory rather than a hand over the microphone. But she vividly remembers being 'rescued'. She'd gone back to Smith and Carroll's flat at Kingswood Road to find no one home, but a woman called Karen arrived and took her to her parents.

'I remember it being brilliant sunlight on the motorway,' she says, incredulously. 'In fact it was dark, at night . . . When we got to the house I thought the floor was made of music and she was the angel Gabriel . . . I can remember it in graphic detail. I thought I'd gone to the four corners of the earth. Really weird stuff!'

The path of The Wonderful and Frightening World had led her to a 'hospital'. Here, she shrouds the details, but remembers that for ages it felt like her whole personality had 'shattered into pieces'. She remembers a visit from her father, but the rest is just . . . fragments, moments grabbed on the long road to recovery. But she feels lucky, and believes the breakdown probably saved her life or at least stopped her becoming an addict. She giggles. 'Not that I chose it.'

According to Baines, her state of mind was the reason she became the third to leave The Fall: 'Contrary to Mark's claims, he never sacked me. I was just too ill.' She says Smith invited her to play more gigs, during which she would stand gazing at the keyboard, which the audience thought was all part of the 'act'. When she first left, Smith dedicated the song 'Mother-Sister' to her from the stage, so if he's since rewritten history, it may be an act of revenge for Baines subsequently taking up with Martin Bramah (they split years ago, but are still friendly and have a child) and forming Blue Orchids, who won much critical acclaim.

'Mark had this weird idea that I'd betrayed The Fall.' According to Baines, she was in Manchester club Rafters one night talking to journalist Paul Morley and made a joke that if she formed a band with Brown they'd call themselves The Lunatics. She thinks Smith overheard her and suspected an act of treachery, 'when it was just this ridiculous line'.

But either way, that was that.

Baines – now a mother-of-three who has worked in community housing – insists she has no regrets.

'I am strong now,' she smiles. 'I was extremely paranoid in those days. There was a lot of acid around The Fall. I took too much. I wanted to break down barriers and I thought that was the way to do it . . . it's not the way. You go to a counsellor and you stop taking drugs! But I survived.'

These days, Baines still dabbles in music – her latest band are HM Poetic Terrorists, a curious blend of intricate guitars and shouty punk rock vocals who do sound at least a bit like early Fall. She says she still goes to Fall gigs and meets up with Smith 'every few years, for a pint and a catch-up'. She says that contrary to belief he's not an 'ogre' and 'far, far more complex' than anyone has ever known. They weren't lovers for long but she got to know him better than most and particularly loves the 'priceless' sense of humour I'd enjoyed during a rare public outing in Malmaison. 'There's what Mark wants people to know, and what is real,' she concludes, beguilingly, as I prepare to exit Chorlton and head elsewhere in The Wonderful and Frightening World. Just as a journalist can encounter various versions of Mark E Smith, I feel like I'm discovering a different side of the man with everyone I encounter. It's like walking into the world depicted by The Fall's 1980 single 'How

I Wrote "Elastic" Man' (in which Smith assesses the impact of becoming a celebrity) and where the only reality is waking up and rubbing your eyes.

CHAPTER 9

'There was an outbreak of fleas.'

I'm starting to realise looking for former members of The Fall is becoming almost as peculiar as life in The Fall. Some afternoons, I find myself sending off pointless letters to houses in Salford that have been knocked down. When I type 'Mike Leigh' into Google in a final quest to unearth the band's late 1970s, jazz-cabaret, PC World-shopping, insurance-selling drummer, I get 4,500,000 entries relating to the film director. A similar fiasco follows an attempt to find Chris Evans – not the famous DJ and broadcaster, but a drummer who apparently filled in for one gig in

Bristol in 2004. I get so obsessed about finding him I even consider, briefly, securing an interview with *the* Chris Evans and asking him if he could pretend to have joined The Fall.

Then there's the peculiar ritual of a daily conversation with Suzanne that goes something like:

'What have you done today?'

'Fired off 75 emails trying to track down members of The Fall.'

Even as a Fall fan herself, Suzanne is starting to bristle at the extent to which it's taking over my whole life. Friends are similarly growing used to a weekend chorus of 'I'd like to come out, but I've got to spend all weekend researching people who used to be in The Fall'.

Meanwhile, my dog, Guinness – who prefers Elvis Presley to The Fall – is starting to bark at me for not taking him on his usual walks. In these really low moments, I naturally stick on an old Fall album for inspiration and fire off a missive to someone like Yvonne Pawlett, who replaced Una Baines in 1978 but left within a few months, allegedly to look after her own dog. Simon Ford, author of The Fall biography *Hip Priest*, kindly gives me an old address he has for her in Doncaster, but I don't expect a reply.

I particularly want to talk to Pawlett, who advertised a cassette of music in the *NME* classifieds in the early 1980s but then disappeared. In old photos she looks as young and innocent as a choir girl, and I wonder what on earth would happen to someone like that in the barmy cauldron of The Fall. Would it be like a Christian being thrown to the lions? Or Mick Taylor who replaced deceased Brian Jones joining the Rolling Stones? He went in a clean-living vegetarian and came out a few years later a chronic junkie.

Equally, Kay Carroll had paid tribute to Pawlett's brief but significant contribution.

'Yvonne was wonderful. I loved her stuff,' she said. 'She had an incredible knowledge of music. We had to rough it a lot but she never compromised. She was very sweet . . . enchanting . . . I liked her a lot.'

The story goes that Pawlett left her German Shepherd behind to join The Fall through an *NME* advert and audition – the only time to my knowledge Smith has adopted such a normal tactic. The keyboard player, from South Yorkshire, was dropped off outside Smith's house by her father. Pawlett's strident, garage rock notes are all over the first Fall album,

1979's *Live at The Witch Trials*. Perversely, this wasn't a live album at all, having been recorded and mixed in two days in a studio in Camden, London, by producer Bob Sargeant. However, it is a quite brilliant document of the early Fall – who skip from punky jazz to jazzy punk in the quirky, compulsive rhythms of 'Futures and Pasts' and the hypnotically splenetic 'Rebellious Jukebox', the title of which still sums up The Fall's stance against prevailing trends.

Pawlett's playing, especially her atypically accomplished introduction to 'Frightened', had been noted in reviews and she appears to the fore on the brilliantly unconventional, mantra-like single 'Rowche Rumble'. But once leaving Smith's tutelage, her musical career stopped dead.

Either Smith had coaxed something from her nobody else was able to tap into, or she really had given up to look after her dog. Simon Ford is under the impression she's some sort of biologist.

I've just about given up on her when the phone rings in the middle of *Coronation Street*. "Ello, it's Yvonne,' she begins simply, sounding not unlike one of the soap's characters. 'Yvonne who used to be in The Fall.'

For the next 30 or so minutes, I further incur Suzanne's wrath by turning *Coronation Street* down to listen to the peculiar words of one of The Fallen.

She explains she'd love to be able to answer my questions but she doesn't really have the time. Her son has just gone away to university and all her spare moments are going into decorating his student residence.

She spends so long talking about this I start to think we could have had time to talk about The Fall. I want to discuss *Live at The Witch Trials*. She keeps returning to paint and soft furnishings. Not unreasonably, she suggests The Fall was 'such a very long time ago'.

After a while, minor details and memories filter in between talk of brushes versus rollers. Yes, her dad did drop her off, it seemed like a big adventure at the time. The Fall were still listening to bands like The Velvet Underground and Can. But every time we edge nearer the thorny subject of what it was like for an unworldly South Yorkshire teenager to be in such an odd band, she seems to clam up and veer off on another tangent. But she's charming, in her way: soft-voiced and motherly and definitely an unlikely recruit for The Fall.

Still, being in The Fall had left her with her a quest for exploration she'd directed back into her love for animals. She'd done a BSc and a Masters in horticultural and environmental sciences, then ended up working in investigative biology: perhaps the ideal profession after what Ben Pritchard suggested was The Fall's 'psychological experiment'.

Pawlett suggests she'll 'think about' my questions and see what she can remember. A few nights later, she calls to say the questions are still propped on the mantelpiece, she even has a scrapbook from her time in the band somewhere and her son – who is awestruck that his decorating, dog-loving mother was in such a famous group – keeps urging her to help. But I never hear from her again.

Before she disappears forever, she does tell me she didn't leave to look after her dog at all – even though the creature was sick at the time – she simply 'never fitted in' and left to pursue biology and breeding German Shepherds. This explanation delights Kay Carroll, who fires off another anecdote concerning Pawlett's mysterious exit.

'I think she got homesick,' she says. 'There was an outbreak of fleas at the [Kingswood Road] house and that really freaked her mother out! It never got nasty with her, she just was like, "I'm going to have to go".'

I can't help wondering if Smith – one of Britain's most avid conspiracy theorists – suspected any connection between the keyboardist's love of German Shepherds and The Fall going down with fleas.

A couple of days later, I'm listening to 'Mess of My', the Fall song from 1978 which contains salty Smith diatribes about being as strong as your weakest link when an email arrives from Martin Bramah, founder Fall guitarist.

That's the good news. The bad news, he doesn't want to talk to me. 'It's all well documented,' he says, via his other band Blue Orchids' virtually dormant website. But it isn't, really. Little is known about Bramah apart from his two spells in The Fall, which included an unexpected return in 1990 for *Extricate*, one of The Fall's most successful albums. I saw his comeback that summer when he strode onstage unannounced at Sheffield Leadmill wearing the sort of silver shirt you'd usually see in a glam rock band. This curious apparel aside, his brilliant, short bursts of jaggedly sweet guitar melody suggested he'd never been away. Since then, all I had to go on were rumours that one of the all-time great Fall guitarists was now driving a bus.

Undeterred, I fire off a load of questions about The Fall's demented dynamic and what he's doing now. This time, his reply is a little more forthcoming: 'Sorry to be so awkward. Your questions are very interesting, but it's all too personal to be put in the public domain.'

I can hardly argue. Apart from his two spells in The Fall, Bramah has also been particularly embroiled in the group's complex romantic history. He first left The Fall to form Blue Orchids with Una Baines, Smith's former squeeze and the mother of Bramah's child. On returning he embarked on a relationship with another keyboard player, Marcia Schofield. It's often rumoured Smith takes a dim view of such behaviour – like any office, perhaps romances are a privilege of the boss. Either way, Bramah's exit the second time was painful. He was abandoned at a foreign airport exactly as Paul Hanley had described one of Smith's favourite pranks – taking members abroad, just to send them back.

Bramah can't be persuaded to break his silence and I respect that as much as I respect anyone who has survived The Fall, but an unexpected ping in my inbox brings an email with this short but significant message: 'I bet you haven't talked to Eric McGann.' And there's a phone number.

'You've got to be a hard case to be in The Fall.'

He's right. I haven't talked to Eric McGann. I'm not as Fall-encyclopaedic as some of the Fall fans out there but I like to think I know my former members. I confess I have never heard of this one who, it appears, replaced Jonnie Brown on bass after Brown replaced Tony Friel. The situation is further muddied when Bramah says he also goes by the names Rick Goldstraw, Eric Echo and even Eric the Ferret. I phone the number and a soft Salford voice answers. He's never given an interview about The Fall since leaving in 1978.

When McGann exited, the charts were full of the Bee Gees and Village People, punk was fading into the new wave of Squeeze and Elvis Costello, and Son of Sam killer David Berkowitz faced 25 years in jail. McGann/Goldstraw/Echo/Ferret says he'll do an interview but only over the phone and he doesn't want his photo taken.

However, we've hardly begun talking when it becomes obvious he was definitely in The Fall. He begins by describing one gig where he was hit by a flying chair.

'My daughter was in the front row and she was getting a lot of hassle from some National Front skinheads,' he explains, bringing up an unfortunate feature of punk-related gigs at the time. 'I had to stop playing to help her.' However, like Fela Kuti, Smith took umbrage at this development and told Ferret in no uncertain terms to 'Start bloody playing'. Then he threw a chair at him onstage. Ferret, as you would, resumed playing. However, none of this has troubled his undoubted admiration for our leader.

'The Fall never, ever cruise,' he states, awestruck after all this time, adding dutifully, 'You've got to be a hard case to be in The Fall.' What's more, Ferret says actual violence in The Fall was rare – it was more the threat of it, to put the group on its mettle.

However, there were plenty of rucks at live gigs, but between band and audience, not between The Fall and Smith. Smith would often encourage hostility by baiting restless audiences with jibes like 'The difference between you and us is we've got brains' – as immortalised on *Totale's Turns (It's Now or Never)*. While gigs often involved projectiles, actual day-to-day life was apparently quite sedate.

Ferret remembers a certain togetherness, especially as the line-up extended to include South Mancunian Steve Hanley and Craig Scanlon (from nearby Beswick – he moved to Prestwich in 1990). However, he agrees with Ben Pritchard that Fall musicians were never secure enough to feel they were in the group and the difference in those days was that these Fall musicians were fans of the band – big fans, years before Smith decided against employing 'fans of the bloody group'. They'd all hang around at gigs, loading gear, occasionally looking for a smile from our leader.

According to Ferret, for lads with few prospects the attraction of joining The Fall was to be whisked away from Prestwich to see the world – much like early twentieth-century soldiers were excited to be drafted. But, once they went abroad, they'd mostly just sit in pubs. They could do that in Prestwich. No, there was something else. For people like Eric the Ferret, the biggest motivation was the opportunity to view, at close quarters, a bona fide genius at work.

'You really get to listen to his lyrics and when you're in the group you realise you how clever the kid is,' he says, sounding more like a teenager than a 50-something. In fact, like Una Baines, he reveals he still follows The Fall.

'Mark's fantastic,' he says. 'I've watched him create soundscapes. People assume he's just trying to wreck the amps, but he creates these collages of sound and voice. Mark is a musician who doesn't play an instrument. But he's sharp, musically. I don't know anyone else who is as relevant. The Fall are the one thing Britain has that America can never have. Most people in music just pose. They have nothing to say except "Look at me".'

Playing onstage with The Fall was a 'magic hour' which they lived for. Ferret says the musicians he played with 'worshipped' Smith and none would ever criticise Smith because he 'made' them. Ferret goes even further, suggesting that among some band members Smith was actually known as 'God'.

Perhaps in the way Jesus instructed his disciples, or Smith's father taught his plumbers, perhaps there is something supernatural or mystical in the way Smith 'takes the crap people do' and turns it into brilliance – the musical equivalent of turning water into wine. Years before Ben Pritchard, Ferret tells how you could join The Fall being barely able to hold a guitar and within weeks be informed by the music papers you were 'the best thing since sliced bread'.

Ferret was an ordinary bass player when he joined The Fall – 'my thing was just to hold down the sound, not that wild thing which they had before' – but realised that by joining the band he subtly transformed the sound. Similarly, cajoled by Smith, he found himself able to write songs, not just 'Mess of My', for which he is credited on record. 'I penned quite a few, actually,' he says, 'but credits are a lottery in The Fall, if you know what I mean.'

Smith defends this charge in his autobiography, essentially saying that he gives credit where it's due. For example, he says that 'Blindness' is essentially a cover of an Iggy Pop song and so Iggy Pop is the only person that can really be said to have written it (although in fact Smith is referring to 'Ibis-Afro Man' from *Are You Are Missing Winner*, which was based on Pop's 'African Man'). But maybe this also explains why Fall musicians subsequently seem to fail. Without Smith's life-force, they are bereft. Or perhaps they are never great musicians, just great Fall musicians. Which may explain why even a Martin Bramah – 'the best guitarist in the world' according to the Hanleys – could be suddenly despatched.

We talk a bit more about Ferret's view of Smith, whom he regards as the genuine item, not a rock performer – 'Mark is that guy, 24 hours a day,' he argues. He also suggests Smith wants things to be so good and to have 'that edge' he bears 'a cost' for fronting The Fall.

I'm curious. What is the cost?

'The way he works, the things he uses . . . they take their toll,' he says, but doesn't elaborate. Just as I'm thinking this Ferret may not be about to squeak, we start talking about Martin Bramah, who played with him in Blue Orchids. The pair had another musical partnership backing Nico, at a time when the German chanteuse was hauling herself around Europe's flea pits playing gigs to pay for heroin. However, the Ferret seems as matter-of-fact about this episode as he is when dropping the revelation that he himself took heroin in those days to combat 'stage fright'. It's a tiny reminder that some musical experiences may be even more bizarre than The Fall.

Ferret – who now manages and plays with Salford poet John Cooper Clarke, himself an ex-heroin addict who occasionally supports The Fall –

says he is one of the few people to be in touch with both Smith and Bramah, who did indeed drive buses for a spell in London.

Ferret agrees with the Hanleys that Bramah's short, attack-like guitar defined the Fall sound and suggests, while they were friends, a sense of competitiveness between Smith and Bramah fuelled their music.

The pair had been 'very close', discovering music together around Prestwich. 'And when people are close,' ponders the Ferret, 'when there's a fallout, it's a big fallout.' Perhaps Smith never forgave Bramah for the perceived betrayal of leaving The Fall to join with Baines. Yet, when the guitarist returned in 1989, he was a hired hand, not a cornerstone of the group. Had Smith brought Bramah back in 1989 just to wreak revenge?

He says the backdrop to the second fallout was indeed Bramah's relationship with Marcia Schofield, but the final showdown was over matters musical.

'Martin fell for all that big shot stuff. "Here I am, back in the band..."' suggests the Ferret, and that silver shirt at Sheffield Leadmill suddenly seems significant. Bramah had broken Smith's most cardinal law – in acting like a rock star, he 'played into Mark's hands'.

Ferret relates how Smith didn't just abandon Bramah thousands of miles away from home, in Australia, but dumped him just before they went to Japan, a country Bramah had wanted to visit all his life. This seems extraordinarily cruel; maybe it's just comical.

'Fair play to Smithy, he kills me!' the Ferret laughs. 'He should have his own TV show.'

These days, Smith and Bramah are at an impasse. Bramah 'will not sell himself off the back of Mark' – perhaps another reason for his silence. Meanwhile, Smith refuses to work with his founder guitarist because, in more football parlance, he's 'got the ball, and refuses to pass it'.

Pranks aside, perhaps the collapse of the Smith-Bramah relationship – the Jagger-Richards of The Fall – is genuinely one of the group's forgotten tragedies. If that competitiveness spawned the music, what sounds could they unleash now, after three decades of rancour? The Ferret believes – while The Fall could have been 'massive' with Bramah, their most pop-oriented guitarist apart from Brix Smith – if they'd carried on together The Fall would not exist. Another cruel paradox.

Ferret adores Bramah as much as he reveres Smith and he's trying to coax Bramah out of retirement. He breaks off to play me a blast of Bramah's new guitar sound down the phone. It's raw, psychedelic – and nothing like The Fall.

'Martin says he doesn't want to sound like The Fall,' suggests the Ferret, audibly exasperated. 'I tell him, "We were the bloody Fall".' But not for long. Despite the Ferret's reverence, he only lasted three months himself.

What happened?

'We were driving to do a Peel session and the van suddenly stopped to pick up this bloke,' he remembers. 'Hawaiian shirt. Bloody bongos! It wasn't what I thought The Fall should be.' The Ferret resigned on the spot. He's regretted it ever since.

I need to find that bongo player.

CHAPTER 10

'I was living this incredible double life!'

Y ou never really quite know when you're going to encounter a ghost
from The Wonderful and Frightening World, and for Steve Hanley
a spirit from the past arrived when he was sat down watching telly.
The programme on the box was Peter Kay's *Phoenix Nights* and Hanley found
himself captivated by a character onscreen. 'It couldn't be,' he asked himself
... but he was sure it really was: the very same bongo player who caused
Eric the Ferret to walk out in disgust in 1978.

That bongo player was the sixteenth disciple – the sixteenth to join The Fall.

All I have to go on is a name. Unfortunately, it's a very common one: Steve Davies. There is a Stephen Davies listed on the *Phoenix Nights* cast list but with no other information, so maybe it wasn't him. A search on Google for 'Steve Davies' throws up 1,420,000 entries. There's Stephen Davies, a 'Pr/blogger', Professor S G Davies who works in chemistry research, and Stephen Michael Davies, a professional left-handed wicketkeeper/batsman. It could be worse. He could be called Steve Davis, which would give me 50,600,000 items relating to the snooker player.

However, the Fall website – which has barely any details about crucial founder members – turns out to be a relative mine of information about the disappearing and reappearing bongo man.

He first appears in Fall history adding congas to the first Peel session in May 1978, which an old interview with Marc Riley suggests was a ruse by Smith to up the BBC session fee by taking an extra member.

Then Davies disappears for two years, abruptly making a reappearance on the 1980 Dutch tour as a stand-in for Paul Hanley who – aged just 16 – is taking time out to do his O-levels. After the Dutch tour, during which he borrowed and managed to demolish a drum kit, it appears he took up Afro-Cuban and Brazilian hand drumming. He now runs a percussion and dance workshop with the hefty name Baba Yaga Global Percussion & Arts Workshops, which is how I find him. Davies is another forgotten cog in The Fall's demented past, but is about to break decades of near-silence. An email returns within days of my contacting the Baba Yaga website: 'Sure, I'll talk about The Fall.' He immediately confirms Hanley's suspicions. He was indeed on *Phoenix Nights*: 'I played Darius.'

The solitary photo that exists of Davies in his Fall days isn't like Darius or anyone else on *Phoenix Nights*. It depicts a crop-haired, mischievous-looking youth. Now in his fifties, he's greyer, bigger, with a ruddier complexion and a hazy, rather absent-minded demeanour reminiscent of a seasoned dope smoker.

'Some American guy in the Far East turned me onto Lebanese weed and that was it,' admits Davies. Later, when a number of The Fallen are photographed for the newspaper, the percussionist turns up wielding a feather duster. With the possible exception of the Pope, Rod Hull's Emu or Yvonne Pawlett, he's the last person you'd expect to have once been in The Fall.

'It's very hazy,' he sighs. Yet, he says, when he was in The Fall he adopted a 'very healthy' lifestyle – far removed from the usual Faller diet of beer, more beer and speed.

But the bongo man wasn't a usual Faller.

For a start, Davies was older than the line-up he joined and thus wasn't another willing indoctrinee who would put up with all manner of psychological assault courses just to escape the snugs of Prestwich. By the time he joined up with Smith's barmy army, he'd been in the navy and had been in prison – which is where he often is today, but providing percussion for workshops rather than doing time for some mystery offence. In the 1960s, he travelled around the States and even worked for the Kennedys, another experience he insists must otherwise remain a secret.

'I'd taken myself to the edge,' he admits. Which perhaps aroused the interest of the boss.

Crucially, Davies lived in Prestwich, which often seems to be the only qualification needed to join Britain's most parochial band. Once again, the bongo man just seemed to career into Smith's orbit. He had a mate who knew Kay Carroll and their paths crossed in the grounds of Prestwich Psychiatric Hospital, where various undesirables including Baines and Carroll gathered to smoke pot.

The mental hospital loomed large over Prestwich back then. Not least because, according to Davies, its inmates often roamed the streets. 'In those days they used to just let them wander around,' he says. Thus, in 1978 and 1980, Prestwich was crawling with chemically enhanced nurses, the mentally disturbed, and past and current members of The Fall.

'We'd live alongside each other really. There were some wonderful characters,' sniggers Davies, 'and that's how I met Mark.' Davies smoked pot, and was into Can, the seminal German band whose doctrine of Repetition so strongly influenced The Fall.

Davies suggests his involvement was much earlier than is actually recorded – he says he was 'there or thereabouts' at the beginning, jamming in rehearsals with Bramah, Smith and Baines, but not actually joining the group.

But maybe that was the point. Gradually, Davies seems to have been 'moulded' as effectively as Ben Pritchard. Before he joined, he listened to jazz legend Miles Davis, admired the 'competence of musicians' and when not puffing on spliffs spent nights doing gym work and Thai boxing, in the belief it would make him a great drummer. All these notions would be beaten out of him in The Fall.

The Peel session appearance notwithstanding, it's likely Smith decided to actively recruit Davies into the Fall live line-up after watching him around Manchester playing in bands like Victor Draygo (who possibly partly inspired Fall song 'Draygo's Guilt', in which Smith talks of guitars that turn and stab you) and Victor Brox And The Blues Train. The latter combo's singer was described in the British Blues Review of June 1989 as having a Smith-like "Edwardian impresario" approach to musicians he deemed "fortunate enough" to play with him.

'We used to back all the American blues artists like Johnny Guitar Watson and Jimmy Witherspoon,' says Davies, providing a vocal snapshot of the forgotten, godforsaken live circuit The Fall were up against at the time. The *NME* were writing about Joy Division and Siouxsie and The Banshees but most clubs up and down the country were still hosting hippie bands with beards and jobbing blues guitarists. The spiky Fall sound wasn't exactly what Davies listened to, but that night he grasped their indefinable appeal.

'They were so refreshing after all that 1970s rock stuff, Pink Floyd and that, which had dragged on too long,' he says, remembering how he'd seen Pink Floyd at Knebworth a year earlier and the prog rock legends were so out of tune he felt 'embarrassed' to watch them.

Watching other people watch The Fall, Davies realised there was 'this wave of tremendous energy which the hippies hated'. He remembers Smith's group then as being very experimental – Smith's vocals were more like a 'collage of ideas' than singing – and so he felt honoured when the singer finally asked him to join.

However, there was a twist – Davies was an aspiring percussionist, not a drummer. He'd never owned or played a drum kit in his life. Displaying just the sort of dementia or genius that holds Fall fans in awe, Smith suggested this wouldn't be a problem, he could just borrow a kit and play 11 dates in 14 nights in a foreign country.

Davies remembers the tour of Holland he was thrown into as being 'absolutely crazy'. Using the borrowed kit, he had so little technique it gradually fell to pieces every night while all he could do was 'whack the hell out of it and hope it was in time'.

Kay Carroll remembers the night the drum stool collapsed, leaving Davies slowly shrinking behind the kit while his knobbly knees came up over the snare drum. 'It was the funniest thing I've ever seen,' she shrieks.

Typically, hazy Davies can't remember the specifics, but suggests there were so many things like that they all blur into one. 'Um, ah . . .' he begins, and trails off once again. Luckily, one or two tapes survive from that tour. In one of them – recorded at Eindhoven Effenaar – Smith introduces 'City Hobgoblins' by telling the crowd, 'We'll stick punk rock up your fucking arse. Right, here's a good one – it's a bit of fucking culture for you. Right, Hobgoblins! Davies! Hit the fucking cowbell quick!'

And he does. The insanity was compounded by Davies' driving between gigs, which he says 'terrified' the musicians almost as much as Kay Carroll. 'I was doing *French Connection*-style driving.' He's laughing loudly. 'They were very dull, y'know!'

There were a lot of capers, but Davies admits he didn't really bond with the 'Jesuit lads' – a name coined by Smith for a mythical (not actually religious) group of Fall musicians, also including Craig Scanlon and Steve Hanley, who were known for their particular devotion to the cause and unstinting dignity of labour. They were so much younger, and appalled by the Hawaiian shirt. 'They must have been thinking, "Look at that shirt",' he laughs. '"What's he doing in the band?"'

Another difficulty was lifestyle. Davies could smoke pot with anyone, but found it particularly difficult to keep up with the apparent Fall requirements of seriously heavy drinking. 'I tried,' he pleads, 'but it was hard!' There were money issues as well.

Because The Fall had a growing following, Carroll was able to challenge the 'pay to play' policy that existed in many venues – and The Fall were able to command large fees – but because it was ploughed back into the group or behind the bar little made its way to Davies, who became the third Fall drummer – after 'Dave/Steve' and the PC World-shopping Mike Leigh – to sell insurance.

'I was leading this incredible double life,' he says, describing playing gigs at night and selling insurance policies to housewives in the daytime, who presumably had no idea what the smiling man in the suit did after hours.

I can relate to this madness. In the 1990s, when I was working for the now defunct *Melody Maker* magazine, I too lived a crazy double life. I could be jetting around the world, interviewing Jarvis Cocker about the size of his penis and spending nights quaffing champagne with Michael Hutchence ('Have you met Kylie? You should.') ... but then I'd go back to a two-bedroom former council house, where I'd receive sackloads of packages in the post to the bemusement of neighbours who thought I was either on the dole or selling drugs.

I lived like that – freelancing, not selling drugs – for years until I sent a review in to the *Guardian*. But for Davies, who had a mortgage, something had to give, and that something was The Fall, although he never asked to leave. Paul Hanley came back, and the incredible double life was over.

'Could I have become a permanent member?' he muses, asking a question which has nagged him ever since. 'Possibly, but Mark never asked me.' However, like Friel and Carroll, Davies doesn't rule out a return either – although I somehow can't see Smith salivating at the prospect of what he suggests would be The Fall with an 'African percussive twist'.

At the time, though, Davies decided he 'never wanted to play with a rock band ever again' and plunged into percussion. Then, following some sort of 'mid-life crisis', he enrolled at the Northern School of Ballet, where he found himself in the bizarre situation of being interviewed by a fellow student who couldn't believe an ex-member of his favourite band of all time was prancing alongside him in class.

Davies never did entirely sever connections with The Wonderful and Frightening World. He reveals Kay Carroll emailed him recently – like me, looking for Karl Burns – but he was unable to help beyond suggesting the drummer may be 'in the hillsides' around Rossendale, Lancashire, where they formed Victor Draygo.

The bongo man reveals that for some time after leaving the group, he was regularly allowed backstage but one day visited Smith at home to find the metaphorical drawbridge being pulled up. Messages were posted through the door to no avail: he'd been discarded like all the rest. He wonders what the reception would be now, if they bumped into each other in the street.

'People get a bit starstruck with Mark, and he's very detached,' he says. Smith's misanthropy is 'a defence thing. Working-class, stiff upper lip.' Davies knew Smith was a big drinker but was taken aback when someone suggested the singer might be an alcoholic, although reasons if this was the case it would explain 'some of the behaviour'. He doesn't wish to dwell on this aspersion from long ago. 'I'm quite protective towards Mark.' That devoted loyalty again – after all these years and that rejection, it's rather touching.

I can't help wondering: could Smith have been an alcoholic as long ago as 1980? After all, he did sing about grappling with terrible urges to drink during the early hours, in 1982's 'Hard Life in the Country' on *Room to Live (Undilutable Slang Truth)*. Were alcohol-fuelled flights of fantasy the source of apparently crazy ideas like recruiting drummers who couldn't play drums? And if he was – or remains – an alcoholic, how on earth has the Fall Factory managed to keep producing output for 30 years?

Maybe my next informant will provide some insight. After all, as Davies was on the way out, another was coming in.

CHAPTER 11

'There are a lot of skeletons in the Fall cupboard, stories that haven't been told.'

Like any classic long-running British soap opera, The Fall has minor characters and major characters, although even the latter can suddenly disappear and the saga just rolls on. In the bewildering Fall cast, few characters have made as much impact with their appearance and disappearance as Marc Riley – who has since gone on to other prominent roles but during his time in The Fall (June 1978 to December

1982) loomed as large over events and music as Ken Barlow in *Coronation Street*.

What I know about Riley is this: he joined after hanging around with The Fall and becoming one of their sporadic road crew. Thus, Riley replaced Eric the Ferret, who replaced Jonnie Brown, who replaced Tony Friel. He became the eleventh disciple to join in the first two years, his reign predating but outlasting Steve Davies. In the month he signed up, cricketer Ian Botham became the first man in the history of the game to score a century and take eight wickets in one innings of a Test match. Albums lining up against The Fall's 1979 *Live at the Witch Trials* debut at the time included Prince's debut *For You*, Dire Straits' first eponymous album, Bruce Springsteen's *Darkness on the Edge of Town* and X-Ray Spex's punky, saxophoney *Germfree Adolescents*. Margaret Thatcher was in power. It seems a world away.

As does December 1982, the month he left, when Thatcher still had years ahead of her, but the pop landscape was changing. Manchester greats like The Smiths and New Order were edging towards *Top of the Pops*. Neil Kinnock was elected Labour leader and Michael Jackson's *Thriller* rapidly became the biggest-selling album of all time. Riley's five-year stint was a relative lifetime in The Wonderful and Frightening World but coincides with the beginnings of The Fall's noble ascent from indie cultdom to national institution.

Riley was one of the 'Jesuit lads' as well. I remember watching these legendary characters at gigs: silent, heads down, trying not to catch any crowd attention or their leader's eye while Smith unleashed his torrents of sarcasm, insight and bile. And yet, Riley was different.

A big, swarthy youth who looked tougher and older than his age, on the rare occasions he did look up to face the audience he had a certain glint in his eye that suggested a man of more individual talents and – perhaps – his own mind.

Riley was just 16 when he began helping shuffle The Fall's amps and guitars into punk clubs and WMCs in late 1970s Doncaster and Preston: not old enough to vote or join the British Army, but man enough for The Fall. His first task in the studio was to provide twangy, melodic bass to Bramah's 'It's The New Thing', the second Fall single and Smith's sarcastic broadside against manufactured pop groups and svengalis which in hindsight, apart from the suggestion of trendy clothing, doesn't sound dissimilar to the way he runs The Fall.

Once Riley started playing lead guitar over the hypnotic rhythms of Craig Scanlon, their twin-guitar soundscapes became the engine room of The Fall's first – and to some best – truly golden period.

Riley's melodic style powered 1979's classic single 'Rowche Rumble' and the *Live at the Witch Trials* and *Dragnet* albums. But once he became involved in song writing, Riley's credits seemed to up the band a gear. He co-wrote a good half of the sinister, compelling *Dragnet* including the classic 'Psychick Dance Hall' and had a hand in 'Rowche Rumble' and another killer single, 'Fiery Jack'. He co-wrote over half of *Grotesque*, every single song on *Slates* and even *Perverted by Language*'s 'I Feel Voxish', which emerged in 1983 after he'd gone. He was also in the line-up I saw at the Riley-Smith in 1981 and at every Fall gig I went to over the next couple of years. Then he too vanished and The Fall never sounded quite the same again.

A decade and a half later, Riley is no longer a Jesuit lad but is arguably equally hardworking – but for the BBC, not The Wonderful and Frightening World. His offices are the Beeb's Manchester headquarters on Oxford Road – a fading, grey epicentre which itself still looks like a hangover from an architect's futurist fantasy of the 1960s or early 1970s. Unusually among The Fallen, since Riley left the nest he has risen to a profile higher than Smith's. Although he enjoyed a stint in his own post-Fall band, The Creepers, Riley's big success has been on British radio.

He first emerged on the *Beeb* in the early 1990s, when he was sidekick to Mark Radcliffe on Radio One FM's cult music show *Hit The North*, where they'd play the latest hot offering by trendy bands like Suede alongside the music that inspired them – in Suede's case Bowie and The Smiths.

Nowadays, Riley is better known as 'Lard' – the DJ and occasional butt of jokes – who, again alongside Radcliffe, became part of a formidable comic duo who fronted Radio One's flagship *Breakfast Show* for six months in 1997. At the time, I was despatched to their Oxford Road nerve centre to file a piece for *Melody Maker*, but to be honest wasn't as impressed by being in the HQ of the supposed hottest and hippest DJ team on British radio as I was to be in a room with the co-writer of 'Container Drivers'. In person, Riley had the same matey, blokey 'boy Lard' persona that works so well on radio but I suspected concealed steel. You can't, after all, spend five years in The Fall without developing some toughness.

It was that toughness or combative edge which probably did for Radcliffe and Riley. They grew more impatient with the constraints of Radio One's infamous playlist and increasingly began making subtle but sarcastic – even Smith-like – comments about the records they were forced to play and somehow it was no surprise when they were moved to a less high-profile afternoon slot, to make way for the more conventionally zany Zoe Ball.

In the parallel universe of Prestwich, Smith was becoming publicly irked by the rise to stardom of one of his former employees. He told an interviewer how he found himself confronted by Riley's enlarged head on an enormous billboard in Manchester city centre and found it 'fuckin' scary. I thought I was going to die and all the people I'd ever known were going to flash before my eyes.'

These days, Riley enjoys a lower but perhaps more fulfilling profile as presenter of BBC 6 Music's *Brain Surgery*, still at Oxford Road. Currently broadcasting for three nights a week, it's another mix of old and new records designed to 'educate and entertain' like the original *Out On Blue Six*. His own Rebellious Jukebox.

Contacting him is as easy as firing off an email to the BBC 6 Music website.

'What exactly are you doing?' comes the surprisingly quick reply. Riley says he is forever getting asked to do Fall interviews and rarely does them because he's got nothing to gain and plenty to lose – interviews by former members do not generally go down well in the Smith household.

I email again, explaining I'm tracking down 40-odd former members of The Fall. 'Ha ha ha ha ha. You're crazy. I'll do it!'

Now a powerfully if not entirely athletically-built man in his forties, Riley still has the gentle, matey voice from the *Breakfast Show* and his conversation is peppered with 'mate's and talk of pints which is a second language to many a Fall fan. However, despite his shift from making records to playing them, Riley has never left The Wonderful and Frightening World. We've barely begun talking when he reveals that far from hanging out at showbiz parties he's yet another member of The Fallen who still goes to the gigs.

I'm starting to suspect part of the reason The Fall are currently attracting their biggest audiences in years is that they're stuffed to the gills with former members of The Fall.

'I've just seen them on this [latest] tour,' chirps the former Lard, explaining that at gigs he still has to adopt the head-down posture, not to avoid the leader of The Fall but the gaze of curious Fall fans. 'They were great,' he says of the band he left behind. It's typical of the way The Fall operate that despite their former guitarist being in a position to help them considerably – and the sort of media figure any other band would schmooze – Riley's name doesn't ever appear on Fall guest lists.

'You're joking, aren't you?!' he splutters. 'He was scribbling my wife's name off when I was still in the band!' Thus, we're onto The Fall's bewildering but effective working methods, which he describes as 'fraught'.

The matey, blokey tones give way to something discernibly harder – he sounds more like a BBC war correspondent than jokey 'Lard'. Riley says Smith's doctrine of tension was so entrenched, even by the late 1970s, when he joined, that whenever things seemed to get comfortable, the boss would 'throw a spanner into the works'.

Not that Riley disapproves. 'He thinks it's creative, and I think he's right.'

Smith's beliefs – often literally drummed into his musicians – are not given up easily even 25 or so years later. Similarly, Riley describes how Smith and Kay Carroll controlled the purse strings to control The Fall – musicians never knew when they would or wouldn't be paid because this kept them 'nervous'. But Riley concurs again.

'We weren't really "musicians",' he suggests. 'We were just kids who were learning to play as we went along.' And to do that meant getting with the programme.

Unlike the Ferret, Riley doesn't call his old boss 'God' but retains respect even after so long apart. He sees Smith as an 'almost Dickensian' character – a one-off in the rock world, 'more Hunter S Thompson than Roger Daltrey', but with characteristics of a harsh but benevolent leader. 'If he ruled the country there wouldn't be people walking round in hooded tops robbing old age pensioners.'

Riley may have been even younger than Ben Pritchard when he joined, but in those days – suggesting Smith has indeed 'mellowed' – there was no great friendship between the Fall leader and his most junior ever pupil. Riley was a worker and Smith was the boss, and, as such, demanded discipline, even subservience. However, in 1982, a heavily jetlagged Fall played a gig in Australia – not a great one, but not a bad one – and, as we have heard, Smith does not do 'average'.

The band relaxed after the show by heading for the dance floor. As the musicians gyrated away to The Clash's hit 'Rock the Casbah', Smith came up and slapped each member one by one. Fatefully, when it came to Riley, the guitarist raised his hand to stop Smith and punched him back.

That punch – an act of resistance unheard of in The Fall – was his P45. One story – given to me by another former member – suggests Riley was sacked on his wedding day because getting married meant he missed a rehearsal, but he says this is only half-true, at best. In Christmas 1982, both Riley and Steve Hanley were getting married but didn't dare mention such a development to Smith or Carroll. Riley was married on Christmas Eve and the first couple to be hitched when the registry office reopened after New Year were the Hanleys. They both announced their new marital status at the next rehearsal, but while Riley was sacked a few days later, Hanley wasn't. However, conflicting accounts sum up the wider confusion that has always surrounded Riley's departure and it seems time to try to set the record straight.

One repeated suggestion is that Riley wanted a career outside The Fall. In 'Middle Mass', on the 1981 *Slates* album, Smith narrates the tale of a hapless young musician seduced by the music publishers of Tin Pan Alley – Riley has always insisted it's about him, something Smith rejects. Either way, Riley denies he wanted to play with anyone else and would never have formed The Creepers if he'd remained in The Fall.

The other line, which he also denies, is that he wanted The Fall to go in a more pop-oriented direction.

'The way The Fall went was the way Mark wanted them to go,' he insists, conceding that while they were 'very influential and totally ahead of their time', the poppiest they got while he was there was his co-written 'Fiery Jack', a torrent of spiky rockabilly. But he also mentions his involvement in The Fall's 'weirder' songs like 'Spector vs Rector', written by Riley and Craig Scanlon, and the accusing 'Hip Priest', 'which we all got a credit for'.

'I never tried to turn them into a pop band,' he says, pointing out correctly that The Fall became poppier without him.

'I loved The Fall after I was booted out. "Cruiser's Creek", "Oh! Brother", "No Bulbs". "Hit The North" is possibly the best record they ever made. In fact as I left they became ridiculously poppy!' He suggests there may have been a 'smokescreen put up to hide the fact that . . . I did write a lot of songs in The Fall but . . .' His voice fades.

It's likely that growing insubordination – typified by that punch – may have hastened Riley's exit. The album credits for 1982 albums *Hex Enduction Hour* and *Room To Live* show very little Riley, but he insists that he was writing better than ever and in fact, uncredited, penned or helped pen all but one song 'Fortress' of *Hex*.

'He doesn't sack everyone and I'm not sure he craves that reputation,' he considers of his former mentor. 'It's not easy being in The Fall, but it can't have been easy working in The Magic Band with Beefheart. Mark has got this mindset and he will always follow it. If you're going to work with someone like that you're just going to have to put up with it, he's made more good decisions than bad ones and more great records than not so great ones.

'It's very possible that he didn't like what I was doing at the time. Mark does like turnover. He'd had some good stuff out of me and maybe it was the end of my time.'

Typically, Smith turned it all into another joke. The cover of The Fall's *In a Hole*, the live album of that Australasian visit, is of a newspaper clipping depicting a smiling Riley arriving at the airport, under the headline 'Happy Fall guitarist'.

Two years later, The Fall were performing a song called 'Hey! Marc Riley', which refers to Riley as a 'dancer' and calls him a 'pillock'. However, the future Lard fired his own joke back, using The Creepers as the launch pad for a song called 'Jumper Clown, Warts 'n' All', in which the lyrics – 'Dare to dance on an Aussie dance floor/ Bloody nose, bloody poor!/ 'Cos you're a jumper clown' – make reference to the Aussie incident and Smith's idiosyncratic taste in knitwear.

Although there's possibly the slightest hint of regret, Riley insists he has no hard feelings. In fact, years after Riley was fired, the pair 'sort of made up'. A 'mate' of Riley's was having a birthday party and both had been invited. However, Riley found himself surprised to be told by a third party, 'Mark wants a word with you.'

'We got on great,' he reveals. 'I told him I still loved the albums. It was a bit like two drunken blokes saying, "You're great", "No, you're great!"' However, shortly after, a compilation album came out with Riley's songs on it and, needing the money at the time, Riley put a call in asking about payment. Relations went 'back to square one'. Sometime after that, he glimpsed Smith stumbling towards him in a railway carriage. Their eyes met, and Smith walked on. There has been no direct communication since but Riley still plays The Fall on the radio – apart from the tracks he's on – and admits any lingering grudge would be 'a bit sad, really'. Their paths have veered apart – although Riley supports Smith's beloved Manchester City, he's become one of the country's higher-profile vegetarians. Yet, he says the experience of being in The Fall made him who he is – more confident, more single-minded and more able to express himself – exactly the qualities required for British radio. Who would have ever thought – in those dark winters of 1978 and 1979 – the young kid on guitar was beginning an education that would transform the content of British radio?

Riley admits freely the only reason he got on the airwaves in the first place was because various BBC heads were avid Fall fans and – after encountering him when he briefly worked as a radio plugger for groups like the Pixies and Happy Mondays – liked his presence in the BBC enclave and suggested he stay.

'I'll probably look back when I'm 70 and think I've had a charmed life – working on the radio,' he says, not noticeably dewy-eyed, 'but the thing I'll be most proud of is being in The Fall. It set me up for everything that's happened since. It was a start in life, really.'

However, I can't help feeling the man of few Fall interviews has been guarded today, something he admits himself when he says, 'There are a lot of skeletons in the Fall cupboard and stories that haven't been told, and some of them are pretty out there,' making me wonder what I've yet to find.

We talk about the mysterious fate of Karl Burns and he dismisses Steve Davies's assertion that he's alive and well and living in the hillsides above Manchester. 'I'm sure if Karl moved into a village anywhere near you, you'd hear about it!' he says. Maybe you never really leave The Wonderful and Frightening World. Oddly enough, soon after I interview Marc Riley, the BBC announce that several broadcasting departments are being moved from Oxford Road to Salford – a stone's throw from where Smith lives. Perhaps this episode in the ongoing Fall soap opera may have yet another twist.

CHAPTER 12

'I'm not an arsonist, I work for the BBC!'

My colleague Michael Hann has a theory that every Fall fan's favourite Fall album is the one they hear first – because when you first hear The Fall they sound so odd compared to other bands the experience sticks with you forever. The theory makes a lot of sense and certainly applies to me. My first Fall album, *Grotesque*, remains my all-time favourite although I'm not sure if it's actually the best. If I have to put emotions and associations aside and pick the all-time greatest Fall album, it would have to be *Slates*, from 1981.

The odd thing about The Fall's fourth album is that, technically, it isn't an album at all. It's a six-track, 10-inch vinyl record, therefore, when it was released on Rough Trade records on 27 April 1981, it didn't qualify for the single charts because it was too long and was ineligible for the album charts because it was too short. This is typical Fall illogicality it but didn't prevent its inclusion in something we had in those days called the UK Independent Album chart, where it soared to Number 3. Even the cover isn't like other albums. There's a blurred live shot alongside the barmy slogan '"Slates" by The Fall. Incl: Mid-Mass, Lover etec. [sic] Prole Threat Working, Yeah. Slags, Slates, etset. Cap.! Het! cost: two pounds only u skinny rats.'

Which is a pretty good description of its contents and the average Fall fan, certainly this one who is, and was, a 'skinny rat'. However, once the needle hits the vinyl, conventional descriptions are impossible. Even more than *Grotesque*, *Slates* manages to skirt the boundaries of demented Northern rockabilly, experimental rock and *avant garde*, but despite that manages to be insanely poppy. Smith once revealed *Slates* is one of his own favourites and said it was aimed at 'people who didn't buy records'. The 10-inch – recently re-released on CD to rave reviews – has songs weird enough for Captain Beefheart, catchy enough for Take That, and contains some of Smith's most witheringly insightful lyrics.

'Fit and Working Again' chugs along gloriously while nodding to the working-class work ethic and dripping with his curious little slogans, declaring that while religion costs much irreligion costs more, and comparing Smith's state of mind to that of champion boxer Alan Minter after eight tabs of LSD – a reference to the British boxer who both won and lost the world middleweight title the year before.

Another track, 'Leave the Capitol' sums up Smith's diffidence towards London and mutters darkly about a hand on the shoulder in Leicester Square. A succession of negative images of the Big Smoke are then delivered in the psychotic rambled style familiar to latter-day Tube travellers encountering the oddballs who hang about outside Camden Town station.

'Prole Art Threat', another glorious moment in the Fall canon, is almost derangedly fast, a miniature conspiracy theory bound up in an anti-media tirade against a pink press conspiracy funded by 'MI9'.

The sublime 'Middle Mass' coasts along on the kind of economical but instantly memorable Steve Hanley bassline which suggests just why Smith said he 'defined' The Fall. 'An Older Lover Etc.' protests about the difficulties of a monogamous relationship with an older woman and is generally believed to be about Kay Carroll. In fact, the song alone perhaps justifies her lingering love/hatred/bitterness towards Smith:

> Take an older lover
> Get ready for old stories
> Of teenage sex
> From the early sixties
> Under cover
> Behind office desks
> Old divorces
> Children's faces
> You'd better take a younger lover
> You'd better take a younger lover
> Or take an older lover
> You'll soon get tired of her
> (She'll shag you out on the table).

Smith manages to bring a comic twist to feeling wistful: 'You'll miss your older lover/ Her love was like your Mother's/ With added attractions.' Ahem.

Meanwhile, the caustic title track suggests that anyone spilling a pint must pay for the correct amount spilt and sends out a veiled, unmentionable threat to the myriad of Fall copyists who have picked the album up over the years.

Slates is like nothing else in the Fall canon and bears a name that doesn't appear on any other Fall studio albums: Dave Tucker, who briefly joined The Fall on – wait for it – clarinet.

Almost three decades after Smith offered the advice to 'Leave the Capitol', I find Tucker in London, where he lives in a first-floor apartment in Haringey. The door opens and I'm greeted by a bear-like man with a bald (rather than shaven, as he sported in 1981) head and few remaining teeth, which is at least one thing he still has in common with Mark E Smith.

While the dentist's worst nightmare makes the tea, I survey the contents of his flat. There's every instrument imaginable, from a large cello to a tenor sax and a tiny drum kit. A giant Frank Zappa poster gazes down over a computer. The room is littered with CDs, some of which he is using as beer mats which means every time I take a sip of tea a compact disc sticks to the bottom of the mug. Tucker seems completely oblivious. Every so often, a CD will tumble from my mug and land on the table, where I notice it hails from the world of jazz or improvised music in which Tucker now plies his trade (most recently with Scatter, an improvising band of several years' standing). He's clearly not making a king's ransom although he's been successful enough to have played with name musicians like Evan Parker. Rather than the favourite Fall diet of amphetamines and beer, Tucker seems to run on spliffs and Typhoo. We seem a very long way away from The Fall's natural habitat, but maybe that was always the point. Ben Pritchard's revelation that 'the challenge is to take someone not right for the group and make them right for the group' certainly seems to apply to the jazzy clarinet player, even more than bongo man Steve Davies. Tucker has his own take on why he was recruited: Smith wanted an accomplished musician 'to make the other guys nervous'.

It's all a very long time ago, but just talking to him I get a sense of the odd vibes that fuelled *Slates*. I've only been in the flat a few minutes and he's telling me a weird tale about being given a copy of *The Necromonicon*, a fictional occult book of spells and the like, created by Smith favourite H P Lovecraft. Tucker then lent the book to a friend who suddenly dropped dead. By the time the body was discovered, in a state of decomposition, *The Necromonicon* had disappeared.

Still, at least in some ways Tucker is a relatively normal Faller. Like the Jesuit lads, he lived in Prestwich, moving there after spending his childhood being bounced round various other North Manchester suburbs. Once safely in the territory covered by Smith's trusty radar, he was an occasional presence on the punk scene after being 'swept up' by new wave while still a schoolboy. His first band, the Dirty Shirts, were unable to play their instruments. Then he formed Mellatron [sic], who got a good review in *Melody Maker* for a track ('Hunters from Beyond', on a 1978 compilation called *Identity Parade*) he says was a 'mess'. 'It was a psychedelic jam using all the buttons and effects in the studio,' he chuckles, spliff in one hand and Typhoo in the other. In timeless Fall fashion, Mellatron didn't have a drummer so 'drafted someone in' the night before.

They were all set to take off with an EP produced by Buzzcocks' Pete Shelley, who'd just scored a massive hit with 'Ever Fallen in Love (With Someone You Shouldn't Have?)' when it all went badly wrong. The band got into an argument with the label boss, who wanted a picture of Shelley on the sleeve, not them. This all became rather academic when the label manager suddenly stopped returning Tucker's calls. The Mellatron man was then told that the label boss had been suddenly detained at Her Majesty's Pleasure after a serious driving incident: either way, the boss and the master tapes disappeared. This sort of farcical, tragic chaos doesn't just happen to The Fall.

Fatefully, the drummer who was drafted in – for the impressive fee of £50 and a curry – was none other than Karl Burns. Tucker remembers the now missing Faller as a 'seriously good drummer' with an 'incredible sense of tempo', who wore plastic pants and a leather jacket and never changed his clothes. 'He had the sort of rock 'n' roll attitude that should have landed him in Mötley Crüe,' says the almost toothless man. Which is why Tucker is surprised such a big character has disappeared – although he thinks he may have left the country.

'He was always in hot water. He'd either owe someone some money and they'd be threatening to break his legs or he'd be fucking someone's wife. There was always something a bit dodgy with Karl.' He adds that 'bad blood' lingered between Smith and Burns after the onstage punch in New York.

Still, knowing Karl indirectly led to Tucker joining The Fall. Hanging out in Prestwich, he got to know Una Baines and Martin Bramah. One night he popped into Smith's local, The Foresters Arms on the Bury New Road, and ended the evening in The Fall.

'I met Smithy, we talked about H P Lovecraft and Ornette Coleman,' he remembers. 'Two weeks later I was onstage with him at Manchester Polytechnic.'

Tucker remembers Fall gigs in those days as tense, edgy affairs with a mixture of appreciation and hostility between band and audience – a charged atmosphere in which Smith thrived. At one gig, at North London Polytechnic,

The Fall went on stage to be met with Nazi salutes. At another, in Paisley, the atmosphere was so violent they had to make every song last 15 minutes until the police arrived to escort them out.

To place such madness in some sort of context, the music press was full of 'new pop' at the time – fey guitar bands from Scotland, and Adam and The Ants were huge with their Burundi beats, pirate and Indian chic. My school bus often carried a miner who travelled to North Leeds in a shiny-backed NCB donkey jacket customised to read 'Adam' on the back, and he had a white line daubed in make-up across his nose. These were mixed-up times. Hardcore punk was still popular at street level but the *NME* were writing about squeaky pop duo Dollar and the mainstream was being infiltrated by the floppy-haired, make-up wearing but otherwise conservative, materialist New Romantics. Meanwhile, in tension-wracked outposts around the country, The Fall were crafting hypnotic wordscapes that in terms of influence and relevance would outlast them all.

Tucker remembers the Fall line-up that made *Slates* an album 'firing on all cylinders' – where The Fall are often militarily regimented, at that time a big ingredient was improvisation. Songs would be so loose they sounded different every time they were played, and so the recordings on *Slates* document a unique moment in time in the studio. How much Smith encouraged this remains unclear. At the end of 'Slates, Slags, etc.', he cries out, 'Don't start improvising for God's sake!', which may have been directed at Tucker, who, as a 'creative musician, was treated accordingly, with disdain'.

Tucker provides an insight into the way the songs themselves came about. The musicians would arrive at work with songs, which would then be subjected to the site manager's quality control as efficiently as if they were a production line making sausages or radios. The ones that passed the Smith 'ear test' were then recorded in London's Berry Street Studios – chosen because it had just hosted one of Smith's few musical heroes, Jamaican reggae legend Prince Far I.

The other key component was tension, fuelled by the familiar fear of the P45. Like Kay Carroll, Tucker recognises Smith as a master-manipulator who relished playing people off against one another and who, like Brian Clough, knew just when to 'inflate your ego and when to devastate it'. But he goes further, suggesting Smith's mischievous prods and backstabs even made their way into songs about band members. Tucker confirms 'An Older Lover Etc.' is indeed about Kay Carroll – 'You should have seen Kay's face when he sang it.' Tucker suggests one song, the wonderfully rampaging 'Fantastic Life', refers to him, having been identified by the scrutinising Smith as someone prone to exaggeration. The song describes a 'David' who reckoned he'd had a run in with a policeman, but suggests Smith didn't believe him.

'It's true!' pleads Tucker. 'I was in the cells the next day.'

Part of the problem may have been that people in and around The Fall then were often so out of it nobody knew what was real and what wasn't. Tucker paints a vivid picture of The Fall's social scene. Smith 'didn't court close friends' but there was an 'inner circle' of drinkers at The Foresters who'd go back to someone's house – often John Quays' because he had a mammoth record collection – take drugs, drink beer and listen to music (rockabilly giant Charlie Pride for Smith, industrial weirdos Throbbing Gristle for Tucker).

To this day, music, work and stimulants seem the primary components of Smith's social life. He doesn't drive, eschews materialism and pours scorn on traditional rock lifestyle perks like cars and yachts. Dave Tucker suggests this is because of his background. Tucker, like Smith, was from a lower middle-class/working-class family in Prestwich.

'We didn't have that many choices,' he comments. 'You had to make your own fun. At the docks he was making 17 quid a week. It was the same for me in the late 1970s. I landed this job where I was earning 40 quid a week, it felt like a fucking fortune. I was going to see Sham 69 one night, Wire the next. It was a different age.'

'You've got to think of Manchester in the late 1970s,' he expands, lighting another spliff. 'It was a depressed area, no one gave a fuck about it. You could still see the remnants of textile mills or whatever. That's totally gone now, it's all business parks, malls. I don't recognise Manchester any more, although you can still go to some pubs and get bladdered on a tenner. Mark's a big drinker, always was. He's at his happiest when he's getting out of it. I've never seen him straight. We were either popping speed or smoking or drinking ourselves stupid.'

Tucker suggests a lot of Manchester folk are still content with a pie and a pint, although in Smith's case you can usually skip the pie. Bizarrely, he insists that in his two years in The Fall he never once saw Smith eat: 'I never saw him put anything in his mouth that didn't have a filter tip or roach attached to it.'

The phone rings and we're blasted back to current reality.

'Yeah, yeah, we won them over at the Union Jazz Festival,' he breezes down the receiver. 'I thought we were going to get fucking lynched.' As I gaze at him quizzically, he says 'Look, can I call you back? Someone is "interviewing" me.'

And we're back to early 1980s Prestwich.

When he picks up his thread, Tucker relates how popular speed was at the time, because it was 'the anti-hippie drug'. 'It gave you an edge,' he says, although he insists amphetamine abuse in The Fall was generally limited to himself, Smithy, Carroll and – alarmingly – one of the band's drivers, who ferried them all to gigs. This is confirmed by Carroll, who says the driver, 'a really sweet guy, got into speed amphetamines with us a bit but wasn't a major addict'. One hopes he wasn't done for speeding.

Tucker says that the Jesuit lads didn't dabble – unless they had been recording all night and had a gig the next day, in which case one of them might pop a 'bluey' – whereas Smith, Tucker and Carroll would go 'apeshit'.

'You've gotta remember that this was an era when the record companies were giving their bands drugs,' says Tucker. 'Maybe some still do. But there were guys turning up at the recording studio with gear, [speed] wraps everywhere. It wasn't party time, because we were working, but it did give you a certain front.'

And that front came out in the music and Smith's sneering performances, which may explain *Slates* and other Fall albums' slightly unhinged vibes.

What an odd world it must have been . . . travelling the country, crammed into a van, amphetamined to bits, making this brilliant, warped music. With Kay Carroll leading the assault. Tucker explains that, because The Fall's manager was female (unheard of before Sharon Osbourne), Carroll had to make sure she was doubly tough. He remembers her having guys 'up against the wall' in universities in states of abject terror.

'She'd be screaming, "You fucking this and that,"' he laughs. Meanwhile, Smith, like Macavity, would be hovering in the background. 'But he probably instigated it. And you weren't allowed to pick up a girl if you were in The Fall! Kay was very scary, off her tits all the time. The thing is, speed and alcohol make you into a nasty piece of work. If you give Santa Claus a line of speed and Special Brew, he's going to start fighting with the reindeers.'

Not for nothing was The Fall's 1980 masterpiece titled *Grotesque*. The 'gramme' – also the subject of its song 'Gramme Friday' – is amphetamine.

'That's what happens when he takes as many amphetamines as he still does . . . I suppose he still does!' says Tucker, of the post-gramme altered state. 'The last few times I've seen him on TV he's been off his tits but he comes across as eccentric which is why the British public like it. He's still full of piss and vinegar and bile.'

Tucker thinks drug abuse has exaggerated Smith's habit of being different things to different people, suggesting that dealing with everyone from rabid fans to 'slimy bastards' in the music industry requires him to be able to slip into various characters. However, when Kay Carroll left in 1983, Smith was suddenly running The Fall on his own – and that led indirectly to Tucker's excommunication.

As he tells it, Carroll didn't just 'run out on' The Fall in America, she made off with all the takings. When I put this to Carroll she says that – according to the group's tour manager at the time – the musicians had the money but drove into a snowstorm in Canada. The tour takings were all in a brown paper bag, which blew out of the van. Cue a hapless Fall line-up chasing dollar notes around in a raging blizzard.

Tucker hadn't played with The Fall for quite some time – because a smaller band is more viable – but was still around the inner core. He got an unexpected call from Smith in America, asking if he could look after the band's affairs in England while The Fall played enough gigs in America to afford the flights back home.

When the beleaguered group finally made it back, Carroll was long gone but Smith had someone new upon his arm – the American guitarist who soon became Mrs Brix Smith.

'I went to the pub and there she was,' remembers Tucker, rather sniffily. 'Her idea of punk rock was The Dickies and she had one of their guitars. You're talking to someone who saw the Buzzcocks at the Free Trade Hall, never mind the fuckin' Dickies. Mark never said a word all night and then right at the end of the conversation he says, "Oh, Dave, thanks for everything you've done, I'll be in touch", and I was suddenly out of the picture. That's what it's like in that band. Suddenly, you're disappeared.'

He thinks some of the mad behaviour that fuelled *Slates* may ironically have accelerated his own exit: 'I know I blew it because most of the time I was out of it or drunk,' he says candidly.

Because of the manner of his exit, the clarinet man felt rather 'put through the wringer' after The Fall, bought himself a trumpet and left the world of rock. However, within a few years, he found himself being drawn again towards The Wonderful and Frightening World.

He was in London, noticed The Fall were playing at the Astoria and plucked up the courage to put in a call. Remembering his 'friend called David' of 'Fantastic Life', Smith didn't just let Tucker into the gig free but accompanied him for several beers. Another time, Tucker was in Ladbroke Grove when he heard a shout of 'Mellatron!' from a man on a motorbike who couldn't remember his name, just his group. It was Karl Burns – leather jacket, plastic trews and all. The Fall were recording just behind Tucker's house but there was a different dynamic to the one in 1981. By now, he says, drug use was spreading through the ranks. Perhaps it is like Steve Hanley said: 'Mark needs normal people to bounce off but after a few years in The Fall you're no longer normal.'

Tucker continued to see Smith. When the band were about to get hammered by the taxman he got a tip-off from a mate in the Revenue and got in touch to warn him. Thereafter, every time he'd visit his mum in Prestwich he'd pop into Smith's and now reports that the old lack of materialism hasn't changed. The Smith house contains a widescreen TV, CDs scattered on the floor, books and very little else. There are none of the toys or gadgets which you'd find in virtually any other modern home.

'He's got what he needs. He's not a holidaymaker. You can't see Mark getting up at 5 a.m. to sort out the sun lounger. He appreciates being able to get up at 11 in the morning. That's more important to him than driving a flash car.'

In the early 2000s, when Tucker was doing some work for the BBC, the visits petered out. Tucker popped in to give Smith a CD he'd just made in America, but found it difficult to gain admittance.

'His wife never answers the door. "Who's there? Who's there? Go away!" she shouts. I don't know if they get visits from weird fans wanting to breathe the same air as Mark.' Unlike Steve Davies, Tucker did manage to get inside. They shared a spliff and headed for The Woodthorpe, another of Smith's favoured local boozers. Tucker – who had other things to do – thought it would be for a quick pint but instead found himself facing a table full of beers and whiskies, struggling to keep up while Smith kept urging, 'Come on, cock, get yer round in!'

Tucker reports a strain in the atmosphere when he enquired, as unsuccessfully as I had, about the New York punch-up, and that eventually Smith 'stopped making sense'.

'Suddenly, he asked me if I could firebomb this stall in Camden Market for him because they'd been selling bootlegs of The Fall!' reveals Tucker, incredulous. 'I said, "Mark, I'm not an arsonist, I work for the BBC!"'

'I couldn't tell if he was joking,' he insists. 'It was weird as shit.' Tucker left the pub.

Soon after this peculiar experience, he discovered he was appearing on various live CDs from the 1980s and made a few phone calls to see if he was due some money, but the man who tipped off The Fall about the taxman was told that their business affairs had been relocated to the West Indies. He didn't pursue it and admits Smith 'would never set foot onstage with me again'. But leaving The Fall was not the reason Tucker fled from Prestwich – the real reason lies behind those teeth.

One night coming home from The Foresters he found himself jumped by 'several guys'. He insists they came off much worse than he did – he was wearing steel toe caps at the time – but says nevertheless he found himself 'scrabbling in the gutter looking for my teeth!' And at least this bit of the tale is demonstrably factual. He had to leave in the end, he says, because the more Frightening than Wonderful World of Prestwich was 'going to kill me'.

I've never been to Prestwich, but I've often driven past the signs for it and wondered what lies up there. It's time to pay a visit.

CHAPTER 13

'A whole different universe.'

WELCOME TO PRESTWICH VILLAGE PLEASE DRIVE CAREFULLY

I'm driving up the Bury New Road towards Prestwich, The Fall fanatics' equivalent of Beatles fans travelling to Liverpool to see the rebuilt Cavern or Muslims crossing the world to Mecca. Except I don't have a mop top or a copy of the Koran. I have the Fiat Punto and *Dragnet* on the stereo. Winding past the sign for Prestwich, there's no immediate sense of what Smith told me is a 'completely different universe', nor why he remains so obsessed with the suburban area in which he's spent his entire adult life – give or take an early 1990s sojourn in Edinburgh.

'It was pretty much an exile, yeah,' he told me in Malmaison. 'I was single for a start, which is unusual for me. I'd played the Edinburgh Fringe with [contemporary dance punk] Michael Clark, and thought I could really live there. They're not Fall fanatics in Edinburgh. They like The Fall, but they're not die-hard fans like in Glasgow. Moving there would have been hell. But

Edinburgh was actually as cheap as Manchester. I could kick myself actually. I should have kept the house. It was different up there . . . but I liked it too bloody much! I was coming home and that, but I was out of touch with the lads.'

He'd suggested he had considered moving but by the time he got to thinking about it there was something else to do, and it seems unlikely Prestwich's most famous resident will ever get around to leaving now.

Prestwich, which borders and then blurs with Salford, seems nice enough. It looks like a rather cosmopolitan area: lots of trees and plenty of facilities, not least local pubs like Smith's favoured Woodthorpe and Foresters Arms. (Another Smith haunt, The George, has long since been knocked down.) But there are places like this all over the country. What keeps him here? Locality to his remaining family – mother and three sisters – who also live nearby? Or something uniquely Fallesque?

I've gone past the big Woodthorpe but now I'm lost. I'm no longer in Prestwich, but adjoining Whitefield, which looks remarkably like the sort of dark landscape depicted in *Dragnet*'s songs all those years ago, like 'Before the Moon Falls', in which Smith paints a brilliant, evocative landscape of late 1970s industrial decay and social stagnation.

> Up here in the North there are no wage packet jobs for us
> Thank Christ
> While young married couples discuss the poverties
> Of their self-built traps
> And the junior clergy demand more cash
> We spit in their plate and wait for the ice to melt
> I must create a new regime . . .
> Before the moon falls
> I must create a new scheme.

Because so many of our cities have been regenerated, the song sounds like a piece of history, but it's all still here in Smith's childhood landscape: weather-stained Victorian and Edwardian houses and industrial shells like something from science fiction or old Fall album covers. There are no visible 'city hobgoblins' or 'hydrochloric shaved weirds' but the queue for the fish and chip shop stretches halfway down the street, like a soup kitchen. Smith occasionally tells hair-raising stories about such places in interviews, and journalists doubt whether they ever existed in the first place. But in Hyde, they still do.

This may be one of Smith's sources of inspiration, but it's not home.

I wind the car back towards Prestwich village, past TGI Friday's and kitchen showrooms, a Chinese acupuncturist and more old houses. At last, a sign: WELCOME TO PRESTWICH – PLEASE DRIVE CAREFULLY.

There's a businesslike, bustling feel here, a world apart from the mysterious gloom of Hyde. There's a large Marks & Spencers, a Chinese takeaway and a Citizens' Advice Bureau. Caucasians go about their business among a smattering of Asians and an enormous quotient of Orthodox Jews. On the pavement, an older man argues with a younger woman, gesticulating wildly. In the newsagent I pick up a copy of the *Prestwich Advertiser*, from which Smith has suggested he occasionally finds ideas for lyrics, but there's nothing in it today except for tiny news stories concerning Prestwich Heys Football Club and Sedgley Park, a little known Rugby Union team Smith is thought not to support.

But the address I'm looking for isn't here, either.

I head out of Prestwich and over the border into Sedgley Park, where Smith spent most of his childhood and his mum still lives today. It looks much leafier, more sedate, upwardly mobile without being showily affluent. Preferred cars are old Volvos, BMWs and the occasional Ford Estate. Solid, dependable, but never flash.

A mock Tudor near-mansion close to my destination has lions on the gateposts and sticks out a mile because of its flashiness, which must drive Smith wild, being so close to his own humble abode.

I've finally found my mecca. It's a deserted street that reminds me of an old New Order lyric from 'Ceremony' about avenues all lined with trees. I park the Punto in the twilight and wander up the road.

This is Smith's street, the avenue which has been the fulcrum of his life for the best part of two decades, where he lived, a few streets from his parents, first with Brix and now with Elena, the young Greek DJ he met in Berlin.

'She took a step down to marry me,' he told me in Malmaison, implausibly but rather gentlemanly, I thought. 'She was a big DJ in Berlin, ran clubs and all sorts, had her own band, Zen Faschisten. She'd just promoted a gig. She wasn't a massive Fall fan, y'know, we just got on like a house on fire. She joined the group first, then we got married. Oh aye, she knows about the ejector seat.'

He cackled, a wondrous, deep cackle suggesting this was a favourite joke. But now he's on his third marriage and – together since 2000 – it's going 'fuckin' marvellous. Touch wood!'

And this is home.

Smith's house is so anonymous I walk past it twice before realising, this is it, the address given to me in confidence by someone around the band (not, if Smith's spies are reading this, anyone in or formerly in the band).

The house isn't exactly what I'd expected from the imagery in the Fall songbook – I'd expected a Gothic manor or perhaps a tiny terraced house with an outside toilet and a couple of underage chimney sweeps lurking. Instead it's a large but nondescript semi – the sort of abode you'd expect of a teacher or a plumber. There is a huge wooden door that, as Steve Davies and Dave Tucker told me, could definitely offer protection against curious fans and former bassists. Like Tony Friel's house, there is no blue plaque announcing THE MAN WHO LIVES HERE IS A LIVING LEGEND OF BRITISH MUSIC. When I ask a passerby who lives there, he shrugs and says, 'Mad Mark.'

Apparently, that's what the neighbours call him. I wonder if he knows.

I do my best private eye routine and check out the situation. There's nothing in the garden: no car, no toys, no plants, just a concrete drive. Venetian blinds cover all the windows, suggesting the inside is kept dark at all times. There is, as Dave Tucker had suggested, no visible sign of ostentation. In fact, there's no visible sign anyone lives here at all. Which is probably exactly how Smith wants it.

Nothing connects this average semi in a tree-lined avenue to the music of The Fall: it's not amazingly comfortable but it's not uncomfortable, a world away from all those satanic mills and Fiery Jacks. Neighbours wash their cars. Maybe Smith would spend his Sundays doing the same if he owned or could drive a vehicle. Probably not.

I'm reminded of something John Lennon said towards the end of The Beatles era. His theory was that if the artist is hungry, he will never work, and if the artist has enough, he won't work. The ideal was to achieve a level of security to be able to work.

This is what Smith has here. As Dave Tucker suggested, 'He has what he needs' – a position of some security from which to create radical works.

But surely this is too comfortable? Where is the creative tension among quietly whistling passersby and well remunerated tradesmen?

I get back in the car and drive back through the centre of Prestwich, where the older man and the young girl are still arguing on the pavement. I park and wander around the streets. And then it hits me. The tension. You can feel it in the atmosphere as clearly as I can now see the light evening drizzle. The tension between the people, the glances of suspicion at this outsider, the distrusting glances between individuals and communities that Tony Friel suggested once lived happily together but don't seem to anymore. Whitefield surrealism and Prestwich tension – it's not in the buildings but in the environment, the atmosphere, the sparks between people. It's not nasty, but it's tangible with an ever so slightly unsettling undercurrent. I remember what Tucker said about 'unease'.

If I could bottle this and take it with me, I would have one of the principal ingredients of The Fall.

I grow tired of suspicious glances and return to the car.

CHAPTER 14

'Ello, luv. Are you having a nice holiday?'

The journey's now taken me 206 miles from Prestwich, to Rivington Street in London's Shoreditch, where I'm looking for a boutique called Start, which houses another of the Fall drama's cast of major characters – the doomed romantic heroine.

The boutique is easy enough to find because even in a street of trendy shops there's nothing quite like this. In fact, I hear it before I see it. *Click, flash. Click, flash.* The sound of two mannequins in the window, clad in PVC, 'taking photographs' of anyone who passes by the window.

It's a boutique designed to cater for the very rich, extremely hip or straightforwardly famous. Some days, a familiar face to Fall fans is visible in the shop, occasionally spinning discs or helping out behind the counter, but her usual job is helping pick fashion lines to buy and otherwise assisting her husband Philip Start in running the business. Her name now is Brix Smith-Start, but Fall fans the world over know her as a Smith.

What I know is this: she was born Laura Elisse Salenger to a middle-class American Jewish family on 12 November 1962. After her parents' divorce when she was just a baby, she divided her time between the Californian homes of her father, a Freudian psychologist, and her mother, a model who lived in the Hollywood Hills and later became a reputed television producer. One day, a babysitter started the seven-year-old-child on guitar, and although she didn't know it at the time it was the start of a chain of events which would eventually lead her to The Wonderful and Frightening World. As a teenager, Salenger wanted to become an actress, but she became more and more fascinated by British pop, although at first she loved Adam and The Ants, Tears for Fears and Culture Club rather than the challenging music made in and around Manchester. However, while studying at the famed liberal arts establishment, Bennington, in the eastern state of Vermont, she engaged in theatre and experimental music and formed a band called Banda Dratsing. Later, she moved to Chicago with the band's singer-guitarist Lisa Feder, One day, while they were in Chicago's Wax Trax, Feder drew her attention to a vinyl copy of *Slates* by The Fall. And so began a process in which Salenger, by then renamed Brix, would marry Smith and join his group.

Brix's impact on Mark E Smith was musical, personal and notably sartorial, but she had an equal impact on The Fall. As Riley had pointed out, with him no longer in the picture they adopted a distinctly more commercial sound, with killer anthemic choruses. They weren't entirely pop, but they weren't too far from it either. With Brix pouting moodily at the camera and lashing out sweeter pop riffs than anything ever conjured up by Jesuit lads Scanlon or Riley, Fall records infiltrated the unfamiliar mainstream.

The Fall's chart positions illustrate Brix's impact. The first Fall album to feature her, December 1983's *Perverted by Language*, didn't chart but received universal rave reviews. Listened to now, the album is almost a documentary of early 1980s Britain, with phrases like 'Eat Y'Self Fitter' (a track which John Peel once said almost caused him to faint with delight) pilfered from an advert of the time, and forgotten terms like 'Gas Miser' (a budget Cannon Industries gas fire often seen in council houses at the time).

In September 1984, *The Wonderful and Frightening World of The Fall* reached Number 62. For an independent band to chart at all was a significant achievement (best track, probably hypnotic opener 'Lay of the Land', where Smith dispenses sage descriptions of the Britain of the day, from towns in Surrey peopled by crooks and kerb-crawlers, to the Home Secretary with a weird look, and the fact that between the human heart and mind there lies an air-block of wind). The following year's *This Nation's Saving Grace* made Number 54 and is a truly marvellous album, achieving the perfect balance between the new, poppier Fall sound and the old, starker weirdness. By this point, Smith had become a purveyor of uncomfortable home truths. July 1985's 'Couldn't Get Ahead' single laid out the pitfalls of trying to keep up with the rat race, but the album takes this theme further to comment on the wider effects of the consumer/industrial society on human beings. 'What You Need' takes the old 'repetition' mantra to the nth degree – the pulverising melody mimics an industrial process and the brutal mundanity of clocking on or going to work. Britons are depicted as a race of sex-starved heavy smokers. Another track, 'My New House', portrays a defeated nation, imprisoned in faceless anonymous homes. The album's a perfect State of the Union address delivered by what was at the time Britain's finest group on unrivalled form. To this day I'm fascinated by the almost mathematical construction of tracks such as 'Spoilt Victorian Child', where Smith seems to get the group to play what is a jazzy melody but within a rock format, the perfect vehicle for one of Smith's typically curious subjects. He imagines a well-off Victorian household where one of the children feasts on sugar and cakes and pop-up books, but later pays cruel penance for their excess in the form of toxic, disfigured poxes. Utter genius: a morality tale for any time.

October 1986's *Bend Sinister* was another Brix-era cracker which took The Fall into the Top 40, a foreign environment but one they'd subsequently occupy for years. Many of the album tracks became live staples, particularly 'US. 80's 90's', a rampaging assault in which Smith would often adopt a megaphone to bemoan his treatment at the hands of Boston immigration, who objected to him spending time in the toilet.

Gigs at the time were transformed. Venues were becoming bigger and fuller. I remember one show in the late 1980s (15 March 1988, to be precise) at Leeds University where I'd first seen them, but the venue was crammed to bursting, not peppered with large spaces as it had been in 1981. The Jesuit lads' heads were still down, but Brix was stagefront, posing and pouting, with virtually every male head in the room gazing at her, even salivating, as they might do today at Kylie Minogue. Smith seemed to acknowledge she'd revitalised the band. When they played Leeds again, at the Polytechnic on 13 December 1988, the man didn't seem to want to leave the stage, leading The Fall through a rare two sets of encores and a total of 15 songs.

When we talk, Brix has a heavy cold, which she's treating by drinking lots of water, one of many tips she picked up in the heavily touring band. It seems I'm far from the first Fall fan to track her down via the shop. Apparently, they often wander in, pretending to be looking for something and then just stand there gawping, exactly like at those gigs.

'Or bowing!' she shrieks, through sniffs.

Brix's life has been transformed since her days in The Fall, but it seems equally significant she still calls herself, at least partly, a Smith. 'I'm very proud of what we did,' she insists. 'It's a part of my life.'

Brix hasn't changed much from her days in The Fall. As the articles in magazines like *Vogue* or newspapers such as the *Independent* testify with occasional but high-profile regularity, she's still a platinum blonde, glamorous and very alternative American – the antithesis of The Fall. Which was no doubt the appeal, and vice versa.

She remembers how it felt to hear The Fall the first time. 'I just thought it was fucking brilliant. I couldn't understand it. I couldn't get to the bottom of it at all. It wasn't banal. It was so interesting, the way it was all put together and I'm sure he designed it like that.' Even now, she still calls The Fall 'super-powerful' and says their records have 'arteries of subtlety' that can flow right to the core of the person listening. She argues that everyone will have a different idea about the lyrics' meaning because, like a great painting, what people make of The Fall is actually a reflection of themselves. This is a fascinating idea, and I can't help wondering if it applies not just to fans, but to the people who made the records.

Implausibly, it was just two weeks after hearing *Slates* that she 'bumped into' Smith after The Fall played at Chicago Metro. Her initial encounter with her future husband – who was carrying two beers and had powder trickling from his nose – suggests he wasn't the usual character a middle-class Jewish girl would hurriedly take home to meet her mum. But, again in contrast to the public image, Brix says she found Smith 'very sweet, considerate and friendly'. In fact, he wasn't just charming, he was magnetic.

'The way he looked at the world was from such a different perspective from the way normal people do . . . In that way he was a great poet. Because he wouldn't see things the same way, he wouldn't speak the same way. He was brilliant, so fucking smart I cannot tell you.' The pair were married at a Bury registry office on 19 July 1983 with the now AWOL Burns very much in attendance as the witness. Musically, the vows were slower coming. It seems Smith was supposedly going to act as svengali and mastermind her own career. However, she explains the process by which she joined The Fall two months later.

'He said, "I like the songs you write. Can we use them? And can you play on them?"' The 21-year-old LA glamour puss found herself duly immersed in The Wonderful and Frightening World. She agrees that for Smith, The Fall is '24-7', which makes it entirely logical that any wives or girlfriends don't just join with the man, they join up with his work.

She suggests her impact on that work was just 'to bring a little bit of light into the shadows' and emphasises how keen she was not to overdo it. She describes a creative process that was collaborative but retained Smith's position as Fall dictator. She would take the skeleton of a song to the singer; he would add the words and change the timing, 'almost like a duet'.

'In some ways it is a dictatorship because he has a very strong vision, but he is willing to embrace ideas and put things together,' she says, considering herself a 'soft melodic part' who 'made The Fall more palatable'.

She certainly did that, but perhaps it had to happen, because the game was changing. Formerly 'alternative' acts from The Cure to New Order were playing big venues and appearing on *Top of the Pops*, while the older strictly independent culture was on the wane. The Smiths were one of the first bands to not just court the music press but also take up residency in the pop charts. Smith, the venerable site manager, was surely canny enough to realise The Fall had to adapt or die, and Brix was effectively a company streamliner. If The Fall had been a limited company, Brix would have made the share price rocket.

She remembers the culture shock of entering the Fall organisation, in particular the crumbling flat at Rectory Lane in which Smith was living at the time, where the 'refrigerator' was an outside window ledge. When she visited the shop around the corner – suicide blonde and wearing kohl eyeliner – the residents of Prestwich would gawp at her as intently as Fall fans do now in Start.

'It was very provincial,' she says. 'Every time I went in they'd say, "'Ello luv, are you having a nice holiday?" I'd say, "No, actually, I live in a house around the corner."' She remembers appalling struggles to obtain smoked salmon and avocados, and struggling to understand the fascination with fish and chips. The Smiths had a BMW even though Smith can't drive, and they didn't use the local swimming pool because Smith has a phobia of water. However, she says in those days they did have holidays – including one at the Hotel des Bains where they filmed *Death in Venice*. 'It was very glamorous,' she says contentedly, which doesn't sound very Fall.

It wasn't just Brix who was adapting to a different culture. Once she was ensconced, The Fall started looking different too. Out went the image of a bunch of blokes queuing up to clock off at the local mincemeat factory: in came leather coats, trendy shirts. Even, God forbid, mascara.

'I used to dress Mark, a little bit,' suggests Brix carefully, perhaps explaining how she unconsciously sowed the seeds of her new career in fashion in The Fall.

She insists she would never have used eyeliner or – 'For God's sake!' – proper make-up. But an 'element of mascara' gave Smith's already naturally big eyes a 'dramatic look'. Thus, Fall audiences who'd grown accustomed to a man with a beer drinker's pallor were now confronted by a creature whose eyeballs were 'popping from the stage'. Not that the process of remodelling the defiantly anti-fashion Smith was seamless.

'He had these absolutely ghastly shirts with Spirograph all over them. So, so scary! We had to get him into something more appealing, less nerdy.' She took him to buy an Armani suit which cost £700. 'It was the most money he'd ever spent but he wore that suit. He probably still has it.' Smith also refused to wear trainers but instead preferred 'hard' shoes. I remember the 'corrective shoes' he complained of in Manchester.

Curiously enough, the shop where Smith bought his first suit was Woodhouse, the Manchester branch of a menswear chain founded by Brix's current husband. But Brix says these sorts of odd coincidences crop up a lot in The Wonderful and Frightening World. One of Start's principles is an old Smith adage: 'The best companies advertise the least.'

Very recently, she was swimming in the Caribbean and suddenly started to panic. The current was very strong, and she heard Smith's 'pearls of wisdom' in her head – 'Never turn your back on the sea.' Out of the blue, we're discussing whether Smith is actually psychic. She thinks he is, and points initially to the track 'Terry Waite Sez' (on 1986's *Bend Sinister*), for which she wrote the music. Four months after the song was released, the Church of England's Special Envoy was kidnapped in Lebanon, and Brix reveals his family got in touch to see if there was a psychic connection to where he was being held.

She cites the song 'Powder Keg', which came out shortly before the Manchester IRA bombing. Then there's 1992's spiky 'Free Range', in which Smith talks of 'trouble' about to sweep Europe, just months before war and ethnic cleansing erupted in Bosnia-Herzegovina. When I first interviewed Mark Smith in 1997, New Labour had just come to power and everything seemed very cuddly and optimistic. However, contrary to almost everyone in the nation at the time, he insisted the Blair government would be 'the Fourth Reich' – the most authoritarian nanny state we've had for years. He was right.

Brix appeared in the video for 1983's 'Kicker Conspiracy', which I think is the greatest football single of all time, in which Smith laments the 'punishment' of skill and predicted how the beautiful game would be taken away from its working-class roots into gentrification. It came out a decade before the formation of the Premier League and Roy Keane's later famous grumble about fans in executive boxes with prawn sandwiches.

Brix remembers another darker incident of Smith's shamanism. In the mid 1980s they were in London and a particular journalist incurred 'God''s almighty wrath by 'disrespecting' The Mighty Fall. Smith was so furious he informed the journo, 'I fucking curse you. You've got the Curse of The

Fall.' Two days later this journalist was in a phone booth when it was run into and crushed by a car. She still sounds wary – 'Nothing ever happened to me. Thank God' – and I sense a distinctly nervous tremor.

After all, since beginning on this journey I've noticed a car has recently appeared in the village bearing the registration number 'MES'.

Fortunately, I remember Smith can't drive.

Brix relates 'countless' examples of Smith's supposed gifts, remarking on his referencing Baghdad (on 'Guest Informant') a year before the first Gulf War.

We decide to change the subject, and she brightens as she remembers how life around The Fall was more Wonderful than Frightening, at least in the early years. On tour, especially with Salford contemporaries New Order, they'd indulge in japes such as partly sawing through chair legs which would then collapse when unfortunate victims took a seat. A favourite prank of Smith's was apparently to fill cups with urine, with which his thirsty, hardworking musicians would gratefully and unwittingly refresh themselves as they came offstage.

Many of the daftest pranks involved Karl Burns. One night, when The Fall were staying in London's Columbia – a hotel frequented by wilder rock bands in which I've also attempted to get to sleep, to no avail – the drummer took exception to the arrival of a band called The Fabulous Thunderbirds. As the band chomped on – what else? – fish and chips, Burns bombarded them with fireworks, making such a racket he alerted the attentions of the Bomb Squad. 'We got in so much trouble,' grins Brix. 'We were nearly banned from the hotel. But they deserved it. They were dicks.' Shortly afterwards, the hotel's water supply had been turned off and Smith left taps on in all the toilets. When the water was reconnected, it flooded through the ceilings. That time they were banned. When they were finally allowed back in, they were almost banned again for excessive partying (a statement was later released suggesting that being allowed into the Columbia again had been 'a cause for celebration').

Brix reveals other, more bizarre Smith tomfoolery at the time: how he developed an 'absolute hatred' for chubby-cheeked, bookish English singer Lloyd Cole and began a Peel session with the words, 'Lloyd Cole's face and head is made out of cow pat'.

Another unlikely recipient of Smith's peculiar loathing was entertainer Tracey Ullman. Brix reveals, sniggering, he 'despised [Ullman] so much that he wanted to put subliminal messages in the videos: "Hang Tracey Ullman!"'

Perhaps as Ben Pritchard found release through football, these practical jokes were Smith's own method of countering stress. Brix attests that marriage did not dilute Smith's creative tendencies and, if anything, he became even more demanding. By the mid 1980s, the schoolboy who once bullied Kay Carroll's brother was starting to draw up a 'torment list' of people he would pick on. There was no obvious reason for being on the torment list.

'He once fired [sound man] Rex Sergeant for eating a salad!' Brix roars, adding that the latest Fall execution took place in front of over 1,000 people at the Edinburgh Festival.

I remember what Marc Riley said about a 'spanner in the works'.

'When anything would get too good or too big or too smooth he'd fuck it up on purpose,' she says. 'He'd sack somebody. He'd have a huge gig, and no drummer! It was a fucking nightmare. He would do that and it would shake us up all the time.'

While Smith's tactics caused havoc, Brix concedes he was right. 'The group would regroup and rethink, but we'd usually come back better, because we were forced to do it.'

However, other undercurrents were creeping into play. Smith's artistic whims tend to reflect his state of mind and the further upping of 'creative tension' seems to coincide with marital trouble.

It had all been something of a whirlwind – from meeting in Chicago to Rectory Lane and later a new house in the avenue lined with trees, to mainstream Radio One airplay and *The Chart Show* – but something wasn't right. Brix says while she 'never fought with Mark', there was 'stress and aggro'. Like Dave Tucker and Marc Riley, she too suspected Smith was singing about her in songs. Although her ex-husband denies it, she insists 1988's 'Bad News Girl' – a torrent at a 'tiresome' lover – refers to her.

Brix says conflict began when the British media started to pick up on her more visual appeal. Apparently, Smith resented her appearing on magazine covers instead of him: 'I think he felt threatened. He certainly didn't like it and maybe he got a bit competitive. I think that kind of thing made him feel emasculated in some way, even though he had encouraged me. I told him not to worry although at the same time I was pushing for success.'

That doesn't sound very Fall, but Brix confirms she believed The Fall were such a great band they should conquer the world. 'I thought it was the coolest band ever and we needed to get it across to as many people as possible,' she argues. 'I had a capitalistic view but out of the goodness of my heart because the band were fab. But he didn't like it and he'd go after other girls and it got a little bit sad for me.'

Accordingly, cracks grew wider when Brix got a solo deal for her band, The Adult Net. Then suddenly everything 'blew up', exacerbated by Smith's increasing use of alcohol.

She claims he was 'never, ever sober. He was irrational and scary and almost impossible to work with. When you're young you can metabolise it and keep [the lifestyle] under control, but it got out of hand. Maybe inside he was really, really unhappy. I don't know, but there was no way to stop it. I tried but he was deteriorating. It wasn't a life I wanted to lead because it was destroying me.'

She could see how everything they'd worked for was starting to fall apart. As she puts it, 'the ship was sinking'. She knew Smith had always been averse to music industry conventions but couldn't see why he wouldn't give an inch or two, and at least schmooze a little.

'He was fucking up everything,' she says, referring to cancelled gigs and interviews. 'It was embarrassing, and I didn't want to be a part of it because I didn't want to be tarred with the same brush.' Perhaps Smith needed some strong management, but she says he can't relinquish power.

'No manager ever stays. He tortures them and bullies them. What he really needs is someone who understands The Fall and who doesn't want to change anything, just get it out there.' But it was not to be.

'It got to the point where I was sick of fighting with him,' she sighs, now quite emotional. 'You know, "Don't do that, do this interview . . ." Everything broke apart. I had my own career so I decided to go with it.'

In 1989, as Smith hooked up with Saffron Prior (a secretary at The Fall's Cog Sinister office and a face around the Prestwich/Fall set for some years), Brix divorced from both Mark E Smith and The Fall. She hooked up with punk-haired classical violinist Nigel Kennedy just as he was hitting commercial pay dirt with *The Four Seasons*, and once again enjoyed the media whirl. Shortly after, Smith appeared to hex the relationship with *Extricate*'s 'Sing! Harpy', a track which seems to be about the musician and features mischievously discordant violin. The relationship fell apart and Brix disappeared back to America, at one point working as a waitress.

Another, perhaps the best, track on *Extricate*, 'Bill Is Dead', sees Smith in the unusual role of emotional singer, still dripping sarcasm but now using his words to cast a melancholy eye over his life. May 1989 had brought another blow, the death of his father from a heart attack aged 59, a man he'd perhaps never really got to know. Sarcastically describing the period as the greatest time of his life, Smith could not have been more honest.

He'd lost his father, his wife and the most successful Fall musician of them all in the space of a few months. But The Fall's doomed romantic heroine was not written out of the script. Brix would return for another episode. The ship wasn't sinking, it was just changing course once again. There would be more highs and more lows.

Meanwhile, I'm starting to realise another Fall fundamental; if you run a band on creative tension, the only way to keep it going forward is to unleash more, and more, and more.

CHAPTER 15

'It was like some kind of medieval Italian principality. Or a Chinese court, full of would-be sycophants and mandarins.'

When you follow The Fall you get used to travelling around. I've been everywhere from dank pubs in Leeds to stadiums containing thousands of people such as Leeds United's Elland Road, where The Fall played a wonderfully inappropriate set in 1987 supporting U2. I've hitchhiked around the country in cars containing homicidal Container Drivers and spanking headmasters, and at one point was given a lift by what is surely Britain's only team of skateboarding Mohican-hairstyled punk rock Buddhists, who dwell in an old coach with no seats. I've met all sorts of characters – the girl who began our friendship as Amanda but ended it calling herself Susan, by which time she revealed she'd never been the same since ingesting the entire contents of a suitcase full of cocaine. But I don't really travel too far following The Fall any more, I just travel the country trailing The Fall's former musicians.

West Suffolk General Hospital lies 208 miles from Prestwich. It's an imposing building like many NHS Trust hospitals, with an endless bank of windows and expansive, leafy grounds. It's not the sort of place you'd expect to find a member of The Fallen, not employed, anyway, but this is the working environment of Marcia Schofield, the twenty-first musician to join The Fall.

What I know about her is this: Schofield joined in October 1986 and left in 1990, during which she played keyboards and occasionally sang on 1988's extremely good *The Frenz Experiment*, the same year's patchily brilliant *I Am Kurious Oranj*, 1989's *Seminal Live* album (neither entirely live nor seminal) and a thunderous return to peak Fall form with 1990's *Extricate*, one of the best Fall albums ever.

Schofield's input was more than just aural. Dark, striking and leggy, her unmistakable looks brought another twist of glamour to the group. Visually as much a part of the more commercial era as Brix, she always looked slightly more down to earth and approachable. Somehow, it's unsurprising to discover she hasn't married a millionaire but a psychiatrist. The couple live outside Bury St Edmunds, recently voted Britain's leafiest town, where Schofield is stepmother to three children and a little girl she calls 'the elf princess'. They share their household with no less than 21 lambs, 12 sheep, 26 chickens and a disabled cat – an even more bizarre assembled cast than that which makes up The Fallen. However, Schofield has never quite left The Wonderful and Frightening World. She tells me none of her medical colleagues had any idea she'd once been in a famous group for ages. She only knew the secret had got out when she arrived in work to discover every computer terminal 'wallpapered' with images of her playing in The Fall. At the time, she was an anaesthetist. 'I'm no longer putting people to sleep,' she reveals from a functional, computer-peppered office. 'Not intentionally anyway.'

These days, twinkly-eyed and youthful, she's treating cancer patients. Her job title is 'pain specialist'.

Now in her forties and retaining a Fall-like sense of humour, the raven-haired Jewish pain specialist entered The Fall's parallel dimension in time-honoured fashion. Her band Khmer Rouge supported The Fall at Hammersmith Odeon in 1985. Almost two years later, her name obviously having been logged in the same way budding players are scouted for football teams, she was un-expectedly invited in.

Like Brix, Schofield remembers most of her tenure as being a lot of fun, not painful at all. She remembers events like drunken days spent tenpin bowling in Bremen – which she says inspired 'Bremen Nacht' on *Frenz Experiment* – when Smith had been bowling 'in a daze'. A B-side, 'Zagreb', came about when Schofield, Steve Hanley and drummer Simon Wolstencroft started jamming Stevie Wonder's 'Higher Ground' in a sound check, a song which would prove a very successful cover version for the Red Hot Chili Peppers, but not The Fall.

She tells how another *Frenz Experiment* track, a favourite of mine called 'Carry Bag Man', refers to Brix's and Schofield's nickname for Smith because he carried everything in carriers; so he's obviously not above taking the mickey out of himself lyrically.

In fact, Schofield reveals further dimensions to the supposed disciplin-arian's alter-ego as practical joker. She tells how he would often customise cartoons and photos from the daily papers with mischievous quips and the tour bus contained an 'art gallery' of doctored photographs of The Fall.

'Photos of the band were mercilessly customised,' she says, remembering one of Craig Scanlon carrying an unfortunate comparison to the Care in the Community patients in Prestwich – OUT ON DAY RELEASE.

Smith could be equally scathing about himself, illustrating an image of himself in a cardigan with the tag CARDY LAD WASTER. However, just like the song 'What About Us' and its references to Harold Shipman, Schofield remembers Smith's sense of humour sailing spectacularly close to the bone.

As a British Jew, she found herself having to play a song called 'Haf

Found Bormann', an account of tracking down the former Nazi who vanished as effectively as Karl Burns, and 'hating every moment'. When The Fall debuted *Hey! Luciani*, Smith's 1986 play based on the suspicious 1978 death of Pope Jean Paul II, Alberto Luciani, the singer mischievously cast her and Brix as Israeli commandos. 'He's got a great sense of the absurd,' she says. 'Very smart and funny.'

Onstage, Smith would come over to 'bash the heck' out of her keyboards while she was dispatched to 'make a fool of myself' at the microphone. Eventually, as ever on the lookout for insurrection in the ranks, it seems Smith suspected she had dreams of fronting a band herself, which she insists was not the case. Mostly, the late 1980s seems to have been an unusually happy time to be in The Fall. She remembers 'hard-core parties' which, because she was the last to join and thus lowest-ranking member, took place in her room, which was then left to be discovered by disgusted hotel cleaners.

All of this was a side-show compared with Smith's famous creativity. She says he has a 'unique perspective' and is particularly effective at pushing people to do their best. Thus, what initially sounded like 'loose-sounding sound check jams' were somehow crafted into songs that became snapshots of history, reflecting not only the wider world but what it was like in The Fall at any given time.

What is it like, I wonder, to be integral to this process – watching the hypnotic effect on audiences from the stage, night every night, month after month – and then documenting the music flowing out on record?

'When he's on form, backed by a good, tight, powerful band, the experience for the audience and the musicians is electrifying,' she says. 'People never forget a good Fall gig. He's a magician at times.' However, she concedes that when the singer isn't on form, he 'doesn't do justice' to himself or the songs.

I'm intrigued by the innocuousness of this statement and can't help wondering aloud what 'not on form' might mean, thinking back to Brix's mention of heavy drinking and Steve Davies' assertion that people were whispering about Smith being an alcoholic as long ago as 1980.

'I don't really know what to say about that,' muses Schofield, as diplomatically as any doctor. 'Mark is a heavy drinker and always has been.' When pressed for a professional opinion, Schofield says that, according to her training, the definition of an alcoholic is someone who continues to use alcohol in the face of persisting harm (taken from the *DSM-IV-TR* medical diagnostic manual's definition of addiction).

'So, if it is harming him, then that's probably true,' she says. She goes on to say that while she was in the band, Smith's drinking involved levels beyond even those described by Brix: heavy drinking from early morning onwards, and most of the contents of a bottle of Johnnie Walker Red Label whisky 'before three in the afternoon'. By any normal standards, this is an astoundingly high alcohol intake but Schofield suggests because Smith 'always' drank, he may have had a much higher than usual tolerance. As the days went on, she recalls, he became more difficult to deal with: 'We generally had to discuss important things early in the day to get a sensible answer.'

The harm aspect is more murky. Smith has managed to operate The Fall at a fairly consistent level for 30 years, so he can't be in that bad a condition, surely?

'It's hard to say if he's actually being harmed,' she ponders. 'Suffice to say, he's a difficult character. Alcohol may be part of that, but I suspect he'd still be difficult without it!'

Of course, Herculean intakes of alcohol (and other substances) are not exactly unknown in rock. Lemmy, of metal band Motorhead, is reputed to be downing two bottles of whisky a day (often washed down with amphetamine sulphate) aged over 60, and is still successfully running his band after three decades. Similarly, Rolling Stone Keith Richards told a 1987 interviewer his daily diet involved two bottles of bourbon and little else. In comparison, Smith is relatively sober.

Again, like Brix, Schofield's experiences in The Fall seemed to follow the pattern of an alcohol-fuelled bender – hugely enjoyable at first, then drifting into chaos. She remembers times when she felt she was living under a 'reign of terror' such was the uncertainty of living in the Fall enclosure: 'One day you are playing the Tourhout Festival [in Belgium], the next you are blindfolded on a bus.' She compares the experience, one of Smith's more bizarre methods of psyching up his musicians, to Costa Gavras' 1970 film *L'Aveu* (*The Confession*), in which unsuspecting victims are blindfolded, bussed, taken away and beaten – although even Smith at his most demanding would surely never come close to the working methods of the movie's sinister Czechoslovakian 'organisation'.

The 'reign of terror' had other parallels with cultdom, at least in the amount of 'Byzantine subterfuge' going on in and around The Fall. She views The Fall as 'some kind of medieval Italian principality. Or a Chinese court, full of would-be sycophants and mandarins', with Smith operating as 'absolute ruler'.

She alludes to people who are 'attracted to Mark's power, and they often try and insinuate themselves into The Wonderful and Frightening World' – it's weird hearing a former member use this term to describe the Fall environment – 'sometimes by trying to undermine people already in the band. But he always used to see through them. He was a good judge of character.

'He isn't above using intimidation, fear and uncertainty to maintain discipline,' she adds, agreeing with comments from other Fallen members about Smith's inability to share or relinquish power.

'He's a control freak, and he thinks people work better when they are uncomfortable.' She notes that, unlike other bands, The Fall sound like The Fall whoever is in the group. 'It's a management style. Unfortunately, not one conducive to staff retention!' Schofield eventually came to realise being out of the band was part of the whole dynamic. She says maybe everyone will fall out with Smith – not because he is a nasty character, but because his working methods demand it.

'He just pushes and pushes you. I quit or was fired many, many times before I was definitively fired. I don't think he can help it.'

To this day, Schofield is not entirely sure what happened and won't be drawn on Eric the Ferret's view that she was fired for dating Martin Bramah. 'The thing with Mark and Martin goes way back' is all she will say and she jokes that if Smith, who was, after all, married, ever harboured intentions towards her she must have 'always got away'. In any case, she says with a twinkle, she was 'quite busy on the boy front', implying she had other distractions besides Martin Bramah. Nevertheless, she understands the cult-like doctrine of loyalty in The Fall – 'No side projects and no "cheating" on the band!'

Schofield's teaming up with Bramah effectively formed an enemy camp within the group. Soon she was 'answering back', especially when she thought Smith 'might be bullying Martin'. That was a *volte-face*: 'The lads used to defend me when I first started!'

Another factor was Brix's departure. Because she had been her ally –

Jewish, female, and chief dressing room cohort – Schofield now found herself topping the torment list. And, in a manner symptomatic of a cult, she recalls all band members being forbidden to mention Brix's name.

Along with Marc Riley, Schofield admits it's possible, as with so many musicians, Smith may have felt he had exhausted her talents: 'I think Mark may have just wanted to move on.' And he did, although Schofield's work appeared on records after she left.

Once Marcia Schofield exited the enclave, she too found herself the victim of cult behaviour. The 'lads' who had liked her a lot and been so protective were suddenly banned from contact. She says, 'It was like being "disappeared".'

She'd survived four years in the camp. In that period, she saw the music world change dramatically. She joined in the era of stadium rock bands like Simple Minds, while The Smiths were the hottest band in music paper circles. By the time she left, in July 1990, The Smiths had disbanded and The Stone Roses and Happy Mondays had ushered in a sea-change towards dancier grooves.

The decade saw huge changes for all of us. I started the 1980s with a spiky punk haircut and ended it with the sort of ghastly, overlong bowl cut that was an unfortunate side-effect of the onset of bands like Inspiral Carpets. In between there was a disastrous perm, a Morrissey-type quiff, an augmented skinhead resembling a root vegetable with leaves growing out of it and a lot of emotional upheaval. Mum had died in 1984, leaving me alone in our semi-detached council house and on the dole for years, listening to too much Fall, before I sent a few reviews to *Melody Maker* and became a journalist, principally so I could be paid to listen to The Fall. I did listen to other bands – for quite a while developing a parallel obsession with New Order – but always returned to The Fall, like a strict but loving parent you return to apologetically after some act of teenage rebellion. Then I met Suzanne when the Roses played my old establishment, Leeds Polytechnic, and she moved in with that record box containing *Live at the Witch Trials*.

As for Marcia Schofield, she felt 'burned and hurt' by her exit from The Fall and for a long time afterwards turned down all offers to make music for work or pleasure. She even found herself unwilling to go out of the house because there'd always be 'some weirdo asking "What did you do to Mark?" or "Are you and Martin Bramah still together?"'

But now she has her life back, and maybe it's significant her psychiatrist husband had never heard of The Fall. Because of his profession, I wonder aloud if her husband would find Smith interesting.

'Probably not,' she responds flatly, 'because he's not mentally ill. He's got some pretty well recognised morbidity. Other people's perceptions of who he is, his cultural significance and the fact that they love his music, but also are intimidated by him . . . that's what's really interesting about him.'

Oddly enough, I've never felt intimidated by Smith when I've met him. I've always approached him like an Alsatian dog – pat it nicely and it will respond. Show fear and it will bite your hand off. But behind my easygoing approach, I suppose some nervousness must have lurked. Schofield echoes Brix's comments – 'The Fall are a mirror' – and compares Smith to a process used in psychology to determine the mental functioning of patients: 'He's a walking, cultural Rorschach Test.'

CHAPTER 16

'Dependency on the organisation . . . attack the self.'

I'm becoming fascinated by the apparent parallels between The Fall and the controversial world of religious cults. I'm not suggesting Smith has ever led 912 brightly clad followers to commit suicide by cyanide poisoning, as cult leader Jim Jones did in Guyana in 1978, but there are things in common.

I'm reading a fascinating book called *Cults in our Midst* by Margaret Thaler Singer, one of the world's leading experts in cults and brainwashing, in which she explains how we should define a cult. The first aspect common to them all is the origin and role of the leader, usually the founder of the cult and based in its nerve centre. We know Smith founded The Fall in Prestwich (although born in Broughton, Salford) and he is the, perhaps not divine, but certainly absolute, leader of The Fall whom some members call 'God'.

The next element common to cults is a power structure, the relationship between leader and followers, and we all know how that works in The Fall.

Singer's third category is persuasion or 'thought reform'. Ben Pritchard calls it 'moulding'. Smith is more direct: 'I just brainwash 'em'.

Another feature common to cult leaders, according to Singer, is their claim to have 'special knowledge', which is true of Smith. He asserts that he has no musical ability but has 'good ears', which takes his claim of appreciation and knowledge of what makes a good tune into the area of the mystic. And, of course, there are Smith's reputed abilities as a psychic, as described by Brix earlier. Admittedly, he has never claimed to have visited special places in a spaceship – a trait common to cult leaders – but he does talk mythically of Prestwich and Salford, finding the uncanny in the harsh industrial North.

Singer suggests cult leaders tend to be 'domineering and charismatic'. Tick.

They venerate themselves over other leaders and gods, as Smith was quick to do with me in Malmaison: 'These other groups are rubbish'.

Cults tend to be authoritarian but within them important jobs are delegated – which might include the driving and other tasks given to Ben Pritchard.

Singer says cult leaders tend to be innovative, offering something novel. What could possibly be more novel in modern music than The Fall?

Singer also says cult leaders have a double set of ethics, requiring exacting standards which are not applicable to themselves. Members are further required to confess all to the leader and deceive and manipulate non-members. Cults dictate what members wear and where they will sleep (including sleep deprivation techniques). From what I've heard so far of The Fall, they don't sleep very much and Fall musicians almost universally have short hair and basic, functional clothing.

Another characteristic is the emergence of black-and-white thinking. This is good. That is bad. There is nothing in between. There are 'food restrictions'. Cult leaders 'intimidate' critics, as Smith did to that pesky interrogator from *Loaded* magazine, who, incidentally, he also branded a 'fookin' dead-leg cunt'.

All the above characteristics can quite easily be applied to the group the BBC call the 'crackpot garage band' from Salford.

Singer also examines how cult members are recruited. Usually, they are solicited on the street like Tommy Crooks, or in local Rotary Club-type groupings – which would rule in the pubs of Prestwich. Potential members may be depressed, confused by life's choices or seeking purpose – 'I was a terrible guitarist before I joined The Fall,' quoth Ben Pritchard.

Cult members often experience a 'first fatal step'. For Crooks, that fatal step was suddenly finding himself in 'the eye of the storm'.

Singer says that, after the recruitment, cults are often reminiscent of a 'jack-in-the-box – a pretty innocuous container that, when opened, surprises you with a pop-out figure, often a scary one'. Similarly, 'surprising and frightening' things pop out over the course of membership.

However, the most interesting areas of her work for me are the sections where she explores 'brainwashing', or moulding. One of the foremost tactics is for the leader or upper echelons of the cult power structure to 'attack the self' of new or unconverted recruits. In religion, this may involve calling someone a pagan, with no beliefs, creating a vacuum of spirituality in that person within which the cult can grow. In music, it could encompass something like 'You're playing like a fookin' pub band' and 'Get it together instead of showing off'.

In 1950s China, Chairman Mao explored the area of 'ideological remoulding', although this was done not with myths, neo-supernatural methods or 'secrets', but by the simpler techniques of group pressure and careful choice of words.

One of the key characteristics of cult brainwashing is the members having no idea they are undergoing the process – which is opposite to The Fall experience, whose new musicians know full well what is happening to them and are happy to get with the programme. However, Fall musicians certainly seem to develop 'dependency on the organisation', as Singer suggests. In fact, the more I read about cults, I wonder how much the very well read Smith knows about them too, and whether the way his group operates is by design. On the other hand, apart from some cults – financially based, which fleece their members and get them out of the door – members are generally encouraged to stay in the cult at all costs, even if this means taking on authorities. In The Fall, conversely, it's now generally accepted every member will one day be asked – or ask – to leave.

If The Fall is in fact a cult, and not just a pop group, where does that leave you and me? I've read Singer's book from cover to cover because I'm having trouble sleeping. I've become fixated and sometimes irritable. One night, Suzanne comes home while I'm in the middle of typing an email and I uncharacteristically yell, 'Shut up!' at the interruption to my concentration, and feel terrible afterwards. Sometimes, I feel I'm slipping further and further into The Wonderful and Frightening World, and wonder where it will all lead.

CHAPTER 17

'Creative management, cock!'

Everything is a blur before I suddenly realise where I am. There's a mass of equipment. To my right, two guitarists. To my left, a bass player who is shrouded by a stack of amps. All around there is music. What am I doing here? I get a feeling I shouldn't be here at all . . . a feeling forcibly rammed home by a figure walking towards me in a white shirt.

Now I realise where I am.

The Fall's stage.

His stage.

And I shouldn't be here at all.

I feel a shove beneath my ribcage. 'Get off my fucking stage.' Then all becomes blackness.

I wake up to be confronted by another omnipresent figure in my life – it's Guinness, nestled beneath my ribcage. I've fallen asleep and been dreaming about The Fall.

It's happening a lot lately. Sometimes, I remember what life was like before I started on this biblical quest, before almost every waking hour was spent finding The Fallen. But I can't think about that now. I have to get myself together. The Fall are playing 26 miles away at Leeds Irish Centre, which for some reason has become the only venue The Fall ever play in Leeds, and I have to go.

Several hours later, I'm showered, dressed, *Fall Heads Roll*'s on the car stereo and I'm pulling into the Irish Centre car park for my third Fall gig this year, which must be something like the twenty-ninth or thirty-second Fall gig of my life. Soon enough, I'm in the company of around a thousand cult followers. Among the audience are Hells Angels, blokes with strange facial expressions who look like they've been released from somewhere for the day, teenage girls, bald men and, bizarrely, most of the cast of *Emmerdale*. Who would have thought Paddy the vet and Jimmy King the high-rolling, crooked incompetent would spend evenings listening to The Fall? It's exactly how Kay Carroll described Fall gigs in the 1970s and early 1980s – as if a plane had crashed and the passengers stumbled to the gig.

As usual, there is much speculation over whether Smith will turn up, how long he will be onstage, and in what condition. At around ten, a burly guy wanders through the crowd shouting 'Five minutes to The Fall'. I'm reminded of the little besuited black man who used to say, 'Tyson's coming through!' whenever the former champion boxer made his latest increasingly unhinged public appearance. At 10.10 p.m. there's a more familiar voice: 'We are The Fall.'

He seems in good shape, the best for quite some time. For once, even those deliberately misshapen free-associating vowels are crystal clear, which means the crowd notice when he breaks off from the turbulent 'Blindness' – about David Blunkett – to launch into an incomprehensibly withering annihilation of Roy Hattersley. As he works the stage like a comedian, I notice he's wearing the same jacket he struggled to keep on in Malmaison. On 'Pacifying Joint' he starts fiddling with the bassist's amplification so the booming basslines drown out the group, like some kind of peculiar Fall reggae. Meanwhile, the poor bassist – who, as if his art being tampered with wasn't bad enough, has to tolerate the humiliation of various prods and shoves – stares ahead impassively, in the manner of a Buckingham Palace sentry.

Smith's jacket comes off to reveal a zip-up tank top over a shirt – making him look like a businessman who has been dragged by a mad outfitter into the nearest branch of Oxfam – but after 40 minutes the jacket goes back on and the singer beckons the band offstage. They remain in the dressing room for 15, maybe 20 minutes, after which Smith leads them back on, looking rather zonked. But somehow after the break they sound even better. What Clough-like pep talk did the boss give them in the break? Did Smith supernaturally prompt the musicians into playing better by blindfolding them, as Schofield had suggested? Did he attack the bassist with a cattle-prod or indulge in some performance-enhancing substance? Or was he simply dispensing more of those odd instructions we discussed in Malmaison: 'Hit it harder!'

'Mark is the master of the cryptic instruction,' says Simon Rogers. 'Do you take sugar?'

It's a few days after the gig and I'm 200 or more miles from Prestwich once again, in London's leafy Ealing Broadway, where I meet another member of The Fallen. Rogers – the nineteenth disciple – was officially in the cult from 1985 to 1986 but as a producer of The Fall's albums he was in the camp well into the 1990s.

His house, in a quiet street in the busy suburb, looks like somewhere I've previously encountered – Dave Tucker's tiny abode, but times fifty.

The studio at the back of his house contains more instruments than even Smith's ex-clarinet player turned jazz man has probably ever seen. A collection of mandolins hangs on the walls. There are computers and a baffling array of sound equipment. A large elephant's head sculpture overlooks books on Wagner and Lord Byron. There are scores of CDs and DVDs. Glancing through them, every so often I come across something by The Fall.

In a sense, the quizzical 40-something with close-cropped hair – the operatic barnet he sported in Fall days is long gone – is Dave Tucker times fifty. He was, and remains, anathema to The Fall – a technically accomplished and highly trained classical musician.

Rogers was not hanging around Prestwich or lurking in American clubs like Brix. While The Fall were treading the boards in smelly clubs between 1977 and 1980, this tea-making Faller was studying at London's Royal College of Music in London, gaining a coveted ARCM (Associate of the Royal College of Music).

When The Fall recorded *Grotesque* in 1980, he picked up the College's guitar prize. In the early 1980s, he played in the Ballet Rambert's Mercury Ensemble, composed ballet scores and worked on BBC dramas. Somehow, he also found time to form Incantation, who played a form of South American folk and scored hits with music that would normally make Smith retch.

By any standards, Rogers is the least likely musician ever to end up in The Fall. Which may be why Smith invited him in. The process occurred by a familiar, obtuse route. Michael Clark – who Rogers remembers as a 'tearaway' when they were together in the Rambert – was working on a dance based on the Fall song 'The Classical' and asked Rogers to provide the score.

Rogers phoned Smith to ask whether he should use cellos but was simply told, 'I don't know, just get on with it!' At the time, Steve Hanley was briefly absent from The Fall because his wife had had a baby. Out of the blue, Smith phoned the classical musician, 200 miles way.

'He asked if I played bass,' Rogers remembers with a grin. 'I said I had, but only jazz funk.' Thus, inevitably, the mandolin collector who'd only played bass in the entirely different Incantation would pick up the instrument in Britain's strangest group.

Rogers had never even been to Manchester, never mind Prestwich, but soon found himself staying with the Smiths and being inducted into the lifestyle. He remembers days lost to dingy local boozers and nights listening to 'weird records' like Captain Beefheart and Nervous Norvus – the performing name of the Californian Jimmy Drake, who had a smash hit in 1956 with 'Transfusion', a song about careless drivers who receive a blood transfusion after each accident (every stanza ends with the line 'Never ever ever gonna speed again').

As the records played, Smith would rummage through plastic bags looking for misplaced lyrics. Rogers' bed for the night – when he was allowed sleep – was the spare room. He remembers 'speeding off my head', unable to rest and gazing at strange images on Fall posters on the walls.

Induction into The Fall was another culture shock. Because The Fall place intensity above technical expertise, he was required to 'de-learn' his classical training and at early gigs found himself being given a 'hard time' by fans wondering who this odd chap was, wearing a solitary white glove to protect his 'classical guitar fingernails'. Meanwhile, the musicians called him things like 'Wendy' and 'Ottersley Kipling' – apparently viewing him as a 'fat bastard' for the heinous crime of having a 'normal' appetite.

Like Dave Tucker, and episodes such as firing a soundman during the gig, Rogers was another musical 'spanner in the works' – someone to 'shake up' the other musicians and, ideally, amuse the site manager in the process. Rogers reveals Smith's justification for any unusual developments – the catch-all 'Creative management, cock!'

However, as Smith explained to me in Malmaison, Rogers came to enjoy the enormous musical freedom of playing in The Fall. Freed from the prison-like disciplines of his training, he enjoyed 'making some noise'.

He also found a different Smith to the stern public image – someone who was 'very civil' and frequently hilarious to work with, especially if he ever suspected the band were becoming complacent, in which case he'd attack the latest drummer or hurl the keyboards off the stage.

Rogers backs up Smith's suggestion to me that at least some of this was showbiz (among Smith's few heroes are Johnny Cash and Elvis Presley). Along with 'creative management', another of Smith's mantras is, apparently, 'Don't knock The King'.

Another reason he enjoyed working with The Fall was the money, which was comparable if not better than anything he could have commanded in the classical world at the time. He suggests some musicians may feel aggrieved because Smith's approach to wages was haphazard and similar to that of a nineteenth-century employer: if he felt a musician deserved recompense, the musician would find him- or herself the recipient of 'bundles of tenners and twenties, out of the blue'. If not, then there were starvation wages.

Rogers says he wasn't always paid on time but was handsomely rewarded by the boss. In fact, Smith became quite friendly with the classical musician who aroused his intellectual curiosity. Whenever Smith was in London, he'd stay at Rogers' house and Smith became friendly with Rogers' wife, Lucy, who potters in the garden as we talk.

There's a lot of amusement when Rogers tells me about touring with The Fall. He remembers an episode in Rennes when Smith had a boil on his neck and was starting to hallucinate.

'I thought it was the drink but, apparently it was so close to his spinal cord and infected, if we hadn't got him to a hospital he might have died,' he says, explaining how the doctor lanced the boil and Smith came out covered in bandages. Any other musician would have pulled the gig, but Smith took to the stage, looking 'like a mummy'. This curious sight prompted the crowd to throw things at the stage and Burns to hurl them back. When the promoter withheld the fee, Burns smeared his body with pâté from a nearby spread then hugged the promoter, smearing him with food paste. The evening ended with Rogers and Burns wrestling in the mud in the middle of the night and spending the rest of it on wooden floors in the local YMCA.

He has lots of stories of fun on the road. He remembers a Welsh road manager whose nationality prompted Smith and Rogers to spend all night in a Novotel hotel filling in hundreds of comments slips reading, 'Please build more Novotels in Wales, the land of my birth', all bearing the forged signature of the Welshman.

Rogers had even more fun in the studio. Because he was asked to play a keyboard – an instrument he didn't take to, having never played one in his life – he retired from the live band to become The Fall's producer and has more insights than anyone I've yet encountered into The Fall's unconventional approach to making records.

He remembers the studio as being as peculiar an environment as the stage, with musicians being given bizarre instructions. Karl Burns, for instance, was told to play a tom tom – the usual fine presumably having been lifted – 'like a fookin' snake!'

How does one actually play a drum like a snake?

'I have absolutely no idea,' grins Rogers. Neither did Burns, who just took it as a cue to try something different.

For Rogers, some of the most outlandish recording experiences didn't take place in a studio at all. He remembers a song called 'Paintwork' from Brix-era album *This Nation's Saving Grace*. The band had recorded it in at least moderately conventional fashion – a studio was hired, the musicians played and Smith wreaked havoc on the sound desk. The track was finished and Smith took a cassette recording of it back to his hotel, where he placed it in a cassette machine and accidentally sat on the button marked RECORD. The resulting recording – the expensive studio track interrupted by a BBC documentary about stars – ended up on the album. 'And it sounded amazing,' laughs Rogers, still incredulous. He describes another track – 'Crew Filth' on 1992's *Code: Selfish*, a spoof of hip-hop 'crew' culture involving what sounds like a toy organ – being recorded with a microphone in the back of a Transit van at 70 mph, which would explain why Smith delivers the lyrics while howling with laughter.

He says Smith 'never knew when to stop' and unusual approaches to sound even went as far as the cutting room (where sound engineers make the initial pressing of a record), where Smith would decide at the eleventh hour that a certain track needed an extra backing vocal.

He cites the cutting of 1987's single 'Hit The North' – at Abbey Road, the famous London studio where the Beatles recorded – as typical. Engineer Ian Cooper had done a 'fantastic job. It wasn't like The Fall at all but it was brilliant, really clean,' says Rogers. Smith listened intently, then stood up and suddenly declared, 'Right, cock, in the intro put the top end [treble] right up. In the chorus, take the top end right off and put some fookin' bass reverb in.'

'The thing about engineers is that they spend a lot of time on their own and can be a bit weird themselves,' says Rogers, describing how Cooper went into the kitchen, brought out a 'fucking great knife and just put it down on the desk and he said, "Right then, shall we cut the track?"'

In the flash of a blade, Smith decided: 'It sounds great, cock!' And indeed it did – one of The Fall's finest singles, still heard on dance floors to this day. Curiously, I have since heard that Lightning Seeds man and former Fall producer Ian Broudie tells a different version of this story: that it was Smith who produced the knife. So either Rogers' memory fails him, or the Fall leader picked up a useful tip.

Rogers breaks from the interview and starts rummaging in boxes, emerging with a tape of Smith speaking in the studio. The man is delivering his lyrics while adding spontaneous instructions. It's really mad stuff; 'Use Pinky and Perky voices' and the like. The words pierce the comfy environment of Rogers' home studio: 'We're coming, Leo, whoahwhoahwhoah . . . Crusty mystics!' and 'Autobiograph . . . self-pity crap . . . Simon, put that bit in if you like'.

These are Smith's vocals and instructions for the song 'Pumpkin Head Xcapes', a 1992 B-side that's never been played live. After recording all this stuff on cassette tape, Smith had posted the results to Rogers, who had the daunting task of somehow sifting the lyrics from this lot and synching them to The Fall's music. It's a demented way of working but it worked.

In another box the bassist turned producer finds letters Smith sent him welcoming him to The Fall.

One reads: 'Dear Mr Bastardo, mucho thanks for subbing rehearsal fees and for bringing Incantation featuring Algernon Bastardo musicians into the world' and is signed 'the white Christian, let God be your judge'.

Another reads: 'Dear Mr Rogers, welcome to the twilight zone. Are you ready for the disembodied head of Karl Burns to manifest itself in your street?'

I still haven't found Burns, never mind his disembodied head, but Rogers at least has a new tip for me: Burns is currently 'doing post offices'. He remembers the colourful drummer as a 'character' who would go on a US tour armed only with a giant suitcase containing a single pair of underpants and nothing else, and says the reason he was forever being fired and rehired was that unlike the rest he'd stand up to Mark E Smith. Physically, if need be.

'They were always having fights,' says Rogers, remembering one time when the pair of them were punching each other in a moving car. Luckily, neither of them was driving.

The musician tells how one night the whole Fall returned drunk and red-eyed from a US tour and turned up to stay at Rogers' house, where he was hosting a visit from his elderly parents. During the early hours, his ageing mother awoke in her nightie to find a man on the end of her bed.

'I was going, "Er, Mum, this is Karl",' laughs Rogers, who believes Karl Burns may have disappeared from public life because, despite being brilliant on drums, his unpredictable personality simply wouldn't fit in with any other group.

Rogers guesses a lot of members suffer burnout. He mentions 1980s–1990s drummer Simon Wolstencroft who developed a stomach ulcer, possibly from the stress of being in the group. To relax, the drummer took up the hobby of searching for antique glass bottles in fields. One night while he was in a field a helicopter came down with a searchlight and the hapless sticksman was heard to exclaim, 'Oh, my ulcer!'

But another reason is commitment.

'If you're really into The Fall and Mark likes what you do you could, in theory, be in The Fall forever,' says Rogers, oddly enough using the same cult-like phrase as the Ferret – 'the magic hour' – to describe being on their stage. However, similar to what Charlie Watts once said of his first 25 years with The Rolling Stones ('five years work, 20 years hanging around') – there is apparently a lot of downtime in The Fall.

'There's a lot of time in the boozer waiting for Mark,' he explains. 'Obviously, he gets fantastic results like that but it's not for everyone.' Rogers, who saw a stream of musicians flow through in his time, has clearly thought about this a lot and delivers another insightful reason why so many people leave The Fall: in the end, no one can ever be into it as much as Mark E Smith.

His own exit from Fall circles, in 1994, came after a row about a studio Smith had booked. Rogers had mentioned, perhaps wearily, that it was unsuitable. Unusually, there was no big falling out. They just stopped phoning each other.

'Mark says he sacked me,' he says, echoing Una Baines. 'He didn't.'

They haven't spoken since, although listening to the tapes seems to have prompted some fond memories, and he says he 'just might' call his old boss up.

After exiting Smith's orbit, The Fall's unlikeliest musician carried on working in differing musical environments. He produced The Lightning Seeds (including their England football anthem, 'Three Lions'). He's been involved in dance music but has recently turned to TV scores, including the BBC drama *Family Business* and Carlton Television's naval series, *Making Waves*. Never mind the Royal College or the Ballet Rambert, Rogers insists his greatest education was in The Fall.

'It taught me that there are no musical rules. Just do something good.'

He plays me the theme tune he wrote for the BBC's hit crime caper series *Hustle*. As he admits, it sounds very like The Fall, suggesting they invade our culture, and his life, in ways he least expects. He's not the only one.

Because Suzanne can't drive, part of my daily ritual is to ferry my partner to her work, some 500 yards away as the crow flies but difficult to access on foot. Every day at 9.15 a.m. – and again at 6 p.m. – I become a driver. I am Suzanne's Ben Pritchard and, like young Ben, if I am not on time the boss gets very angry. Lately, there have been quite a few times when the boss has been very angry. I feel bad. I feel disloyal. But it can't be helped. I'm on a mission.

CHAPTER 18

'He looks much the same as he ever did – short hair, glass eye.'

Rogers' anecdotes have made me even more determined to find Karl Burns, but my next assignment is finding a much more minor, but significant character in the Fall soap: Kenny Brady, a fiddle player who was the first Fall departure of the 1990s but hasn't been heard of since 1991.

My Google enquiry, 'Kenny Brady and The Fall', throws up a mere 507,000 Kenny Bradys, at least some of whom were in The Fall. The first one is from The Fall Live Gig Repository, a sort of rolling compendium of live shows, which has a few inaccuracies and half-truths like anything in The Wonderful and Frightening World. However, the Repository records Brady's live contributions, ranging from adding fiddle to a 'lethargic' Fall at The Fridge in Brixton on 3 December 1990, to making the instrument sound like a 'demented bluebottle' in Cardiff a week later. Alas, by the time The

Fall play Brighton Top Rank on 26 March 1990, just three months later, Brady has vanished, although you can still hear his fiddle on the bootleg of the gig. Just like Marcia Schofield, Brady still seems to have playing been in The Fall long after his physical body had departed.

The following year Brady makes a surprise reappearance onstage at Amsterdam's Paradiso. The Repository notes how, 'Simply memorable versions of "Bill is Dead" and "The Mixer" dominate the first half of the set – the importance of Brady's violin in this context is never better realised than on the latter.' During 'Life Just Bounces', the author notes how the violinist 'leads the band in a mad jig around the melody – this is simply a wild ceilidh of speedy noise which just has to be heard to be believed'.

Which sounds as if Brady had become an integral part of The Fall – fitting then, that that was his last gig.

After hours of fruitless Googling I throw in a few curve balls after remembering Brady is, or was, if he is no longer alive, a Scotsman. I type in cities like Glasgow and Edinburgh alongside his name. Eventually, this pays off, and I discover he had been in Glasgow Cajun band The Peyote Brothers. But he's now left them, as well. After that it looks like he played with a singer in Glasgow called Electra, who resembles Cher in a particularly ill-fitting fright wig. Again the trail goes cold. Then, a breakthrough.

By curious coincidence, I get an email from a journalist colleague who knows about my quest. 'You'll never guess who my ex-boyfriend has bumped into', she writes. 'Kenny Brady – in the Bongo Club in Edinburgh'. Then her ex-boyfriend emails me too; Brady looks 'much the same as he ever did – short hair, glass eye, just thicker-set'. He's been in another Cajun band called Deaf Heights Cajun Aces and has his own band Starvation Box.

Unfortunately, an email to their website reveals they're trying to track him down as well. 'He left a year ago,' comes the reply, 'and we're still trying to catch up with him. Can you let us know if you track him down?'

By now, my journalist pal's ex has turned sleuth too. He discovers Brady is playing with former One Dove vocalist Dot Allison, and it's confirmed on her website. Then he forwards me Brady's email address, but nobody replies. Several months later, I get a message – from Kenny Brady.

He sends an email – which means I can't confirm the story of the glass eye – and describes how, during Smith's exile in Edinburgh, when he lived just up the road, they became friends. They had already met in London at a do organised by dance tearaway Michael Clark. Months later, Smith phoned Brady out of the blue and asked him to contribute to 1990's *Extricate* album, which The Fall were recording in Oxford. Brady fulfilled Smith's requirement. He told him he wasn't a Fall fan (although he now admits he loved 'Totally Wired'). He supplied off-kilter fiddle to *Extricate* and 1991's *Shift-Work*, sang on a track called 'Book of Lies' and toured for about three years.

'The gigs were always great . . . great energy,' he says, and that particular band – 'I know there's been a few!' – were incredibly tight musically, which allowed Mark free rein. Brady says he 'felt privileged to be part of what was and still is, I think, one of the biggest cult bands in the world'.

So why did he leave? For once, an exit that's almost normal. Brady is under the impression he was the only one who wasn't sacked, which isn't true, however, he explains that he left of his own accord because his domestic life was suffering from going all over the place with The Fall.

'Also, the band were having financial problems and I thought it would be one less thing for Mark to worry about if he didn't have me on the payroll,' he says, reasonably. He adds, 'Mark himself was really stressed out and it led to a lot of tension within the band, so it wasn't as enjoyable.'

Although he refuses to be drawn on what these tensions were, Brady says he took the unusual decision to step out of the fray because he didn't want to end up with Smith and himself hating each other. As a result, he's one of few Fallen musicians who can say he counts Smith as a friend – even though they haven't seen each other for a long time.

Like Eric the Ferret, Brady has unstinting respect for the leader, admiring Smith for carrying on through various adversities and admiring his 'amazing' body of work. One of Brady's favourite lyrics is 'Check the record, check the guy's track record' from 'New Big Prinz' on the *I Am Kurious Oranj* album. 'I think Mark's track record speaks for itself in terms of originality and output,' he says, before disappearing into the ether once again.

CHAPTER 19

'I neither left nor got sacked.'

Ido another email interview with Charlotte Bill, the next 1990s exit, who very briefly played the rather un-Fall instrument of the oboe live and on *Extricate*. I find her via Martin Bramah, because she's played in his Blue Orchids band.

She recounts how she ended up in The Fall via Una Baines. They met at a music session in Manchester in 1982 entitled 'Women Make Noise', where Baines noticed Bill playing the flute and liked her sound enough to invite her to play in Blue Orchids, where she switched to oboe. Curiously, a tape of her playing oboe with Blue Orchids found its way to Smith who wasted no time in getting her to join The Fall.

'Mark liked the sound and asked me to come and record with The Fall,' she says, making it sound as if she was recruited by an insurance company or group of Buddhists.

The way Bill describes Smith's creative process sounds a bit like those old adverts for PG Tips tea, where two chimpanzees dressed as humans sit at a grand piano and one goes, 'You hum it, Ah'll play it.'

'If he liked it, he'd say carry on.' And that was that. No blindfolding musicians or commands to play like snakes. She loved hearing her flute and oboe 'slicing across their sound' and describes the Fall line-up back then – Smith, Hanley, Scanlon, Schofield, Wolstencroft, Bramah plus Brady – as 'loud, relentless'. As for surreal situations, she remembers one when the police boarded the tour bus looking for an escaped prisoner, but otherwise isn't saying much more than Bramah, whom she's worked with, after all. On her departure, she emphasises she was a 'guest, so neither left nor got sacked'. Which is another new one.

Lately, she's made experimental films for a band called Nocturnal Emissions, who released CDs and played shows in Canada, the USA and UK, and made animations and documentaries for the BBC. She took a break to have a daughter, then returned on Blue Orchids' 2003 album, *Mystic Bud*. There are no revelations about Bramah's take on Smith either: 'Martin and Mark have a very deep relationship' is all she'll say.

CHAPTER 20

'He smashed up my keyboards quite often. It was an occupational hazard.'

Somehow, I think I'll get more than I got from Bill out of Dave Bush, the third 1990s departure whose November 1995 exit marked the end of a relative period of stability and continued chart success for the line-up.

The Taplow-born keyboard player joined in 1991 and for a while was a pivotal Fall member. Appearing on *Code: Selfish* (1992), *The Infotainment Scan* (1993), *Middle Class Revolt* (1994) and *Cerebral Caustic* (1995), Bush brought with him keyboards and electronics that revolutionised the Fall sound, without losing sight of who they were, as effectively as Brix had when she'd arrived bearing pop riffs. This was the era of club-friendly and commercial dance music, and, backed up by remaining Jesuit lads Steve Hanley and Craig Scanlon, Bush's keyboards ensured The Fall dipped a toe into club culture while Smith's lyrics, often deriding that very culture, were as ever a step apart.

Bush was the twenty-fourth musician to join The Fall, but Smith's doctrine of 'turnover' was nothing if not successful. Losing both Marc Riley and Brix Smith should have been insurmountable setbacks but, with Bush in tow, The Fall became even more successful than they'd been before. *Code: Selfish* – their last album for major label Phonogram – reached Number 21 before Smith took the contrary route of exiting the label (after disagreements) and scoring a Top 10 smash with *The Infotainment Scan* on Permanent, a smaller indie label. Once again, his perverse instincts were proved right. I love *The Infotainment Scan*: it's one of The Fall's most mischievous, playful albums. Highlights include an inspired version of Sister Sledge's 'Lost in Music' where Smith sounds more like he's lost in a pub cellar than the disco, and a track rejoicing in the title 'The League of Bald-Headed Men', which seems to steal a Led Zeppelin riff despite Smith insisting unconvincingly he's never heard the rock band's music. 'Glam Racket', which just missed the Top 40 when released as a single, sees Smith pouring bile on an unnamed pop star half-wit who eats too much chocolate. 'Paranoia Man in Cheap Sh*t Room' is possibly autobiographical but allays any concerns that Smith was ailing, brilliantly depicting a leather-jacketed man at the zenith of his powers but going down fast. It hurtles along on one of the group's most hypnotic guitar lines – yet another Fall classic.

However, towards the end of Bush's tenure, the *Middle Class Revolt* album seemed overburdened by cover versions (3 in 14 songs) and patchy, although it contained the particularly catchy, insistent 'Behind The Counter' and fan favourite 'Hey! Student', in which Smith threatens violence on 'dead brain' students who wear sneakers and long hair. *Middle Class Revolt* was less successful – scraping to Number 48; the subsequent *Cerebral Caustic* contained just one Bush writing credit ('One Day'), fared even worse at Number 67, and Bush was gone – far from the only departure in what proved to be a period of exceptional turbulence, even for The Fall.

I find him studying web design in Wiltshire, where the voice answering the phone yells, 'Dayyyyyyyyve!' He answers a few moments later sounding breathless and excitable, and 30 minutes later he's still breathless and excitable. For Dave Bush, being in The Fall was 'very tense . . . but hilarious'.

The breathless man joined The Fall by the most tried and trusted method. After learning to operate sound with bands like The Clash and Echo and The Bunnymen, he joined The Fall's sound crew and subsequently joined the group. He wasn't a Fall fan but became one after watching them onstage and dutifully – one expects breathlessly and excitably – informed Mark E Smith.

'I told him he sounded brilliant and I'd do anything for them on keyboards or computers.' In keeping with his professed reluctance to employ fans, Smith ignored him for weeks but then relented. 'He just came up and said, "All right, you're in".' Once ensconced, in August 1991, Bush found he developed a taste for what Ben Pritchard called the 'frame of mind'.

'It's an attitude, and once you've got that it's brilliant,' he explains, describing the process of writing a melody and thinking, 'Is that a Fall tune? No. It's too nice. Let's change it.' Times were good at this point. The Fall may have left their major label, but because less money was spent on marketing there was more for the musicians themselves. He remembers 'good times and good money'.

I'm breathless myself because Bush played alongside Karl Burns – who returned, in 1993, for the first time in seven years – and another drummer, Simon Wolstencroft, in a second hallowed two-drummer line-up. Together, they sounded like Smith was backed by both The Glitter Band and Adam and The Ants. However, Burns' latest stint didn't last too long. He arrived for the gig at Clapham Grand on 15 May 1993 but had already gone by the time The Fall toured America, just four months later.

Bush has a similar tale to the one Simon Rogers told me about the AWOL drummer going on tour with one pair of underpants in a suitcase. In his version, Burns turned up for the American tour with two drumsticks and a hat. 'No T-shirts, no underwear, nothing!' he laughs. Burns was soon sacked for 'stinking the place out!' However, according to Bush, Burns wasn't about to let the minor distraction of being fired from Britain's greatest alternative band get in the way of his enjoyment of America. With The Fall reverting to a single drummer line-up and continuing on tour, Burns hired a motorbike and had 'the time of his life' riding around America. 'Then months later he flew back to Manchester using his tickets for the same flight as the band,' grins Bush, confirming that, as far as his nose told him, Burns was wearing the same underpants as two months before.

Promisingly, Bush refuses to believe Burns is dead, because he has the 'constitution of an ox', although he admits it is a remote possibility. He offers a more reasonable explanation for Burns' apparent disappearance – that without the money from The Fall, he'd be unable to enjoy the same rowdy lifestyle and so could indeed be living quietly somewhere.

He doesn't have any leads for Burns, but pulls an unexpected Fallen rabbit from the hat – the fate of the original Tory drummer Dave aka Steve.

It turns out Bush had come to know the mysterious Conservative, insurance-selling sticksman on the Manchester party scene in the early to mid 1990s. They were both living in Manchester's Heaton Park district, where Bush would often ask him, 'Were you really in The Fall?' The man had a stock reply to such enquiries: 'Yeah, so was everybody else in Manchester!'

Bush remembers him being called Steve. Definitely Steve. 'He was a bit weird. People used to take the piss out of him.' In fact, 'Steve' had become schizophrenic. He vanished from the party circuit and Bush discovered why – the writer of 'Landslide Victory' had thrown himself under a train.

I feel extremely depressed – a member of The Fallen who has, literally, fallen – and find myself hoping a similar fate has not befallen Karl Burns.

Bush brightens the mood with other mad talk of Fall experiences in America, this time involving Smith. Once, according to Bush, the great man fell stupidly in love with a girl he met on tour from Salem, the Massachusetts city made infamous by the witch trials.

Smith was convinced she was a witch. Besotted, he paid for her to fly over to live in Prestwich. Within a week drummer Simon Wolstencroft was employed to despatch her back to America from Manchester airport.

Bush flips into another story, this time involving Smith overdosing on unidentifiable tablets given to him by a girl, where Smith found himself making his way hurriedly to the evening's gig after spending an afternoon in hospital having his stomach pumped.

There was another pharmaceutical-related episode in Switzerland.

According to Bush, Smith thought he was procuring amphetamine sulphate but the substance turned out to be hallucinogenic.

'He started tripping, and it's not his thing, tripping,' says Bush. Apparently, Smith 'thought the floor was opening and he was in *The Exorcist*', a terror compounded by the sound engineer making faces like the Devil at the man some of them call 'God'.

I have my own memories of the comical Dave Bush-era Fall at a gig at York Barbican. Among other mischievous goings-on, Smith concluded the gig by demolishing Bush's keyboards – returning The Fall to a guitar band in one fell swoop.

'He used to smash up my keyboards quite often,' shrugs Bush. 'It was an occupational hazard.' The explanation Smith gave Bush was, 'It's all right, Dave, it's only showbiz.'

The keyboards would usually be fixed urgently in time for the following night's gig, however, one time in Chicago Smith was so 'pissed' he rendered them unusable. The following night, Bush found himself attempting to play a synthesiser with broken keys. Smith threw the microphone at his keyboard player and yelled, 'You have a go! I can't be arsed.' Bush took up the vocal challenge and found himself fronting The Fall – with the crowd going bonkers.

'It was hilarious,' he says, 'He soon came back to reclaim his throne.' However, by the encores Smith had disappeared – they later found him in a corridor, fast asleep, and played the encore without him.

I keep remembering what Brix said about The Fall being a reflection of the person, and perhaps it says a lot about Dave Bush that he views these episodes as comical, where others may find them disturbing. He remembers being told, 'It'll be all right, just hit it!' whenever things went wrong and tells how Smith once fell asleep in the hotel lift, spending the night travelling between floors while guests tiptoed around him on their way to breakfast.

Never a dull moment. So why on earth did Dave Bush leave? Unusually, he describes yet another cause of Fall execution – being undermined by someone on Smith's fabled 'subs' bench'.

As he tells it, another budding keyboard player, Julia Nagle, had started hanging out with Smith: 'She fucked it up for me in the end. She kept telling Mark that I wasn't happy, and I was, but eventually I got kicked out. She was his girlfriend and there was a campaign going on.'

Although, like Schofield and Riley, Bush does concede it may have been time to go. His last album, *Cerebral Caustic*, was uncharacteristically weak – although it does contain the glorious 'Feeling Numb', a pop song so sweet and perfect it could be sung by Kylie Minogue, and the wonderfully spiky 'Don't Call Me Darling'.

Bush suspects that by then he may have emerged as a threat to Smith's authority – through music rather than insubordination. 'There was a lot of the music on computer and that's not what Mark wants, someone with that much input. It had to change. But five years is long enough.'

It was actually four; maybe it felt like five. He was dispensed with by letter but, as with so many, Bush suggests if the opportunity arose he 'might' go back: 'If it was the same line-up, possibly.'

Which, of course, it wouldn't be.

Like Steve Hanley, Bush says he took a long time to become 'a normal person' again after leaving The Fall and the hardest aspect was never quite knowing if it was really the end. There had been several times when he wouldn't hear from Smith only to be suddenly called back into battle, like a soldier given another tour of Northern Ireland. Between such times, he'd still be getting paid and then, exactly as Smith told me he did with Spencer Birtwistle, the singer would phone and ask, 'Where the fuck are you?'

But the call didn't come.

There are no bad feelings though and, like Riley, he encountered Smith again. He'd joined Justine Frischmann's Britpop darlings Elastica, who were recording in London when Bush bumped into Smith in the nearest pub. He cajoled him into joining the recording session, which he did until the beer ran out. Smith delivered spontaneous performances on 'How He Wrote "Elastica" Man' and 'KB' (Karl Burns?!) – maybe this was a rare instance of Dave Bush and pals 'moulding' Mark E Smith.

More recently, Bush (as 'Elastica Man') scored a techno dance hit – a personal ambition – but he admits he misses The Fall, even though he may occasionally look back with rose-tinted glasses.

'For a few years, I was glad to be away,' he confesses, 'because it was so tense. But now I look back and it was brilliant music and we went to some brilliant places. It was a lot of fun.'

These days, Bush's activities are more ordered. Because keyboard players aren't in fashion anymore, he's considering buying himself a bass.

Lately, he's been buying and selling stuff on eBay to help fund the web design (he ran a similar business selling hippie trinkets while in The Fall). Unusually, it appears Bush's post-Fall direction is unrelated to The Fall, until he mentions he's 'learning about courses and databases. I just want to work at home with nobody shouting at me!'

Sometime after speaking to him, I'm browsing eBay when I come across Bush's ID. It seems he has now purchased a bass – a Westfield metallic titanium model costing £37.

I guess you never know when a vacancy might come up.

CHAPTER 21

'It was like your last tour of Vietnam, with appropriate flashbacks and nightmares.'

With Dave Bush departed and record sales faltering, there was a lot of tension around The Fall. Except now it wasn't quite so creative.

From the outside, with Brix gone and The Fall making more and more uncommercial music once again, it seemed as if Smith had almost deliberately sabotaged his own success; as if he'd started to fear that too much was beyond his control, or that existing in the ultra-mainstream wasn't very Fall.

I asked him about this in Malmaison, and he described pop singles – which don't make money but act as advertisements for groups' albums – as 'a lot of hard work for very little return'. He suggested that he was more concerned with the bigger picture: crafting art, not pop.

'I'd rather get the LP right, you know what I mean,' he said. "Cos an LP is a piece of work, you know. The amount of time I spend with the flow [running order] of an LP and the record company's trying to do it all by market research. They go, "You want all the big tracks at the beginning", and I go, "Well, by side two you'll be bored off your tits".'

'They go, "Ooh, you are funny about your work, Mark". So you have to fight to get your own fuckin' tracklisting, so imagine what it's like with a single. They'll have about eight people with a clipboard. There's a lot of clots and clever dicks. I'm sorry! I hate things like that.'

But, for the first time, the albums were declining in quality. In Malmaison, he'd offered an interesting notion; that for all the chaos around the band he makes his best music when his personal life is settled. And in the mid 1990s, Smith's personal life wasn't settled at all.

After divorce from Brix, he'd recruited not a musician but a second wife – marrying Saffron Prior, the Cog Sinister secretary from Prestwich he'd taken up with after Brix. The marriage floundered and after their divorce in 1995, Prior kindly gave away Smith's typewriter to a fan on the internet. In 1995, he dated Fall fan club organiser (and, briefly, backing vocalist) Lucy Rimmer. There were other band-related problems. Smith sued one ex-manager, suspecting fraud, but was unsuccessful (Smith's suspicions inspired a very bitter song, 'Birmingham School Of Business School'). It perhaps isn't surprising that Smith seems to have drowned his sorrows in drink. Even more than before.

A fan called MadVespa posted on the Fall forum about seeing The Fall in Glasgow at the time:

I was standing at the bar near the door when it swung open violently and Mark E Smith staggered through, bounced off the wall and fell through the bar hatch. On standing up he found himself facing the queue at the busy bar (all of whom were there to see the band). I don't know who was more surprised – Smith or the crowd. A cheer went up, he muttered, 'F*ck', and exited out the front door.

Other live reviews of the period comment less humorously on Smith's condition, noting how he was suddenly looking aged and was often visibly drunk while performing. Shortly after Dave Bush's departure, a sense of imminent explosion in The Fall erupted with the loss of one of their most precious ever members.

I'm staring at one of the most perplexing names on my list, Craig Scanlon, who has been 'missing in action' even longer than Karl Burns.

What I know is this: born on 7 December 1960, The Fall's most venerable guitarist was the ultimate 'Jesuit lad'. If Steve Hanley defined the Fall sound, Scanlon's rhythm guitar built the chassis and in person he typified their spirit. From 1979's *Dragnet* to 1995's *Cerebral Caustic*, his trademark low-key style – memorable but subtly, beautifully underplayed – formed The Fall's finest music.

In the early days, his rockabilly rhythm powered the likes of 'Fiery Jack' and 'Container Drivers'. When The Fall were at their most commercial in the Brix period, Scanlon was always there – quietly sculpting the sound and happy to let Smith's wife take the spotlight. Onstage, Scanlon's posture – head down, grim-faced, holding his guitar like a piece of industrial machinery – was quintessentially Fall. Even the name Scanlon sounds like it should be written on a big sign above a firm of building contractors.

His was the most abrupt departure of that turbulent time, when after 16 years of hard labour he was suddenly given the boot in 1995. Smith insisted his most loyal servant was sacked for his 'slovenly appearance' and the crime of 'failure to maintain amps'. He later changed this explanation to 'trying to play jazz or Sonic Youth-style stuff over good simple songs that he'd written himself'.

Since then, more debate and discussion has centred round the mysterious disappearance of Scanlon than any other Faller. He's never given an interview. Even the BBC's *Wonderful and Frightening World* documentary failed to coax him from wherever he is hiding. He may or may not be holed up with

Karl Burns, but at least Scanlon can claim the dubious distinction of being the only Fallen musician mourned by Smith – publicly at least.

Our leader admitted in a rare 2001 moment of candour that sacking the Jesuit had been a 'bad decision'. 'I still see him knocking about in Manchester,' he said of his once loyal henchman. 'I miss him, actually.'

If Smith was really bumping into Scanlon in Manchester city centre, he was doing better than anyone else. Since 1995, Fall fans have had to feed on mere scraps of rumour and purported sightings: Scanlon going into council offices, or a man who possibly could be Scanlon emerging from a supermarket with bags of beer. Some reports had him working for the council, others in the dole office. Eric the Ferret told me he had spied him and he was looking 'like a broken kid'. Ominously, Marc Riley told me that even if I were to find his fellow ex-Jesuit, 'no way' would Scanlon talk.

Having so far drawn a total blank with Burns, I'm wondering what to do about Scanlon when an email arrives from a similarly frustrated Simon Ford, author of *Hip Priest*. He's just spotted Scanlon.

'Our eyes met and he had that look which said, "I do not want to talk about how I used to be in The Fall", so I walked on by' is how Ford describes the encounter in Manchester city centre. Then he explains how he 'almost' got to interview him for his book: 'First of all, he told me to get lost, then he said he might talk to me and then it was too late. It was a shame 'cause I rate him so highly and he hardly did any interviews when he was in the band. Anyway, I guess this is all no use to you, but, surprise, surprise, he looked older, had grey hair and was quite tubby.'

I've given up all hope of ever reaching him when Marc Riley gets back in touch to say he might know someone who knows someone who might be able to get in touch with Scanlon. I'm starting to feel like an agent in MI5.

Over the next few days, this feeling increases as I take several peculiar phone calls from someone called Moey who also says he 'might' be able to get me to Craig Scanlon. I'm asked to email any questions and then wait – for what, a demand for ransom?

I'm then told the guitarist is now in 'top secret government work'. A couple of days later, an email arrives from the Department of Work and Pensions.

Although Scanlon first suggests he might be 'too traumatised' to answer questions, he's surprisingly forthcoming. Mind you, he says he can only do this by email and won't have his photograph taken because 'my hatred of cameras is up there with my loathing of phones'.

The first question on my list was musical. I ask about his trademark guitar style, which was supposed to have been learned by him from his predecessor, Martin Bramah.

'I taught myself,' he replies. 'Steve [Hanley] and I were in a band before joining The Fall and I wrote most of the songs [The Fall poached one – "Chokstock"]. When I first saw the band I thought he [Smith] had a great, distinctive sound but this "mentor/idol" thing is nonsense.'

So not all The Fallen view Mark E Smith as 'God' then.

The obvious next question is to ask what it was like being in The Fall. I mention that so far accounts have been diverse, ranging from 'a professional, hardworking unit' to 'really weird', with tales of fights and paranoia.

Scanlon agrees all these views are true, adding, 'when we were on form, there was no one to touch us'. However, he suggests the latter years 'did deteriorate into a negative chaos'. The below-par *Cerebral Caustic* wasn't just Dave Bush's last album. It was Scanlon's farewell too and he isn't the album's biggest fan: he says by this point, Hanley and himself had become 'wet-nurses for some psychotic changeling – it just grew tedious'.

He cheers up when asked about his song-writing input, which even in the maze-like world of Fall song-writing credits seems enormous. Scanlon is even credited with penning the tune for 'Bill Is Dead', which on certain (wistful) days usurps 'The Container Drivers' as my favourite Fall song.

'I wrote quite a few,' he says, admitting he can't remember which ones exactly – 'my memory is shot'. But some favourites were 'The Classical', 'Petty Thief Lout', 'Paintwork', 'Iceland', 'Winter', 'Haven't Found It Yet', 'and, yes, "Bill" is a fave of mine'.

Despite some grumbles, Scanlon remembers good times writing with Steve Hanley and Dave Bush at Bush's house; hanging out with Hanley, Bush, Schofield, Riley and the missing Burns, 'all good people'.

'We were travelling the world knowing we were exporting a different subversive take on most music,' he says, remembering the sheer joy of 'hearing one of my songs after the input of the above people'. He admits some of this was countered by having to cancel gigs, 'sometimes minutes before we were due to go on'. Then there were the '3 a.m. phone calls from a pissed-up paranoid Mark'.

I can almost hear the frustration. 'The whole Jekyll and Hyde thing wore me down.'

I move on a little and ask about creative tension.

'Mark created tension mostly because he was bored, drunk or couldn't hack it,' he writes. 'He was surrounded by a great band who put up with a lot of shit. It was Mark's way of motivating himself – we didn't do complacency.'

The line about complacency was familiar but the rest was something new. In all the discussions with The Fallen about creative tension, neither I nor anyone else had considered this could be Smith's tool of motivating himself, not his musicians.

If Scanlon's theory is true, it undermines everything that has been suggested for 30 years about the whole dynamic of The Fall. I wish I could meet him and talk more, but he's adamant that personal contact is off-limits.

This is my only chance. I ask about the notorious 'torment list' and his place on it, but he says all this is news to him.

'First I've heard about it,' he counters. 'Maybe that's indicative of how crap it had become in that I didn't notice any difference.'

Inevitably, I have to clear up what happened with Scanlon's exit.

Was he really pushed out or was Steve Hanley right to think he'd simply tired of the band and let his exit happen? According to Scanlon, Hanley had phoned him with the news that Smith had fired the entire group. 'This was quite common,' he reveals, 'but it was the first time I'd been included.'

'Then the story was that he'd sacked just me and Steve. Then it was just me.'

Bewildered, Hanley suggested Scanlon go to see Smith to clear the air. Scanlon duly did so to find Smith 'hid[ing] behind his girlfriend' and promising to send a letter. After 16 years' service, the ultimate Jesuit lad felt he deserved more.

'I just thought, "Fuck that",' he says. '"I'm not being treated like that anymore."'

And the stuff about playing jazz riffs and 'slovenly appearance'? According to Scanlon, it was a ruse designed to cover up Smith's *faux pas*. One of the odder stories I'd heard was that Scanlon had acquired a Jazz Chorus amp and Smith hated the sound.

'Crap,' he retorts. 'I'd used a Roland Jazz Chorus for years – it was Mark's suggestion after my old amp died of old age. His "wry" statements were just fodder for the press – to show who's boss – basically a cover-up for the shoddy treatment.'

Scanlon has another revelation: Smith didn't just regret jettisoning his loyal servant, he asked him back: 'I had a drink with him a few years ago and he asked if I'd like to come down with him to a Leeds gig the band were playing.' He turned Smith down.

'After the three hours spent with him in the pub, it brought it all back home how fortunate I was to be out of all that,' he says. In what could almost be a line from one of Smith's own time-honoured mantras, he insists he 'will never go backwards'.

I wonder how it affected him, all those years in such a bonkers band. Only Steve Hanley – with his 19-year stretch – served longer than Craig Scanlon in The Fall and he'd told me it had taken him years to recover.

'It obviously turned me into a bitter old man, going by the above answers!' says Scanlon, suggesting that, after all, his sense of humour has emerged intact. 'No, it was a fantastic trip most of the time, working with some good, twisted people.' He has a description of The Fall that tops Hanley's 'house of horrors': 'It's like your last tour of 'Nam, with accompanying flashbacks and nightmares.'

I ask him what his job is now and he repeats the line about 'top secret government stuff!' but, yes, he did put '16 years, guitarist, Fall' on his application form. 'That is exactly what I put. It was the truth after all.'

He says he has no regrets, pointing out that 'unless you're in a blues/lounge/folk band' it's 'rather tragic' performing onstage after hitting 40. But, contrary to rumour, he is playing guitar.

'I have various snippets of music that will eventually become "The Coalman's Song",' he says – it's unclear whether he means an album or a single – 'but I'm not exactly feverishly pursuing it.' His next statement throws down a gauntlet for any music industry Fall fans: 'If I had free access to a studio I would dabble for my own entertainment.' So, somewhere, wherever he is living, when he's not in the Top Secret Department of Work and Pensions, The Fall fans' favourite guitarist is still working with his guitar. I don't know whether to laugh or cry at the loss to British music of one of its most enduring talents. But Scanlon insists people shouldn't get the impression he's bitter or twisted. Most of the time, being in The Fall was 'a fantastic life journey. A very strange upbringing.'

I have one final question. Where is Karl Burns?

Inevitably, he doesn't know. 'Sorry, I last saw Karl in the village quite a few years ago – big-bearded, bit scruffy. I thought he was a tramp at first. We did the usual, "Yeah, keep in touch etc", but nothing since – which is a shame, he's a nice, funny guy.'

And with that, Craig Scanlon retreats back into silence – which, after all, is an essential job requirement of 'top secret government work'.

CHAPTER 22

'He had a face like a mouse's snout.'

At least the blow of Scanlon's departure was partially softened by the prior return of another of the Fall soap's principal characters – Brix. In Malmaison, Smith had talked of a 'two-year gap' between people leaving and wanting to return, although given there was a divorce and a dollop of acrimony in between, it's perhaps unsurprising that the former Mrs Smith took five.

The first I knew of Brix's return coincided with the first time I wrote about The Fall in the *Guardian* – which I joined, as with the music press, by sending in an envelope of reviews. I was as excited about joining a broadsheet as a musician would be joining The Fall, although I had only penned a handful of small articles when I received my favourite journalistic assignment – writing about The Fall.

Not that it was straightforward. Usually, when a journalist wants to review a band, the record company or publicity person simply puts you on the guest list. In February 1995, my innocent request was met by an unusual enquiry from the person representing The Fall at the time: 'Have you ever had a run-in with Mark E Smith?'

No, I hadn't had a run-in with Mark E Smith – not then, anyway – so I was allowed on the guest list, only the second time I've been granted this privilege (the other being the Bramah-in-silver-shirt gig at Sheffield Leadmill).

I loved the gig at York's inappropriately sedate Barbican – the same venue where Smith wreaked havoc on Dave Bush's keyboards – comparing The Fall as I often do to a classic soap opera and perhaps rather cheekily comparing Smith to *Coronation Street*'s irascible pensioner, Percy Sugden. There, unannounced, was Brix. I've still got the review in a bunch of Fall clippings in my garage.

Seemingly recovered from her dalliance with Nigel Kennedy, she smouldered like a rock-chick Elsie Tanner and her brittle riffing added an extra tension to their already compelling Northern rockabilly, which often recalls The Velvet Underground as if they'd been reared on flat beer and working men's clubs . . . [I wrote, describing how this time Smith was wearing a silver shirt which made him look more like "an awkward Man at C&A" than a rock star, as had Bramah's. But then] . . . spanners flew into the works. During 'Free Range', Smith hurled his microphone to the ground and took over his wife's equipment, getting tangled up in all manner of leads. A hapless roadie attempted to sort it out and was immediately admonished, Smith delighting in hurling the mic stand next to where he stood.

We were then treated to several scenes of which any director could be proud: Smith clatters microphone again, Smith manhandles security man from stage, Smith cuffs roadie round ear, Smith removes microphone from bass drum (rendering them inaudible), Smith rearranges keyboard monitors (rendering them unworkable), Smith storms off, and on, and off. And so on, ad infinitum.

His lyrics were by now almost indecipherable ('Your mother is a Communist!' he seemed to sneer at one point), while the band stared resolutely at the floor and Brix gave the impression she'd seen this act a good few times before.

None of this, though, overshadowed the music. 'Glam Racket' in particular was a brilliant parody of a Glitter Band stomp. The instalment ended with the unforgettable sight of Smith as Hero Wronged, ranting through 'Big Prinz' and its chorus 'He . . . is . . . not . . . APPRECIATED!' A point with which one might tend to disagree. But then, one wouldn't want a run-in with Mark E Smith.

One of my favourite Fall gigs ever.

Brix was in Los Angeles, not Manchester, when she heard the calling to return. The thing was, The Adult Net hadn't worked out, nor had a relationship with another boyfriend. She'd studied acting and had been in a real soap opera, but was playing bass with her friend Susanna Hoffs from The Bangles when the phone suddenly rang. Hoffs shared management with Courtney Love – the late Kurt Cobain's wife and singer with LA band Hole – whose bassist had just died. Love's idea was that Brix should play bass with Hole, but Brix had been thinking about The Fall.

She'd even left a message on Smith's answerphone saying, 'I've been thinking about all the stuff we did together. It was great. Good-bye.' She was in Seattle dealing with Love when, out of the blue, Smith returned the call.

'He just said, "Would you come back?"' she remembers. '"We need you to kick ass. I'll pay for you to fly back and forth from LA. Anything you want. Just come back."' An offer she couldn't refuse.

Brix had the choice of joining Hole – and being subjected to the strict working demands of Courtney Love – or 'going back to The Fall, which is the grand-daddy of everything. To go back and not be his wife . . . but to go back as a guitar player and writer, having power again and not being in the same position where we're married and it's fucked up. So I thought, "Fuck it, I'll go back!"'

To begin with, Smith was on his 'absolute, best, best behaviour' and Brix tells how she was 'really happy' to be back and 'everything clicked again'.

'Everything was perfect,' she says. 'There was enough money that we were touring in a nice style. We wrote some good songs . . .'

However, very quickly, 'things began to deteriorate with Mark'. To be fair to Smith, while his idea may have seemed a good one, it can't have been easy in practice sharing the stage with an ex-wife, especially one who was dating millionaire Philip Start after meeting him in a lift at designer store Harvey Nichols. Every time he looked side-stage, there was the thing he hates most – a reminder of his past. Perhaps, even, something he'd lost.

'He became more irrational, more difficult,' Brix remembers, describing how touring with The Fall again quickly turned into a 'fucking nightmare'. She remembers how Smith would be passed out, drooling, before gigs: 'We'd be 45 minutes late and having to get him on the stage,' she grumbles. 'It was awful.'

She mentions 'various incidents' but doesn't wish to elaborate, although she does add that like Marc Riley she'd started standing up for herself. For a start, there was going to be no subscribing to the carrot-and-stick treatment. A further development was that, although Brix was no longer married, she found herself in a bizarre romantic square involving Smith, Lucy Rimmer and Julia Nagle.

'The two of them [Rimmer and Nagle] were at each other's throats with me in the middle,' she complains, making this episode of the Fall story sound more like a romantic farce. 'So, Lucy would book the rooms in the hotels but make sure I slept in the room with Julia!' she shrieks. Finally, something occurred which was so 'bad' she literally 'couldn't take it'.

Brix doesn't want the precise details of what took place made public, but it's enough to know The Fall were playing at a Danish festival, by which time Smith's drinking had again degenerated to the point where he'd begun having epileptic-type fits. Before each attack he would become 'unreasonable' and in this instance he managed to get into an awkward altercation with a hip-hop band who had become so irritated by his behaviour they beat him to a pulp. Ironically, the singer was booked into an establishment called The Friendly Hotel at the time.

'I was calling my boyfriend on the phone saying, "You've got to get me home",' remembers Brix, describing how Smith was nowhere to be seen and they began the gig without him.

'Eventually, he turns up, badly beaten, and his face is so swollen he had the snout of a mouse!' she remembers. 'He could hardly speak. It was shocking. We went onstage, him completely fucked up.'

Any other performer would have pulled the gig. Smith is not any other performer.

Amazingly, 'it ended up being a really good gig,' remembers Brix. 'He pulled it off. Again!'

I'm reminded of an ironic heckle from 1980's *Totale's Turns*: 'Call yourselves bloody professionals?'

Smith may not have been a professional, but he was certainly bloody. However, for Brix, this was 'the clincher'. Incredulous at what it now meant to be in The Fall, she decided, again, to leave.

'I left three quarters through that tour before it broke me,' she sighs, going on to describe a night in Glasgow: 'It was a huge Mecca ballroom place. We went to do the sound check. He was nowhere to be seen, then he started berating everybody and breaking stuff. He screamed at the monitor guy and I said, "Please don't speak to him like that." I held my guitar up to hit him. Steve Hanley took me away to have a chat and I said, "What's wrong with him? I can't deal with this any more."'

When I'd asked Smith about this period in Malmaison, he'd been unusually candid. He had been desperately unhappy: 'Losing it? A bit, yeah.'

'He was completely crazy,' she concurs, remembering the next gig where Smith was so drunk he didn't notice somebody had tied his shoelaces together until he tried to walk. The promoters 'begged' Brix to do the London show and it was 'really good'. However, she last set eyes on Smith onstage at that gig – London's Kentish Town Forum, October 1996. Fan reviews on the internet are mixed, but Gavin Eastley sums up the mood when he writes – somewhat disjointedly – 'What a bad gig. A muddy beat combo no less and Brix crying through and some embarrassing bloke coming on and mumbling something about "Sing along you know all the words". Silence from the cringing audience as they checked their incontinence knickers. First time I can remember that they sounded better on record.'

Instead of Brix's usual 'Good night', she said 'Goodbye'.

Almost a decade later, she's again almost tearful – it's not just the cold – reliving this stuff, and reveals she has contacted Smith since.

'I've written to him and said, "If you ever need me, we'll always have something together". But he hasn't responded.' Despite everything, she feels considerable affection for her ex-husband and her loyalty is clearly very personal. She frets that he should be making more money, be more comfortable in life. As Dave Tucker remarked, Smith has what he needs – perhaps comfort would remove the edge of The Fall that has always set them apart. But Brix worries.

'He's not a businessman,' she states. 'He does deals with people that aren't kosher and they know that he's an artist and take advantage. People are greedy. He's been ripped off a lot. When you're so busy being artistic and making up stuff the other part of your brain which should be counting the money is switched off.' Another sniffle. We've been talking for an age but she wants to carry on, while making it clear, as with Craig Scanlon, this is my one shot at an interview.

I change the subject to her much less taxing life now.

After leaving The Fall, Brix gradually abandoned music although she tells me she recently recorded a low-key Adult Net album with The Fall's 'Glam Racket' – a song she says she wrote (it's credited to Smith/Hanley/Scanlon – Scanlon says the credits are correct) cheekily 'reverted to its original state' and titled 'Star'. The very tuneful track subsequently appears on 2007's *Neurotica* album, released as Brix Smith. She giggles at the lyrics: 'They say you're a star but I don't give a fuck/ I watch your head expanding as you're running out of luck'. It's meant as an amiable swipe of the Smith variety, rather than anything nasty.

'That's got him back for "Bad News Girl",' she laughs. Otherwise, things are going well. There's Start, 'which people say is one of the best shops in London', there's the pilot for a comedy series where she plays herself as the manager of a rock band and the fashion shoots in *Elle*. But I can't help getting the feeling Brix seems slightly troubled, that what she really wants is to be able to revisit The Wonderful and Frightening World.

'I'd like to see them live but it would bring back so much emotion. I wouldn't like to go unless I was completely welcome, or embraced, really. I mean, I'm happy. I don't want to tour any more. But I miss it.'

And The Fall miss her.

CHAPTER 23

'Dear Mark, you're my hero. Maybe when I'm of legal drinking age we could go for a drink?'

Adrian Flanagan was the twenty-sixth musician to play live in The Fall. I find him via his current band Kings Have Long Arms but nothing about him seems straightforward. Despite not having been heard of for a decade, he says he's 'flat out' busy and can only answer enquiries via email. Then he goes AWOL because his phone connection has been lost owing to moving house from Manchester to Sheffield. When contact is resumed, he says he was a 'triangle player' in The Fall.

Then he sends a photograph of 'himself' – a small plasticine doll. 'I can only be seen in clay. I am not human, Dave,' he explains, curiously evoking Fall song 'Horror in Clay'. And so I conduct what is surely the first internet interview with a former member of The Fall who might be rolled up into a ball and made into another shape at any given moment.

Flanagan wasn't in The Fall for long – two months – but he's known

Smith for years, and so has his own unique opinions. One of them, which I haven't really thought much about before, is that The Fall have actually become one of the most vital cogs in the Prestwich area economy as a regular employer.

'He was always the one to give local kids a break,' says Flanagan, who wanted to be in The Fall for as long as he can remember. In fact, unlike so many who stumble into Smith's orbits in pubs in adult life, Flanagan was making overtures to Smith before he was even old enough to go in the pubs that are the traditional recruiting grounds.

'When I was 15, I'd put notes through his door saying, "Dear Mark, you're my hero. Everyone else is rubbish. Maybe when I'm of legal drinking age we can go for a drink?" I'd stick it through his door then run off scared just in case he came out and told me to clear off.' He knows it sounds 'pathetic' but he is unbowed, pointing out that at the time, 'he really was my hero'.

The only clay guitarist to ever join The Fall went to a tough school in Salford, where one can only imagine the treatment meted out to someone so quirky. Unsurprisingly, he reveals he was an odd one out. Everyone else liked Duran Duran and Wham!, with their songs about yachts and Club Tropicanas, all of which sounded very exotic if you grew up in the shadow of Prestwich Hospital. Flanagan, against all odds, appreciated The Fall because they did what no one else would do: 'They sang about my area.' While his New Romantic and 1980s pop-loving schoolmates got their education at Salford's toughest, Flanagan was educated by The Fall.

A couple of years later, he was offered a sort of apprenticeship at The Fall factory when Smith offered Flanagan's teenage band some Fall support slots, which he thought was 'amazing' even though his band were 'crap'. Subsequently, he became friendly with Smith's sister, Caroline.

'We got talking in our local,' he reminisces, describing how he became friendly enough with the Smiths to be invited to family occasions such as birthdays and weddings, which would usually end up in post-pub singsongs at Smith's house. He remembers 'fondly' playing Smith's guitar and singing Kinks' songs together, during which Smith would regale him with funny stories and correct the position of his elbow as he played guitar.

So, when 'Whatsherface' – as Flanagan calls Brix – left for the second time, he suddenly received the call.

'I was at me mam's doing my washing,' Flanagan recalls, via email. 'He said, "All right, cock, it's Mark. I want a word,"' and suddenly the clay man found himself agreeing to fill Brix's slightly more fashionable shoes on a 30-date UK tour. That was one problem. The other was it began in two days' time.

Rehearsals consisted of going through 80 songs from 'random' albums with Steve Hanley. Then Smith rang to say Brix hadn't left after all, but could Flanagan tag along for the tour as a 'sub', in case of further upheaval. He opted to stay at home, but said, 'I'll be there if you need me.'

Sure enough 'Whatsherface' did leave again and Flanagan ended up standing in for half a dozen shows in the space of five months. He recollects The Fall being between labels. Flanagan wasn't given any instructions – although Smith would still wander past and reposition his elbow as he played. Comparing the experience to a 'Youth Training Scheme in rock 'n' roll', Flanagan says his only instructions from Smith were to 'Come along and give that bunch of oldies of a group of mine a kick up the arse!'

Flanagan may not have been a great musician but in many ways he was a perfect Fall guitarist. He understood he was there to do a job, and as such harboured as few pretensions as a bricklayer or plumber.

'I'm not going to say he shouted at me or anyone else,' Flanagan considers. 'The group were being paid a lot of money by Mark to sit around on their arses all day, then occasionally they'd have to rehearse or do a couple of gigs. He's every right to shout. He's the boss.' Flanagan says he understands the Fall mentality a bit more because, like Smith, his family came from the professions. The Flanagans were builders and, like Smith, he'd often worked for his 'old fella'. He insists there isn't much difference between making music in The Fall and making a wall for a team of brickies.

'You'd get the hairdryer treatment whenever you were not pulling your weight and I'd constantly get told how to hold a hammer,' he says of his building days. 'I think his musicians at the time' – the long-serving Jesuit lads, now minus Craig Scanlon – 'might have been a bit complacent.' Which, of course, in Smith's eyes will never do.

Flanagan describes Smith's musical input as one might a foreman, rather than a musician. The band would 'hammer out' ideas; Smith would have the final say. 'He'd say, "No, that's shit, try this",' he recounts, adding that The Fall work best when it's stripped-down music with unpolished vocal melodies.

'The hooks come from [Smith's] voice, far more than anyone gives him credit for.' Which is true.

Asked about the best thing about being in The Fall, Flanagan isn't sure the word 'best' is even appropriate. 'It's not a showbiz band, its a working rock 'n' roll band,' he says. 'It's not about pop ditties or doing silly dances whilst dressed as a lion' – which apparently his own band, Kings Have Long Arms, is.

'But the experience taught me you can't replicate The Fall,' he says. He confesses to once making the *faux pas* of moaning to Smith that his own group needed a break. Smith's response was typical and very Cloughie: 'You don't deserve anything. Just get out there and do it.'

'I just realised I was going on to this bloke who for years of my life had been fighting to get out these great pieces of uncommercial art and how pathetic I must have sounded,' admits the man of clay, adding that Smith always looked out for him. He'd read the 'nasty stories' about Smith but insists he was always 'very good to me, very generous and wise'.

In fact, Smith – who Flanagan regards as 'a man amongst musicians, the only true original English rock 'n' roll poet' – did the job for Flanagan he'd expected done for himself. 'He was the oldie who gave me the kick up the arse to do it myself. So that's the best thing for me about once briefly being in The Fall.'

He reels off his recent activities: six singles in the last couple of years; 'cult status' in various countries; working with The Human League's Philip Oakey; and a spot as a 'face' in *Harpers & Queen*. A Prestwich boy made good, and like Marc Riley years before him, the crucial kick came during Falldom.

CHAPTER 24

'We'd had abuse and death threats!'

Early 1997 saw another fleeting guitarist – Keir Stewart. I track him down at Inch Studios in Manchester, where he's working on an album with fellow Mancunians, old school veterans The Durutti Column. In fact, it was Inch Studios that indirectly led to him to The Fall.

As Stewart tells it, he and studio partner Simon Spencer were desperate to produce the Fall album which turned out to be 1997's *Levitate*. They worked with Smith as DOSE on a track called 'Plug Yourself In', which was extracurricular to The Fall. When asked to join the group – as the twenty-fourth member – Stewart said no, but he was coaxed into accepting by Spencer, who thought it might land them the job of producing an album.

Even as a veteran of studios and the peculiar habits of musicians, Stewart says he has never worked in a band like The Fall. When he joined, they were bang in the middle of Smith's phase of heavy drinking and 'losing it' (Smith's words).

Stewart remembers rehearsals as 'structureless': 'Mark wouldn't turn up, or he'd turn up and refuse to do any vocals. He was very paranoid at the time. It was pretty odd.'

With young Flanagan out of the picture, Stewart describes the group as divided into two battalions. Mark and Dave Bush's replacement, Julia Nagle, formed one camp; recent recruit Tommy Crooks along with veterans Simon Wolstencroft and Steve Hanley formed the other. Stewart found himself 'stuck in the middle' and shot straight to the top of the torment list because he was a 'studio nerd'.

Stewart seems to have encountered particular difficulty being paid and has some surreal reminiscences of the way The Fall – yet again constantly switching labels – undertook business at the time.

Early recordings took place in West Hampstead at a studio owned by Scottish solo artist Edwyn Collins. Stewart and Spencer negotiated a producers' fee, but Smith never signed the contract.

'He kept saying, "I'll sign it tomorrow",' remembers Stewart, 'but he never did.' Instead, Stewart remembers Smith doing vocals while reading lyrics off a bit of paper and then disappearing to the pub.

'As the week went on we were getting more pissed off over the lack of money,' he says. 'By the Thursday, I said to Simon, "If he doesn't sort it out tomorrow, I'm off"'. However, Stewart says when this news was relayed to Smith, the boss seemed shocked.

'I phoned him and he said, "What do you mean? It's going really well",' he laughs, still astounded. 'This was after we'd had abuse and death threats!'

Death threats?

'He was doing a vocal and he was terrible,' he says, admitting the great man's wrath may have been provoked by the production pair playing 'sneaky' tricks like recording Smith's conversations unbeknown to him and then playing them back over the studio loudspeakers. But he remembers recording 'take after take' of Smith's vocals. 'He'd say, "I tell you what, lads, the track's going really well but I know lads in Salford who will kick your heads in".' Stewart could have found this terrifying, however, he admits to thinking it was 'hilarious, actually'.

According to Stewart, Smith called him 'Short arse' and dubbed Spencer 'Fatso', and was so vociferous even the long-suffering Steve Hanley was taken aback, while drummer Simon Wolstencroft confided he'd 'never seen him [Smith] that bad'.

Drama turned into farce when Spencer and Stewart wiped all the tapes they'd been recording. And they couldn't resist one last practical joke. They'd recorded a track called 'Inch' with Smith. Packaging it carefully, they mailed the track to John Peel and various major record companies, along with a covering letter purporting to be from Mark E Smith, using language more likely to come from a band Smith hated, like REO Speedwagon or The Eagles.

'We wrote, "Hey guys, check out the sound of my new album",' says Stewart, still laughing about it all these years later. '"This is the brand new Fall sound and I think you'll agree − it rocks!"'

As Stewart tells it, the confused Fall leader then arrived home to find his answerphone full of messages from the music industry, but didn't know anything about any new record. Stewart claims they then found themselves getting visits from 'black BMWs in the middle of the night'. It all sounds very weird, even for The Fall.

'I don't think I'd have been killed over a tune,' insists Stewart, 'but it was pretty mad.'

Stewart and Spencer got a deal for the track themselves with EMI − inked by the A&R man who signed Coldplay − and a meeting was arranged with Smith in a Manchester bar, to iron out the details. Therein, things got even stranger.

'He brought this absolute nutter with him, a complete psycho,' says Stewart, describing a man who looked like 'Bobby Ball on crystal meth'. In these perhaps less than desirable conditions, a deal was struck, but perhaps inevitably Stewart never laboured in The Fall again, after just a handful of gigs.

The Spencer-Stewart-Smith tie-in had another unfortunate twist. One of the tracks they worked on ended up on *Levitate* as 'Spencer Must Die'. In 2003, Simon Spencer died of respiratory failure while waiting for a lift at the end of the Glastonbury Festival.

Yet, when Stewart subsequently ran into Smith, he saw a 'different side' of the Fall frontman: 'He was very humane, in the things he said. A totally different Mark E Smith, really.'

When I mention the elusive Karl Burns, Stewart says he did spot the missing drummer – four years ago. The mythical Faller was on the street in Manchester city centre where, Stewart reports, he 'wasn't looking very well'.

1997 – the year Flanagan and Stewart joined and then departed – was, elsewhere, a year of fallout, change, upheaval and death, especially in August. On 2 August 1997, Fela Kuti, whose drummer Tony Allen had told me about discipline, died of an AIDS-related illness. His funeral in Lagos was attended by two million people. In Paris, on 31 August 1997, Princess Diana was killed in a car crash. Death was in the air – even in the boyband-era pop charts, where Puff Daddy and Faith Evans' 'I'll Be Missing You' strode the charts on both sides of the Atlantic, turning a Police sample into a lament for slain rapper Biggie Smalls aka The Notorious BIG.

But, in The Fall, there was another, far more significant exit in August 1997.

CHAPTER 25

'I'm proud that I survived three years before the first punch-up.'

Simon John Wolstencroft was born on 19 January 1963 and occupied the Fall drum stool for 11 years. He joined in July 1986 for that year's stellar *Bend Sinister* album. While he drummed away through classic mid period Fall albums like *Extricate* and *Shift-Work* and so-so ones like *Middle Class Revolt*, The Stone Roses rose and fell, and 1980s yuppie culture gave way to the bleary optimism of Cool Britannia. Through it all, the angular-faced sticksman from Altrincham kept on drumming, never doing interviews or taking the spotlight but acquiring enormous respect in the Fall fan base, who gave him the nickname 'Funky Si' for his nimble drum patterns and long service for the cause.

Wolstencroft had originally worked in Smith's other favoured environment – a chip shop – but had somehow managed to avoid joining two of Manchester's greatest musical exports of the period before joining The Fall.

He'd been in a band called Freak Party, whose line-up included Morrissey, Johnny Marr and Andy Rourke, who went on to become The Smiths. He'd also drummed with Ian Brown and John Squire of The Stone Roses in a band called The Patrol. Wolstencroft had somehow managed to sidestep two of the most charismatic and demanding rock taskmasters of all time only to land a job with Mark E Smith.

Contact is made through Marc Riley, who one evening slips me a cheery email: 'Si Wooly wants to talk.'

A couple of nights later, Wolstencroft describes how he was recruited after Smith had dispensed with Karl Burns for the umpteenth time – apparently this time for having a disagreeable girlfriend. 'Wooly' was playing in a band called The Weeds and they'd supported The Fall. With Smith's eye for talent running over his opening act as usual, the man who became Funky Si was offered a six-month contract that subsequently lasted 11 years.

Wooly loved being in The Fall. He recalls mostly happy times, wonderful music and says, unlike some members, he didn't generally have to chase the money. 'It was really good. I was never a fan, which he [Smith] liked. He basically said, "Keep the drums simple, cock".' Unlike Burns, Wolstencroft was never fined for hitting the tom tom but he recalls similar battles with the singer, which at least didn't appear to have anything to do with creative tension.

'We did actually have fights,' he reveals. Smith would interfere with his drum kit 'all the time . . . knocking over cymbals and so on'. One particular time wasn't very funny. Wolstencroft's mother had just died, and Smith – who a few years previously had lost his own father – suggested, 'Oh, cheer up, it fuckin' happens to all of us.'

'And a cymbal stand went over,' recalls Wolstencroft. He says they ended up fighting onstage. 'Steve Hanley broke it up.' But at least he can laugh at the memory now. 'He didn't sack me!'

In fact, as Smith hinted in Malmaison, Wolstencroft agrees a lot of Smith's colourful onstage antics are part of the show. Some of the time, at least.

'He was really into the showbiz side, microphone technique and so on,' he says, suggesting that underneath everything Smith sees himself as a crowd-thrilling entertainer, like his beloved Elvis. Punching a microphone stand over, for instance, would 'entertain' the crowd. But other foibles are possibly to entertain himself. As Wolstencroft describes it, one of Smith's odder stage preferences was for a single microphone hanging over the drum kit – much like they used in the early days of rock 'n' roll. These days, with more advanced technology, engineers tend to use at least one mic for every drum, so Smith would invariably spend entire gigs knocking over or removing their microphones.

'He really thought it sounded better his way,' chortles Wolstencroft. 'It didn't, really.' He agrees this may have been part of Smith's psychology of keeping musicians 'freaked out', although he insists he never took much notice – the longer he was in the band the more the creative tension became 'water off a duck's back'.

Such complacency would normally incur Smith's wrath. In fact, they became, unusually, 'very close', especially after Smith's break-up with Brix, when the singer and the drummer would often hit the town.

He shares a colourful anecdote from a tour in 1993. The band were in Vienna. On a previous date in Chicago, they'd all been given a 'pentagram, some weird witchcraft thing' by an American fan. Smith had gradually become convinced the objects were bringing evil on the band and instructed the musicians to dispose of them immediately. All complied, except Dave Bush (who was still in The Fall on keyboards at the time). One afternoon, Smith discovered the offending item and was not best pleased.

'Of course, it became another reason to attack Dave,' says Wooly, suggesting another angle to the odd Fall dynamic when he says some musicians – certainly Bush – seemed to perversely enjoy being badly treated by Smith.

Wolstencroft remembers the bad times of 1994 and 1995, when the leader's mood swings were not so amusing. Smith was cancelling gigs through illness and it reached a point where promoters 'wouldn't touch him'.

'Sometimes it would be really bad,' he admits. 'Mark would be like a time bomb waiting to go off. Somebody just had to say the wrong thing. It could have been totally innocent, but in Mark's opinion he was a dickhead and shouldn't be in the dressing room. If you're an idiot, he'll let you know about it.' Thus, Wolstencroft insists he's 'rather proud' he survived three years before he and Smith had their first punch-up. As for his 11-year tenure, he jokes he should have got a 'carriage clock'.

So what went wrong?

Like Adrian Flanagan, 'Funky Si' seems to have viewed being in The Fall as primarily a job of work and says in 1997 the factory was experiencing problems with cash flow. Contradicting Dave Bush, he insists this began once The Fall left Phonogram and reveals the reason for their exit. As he tells it, the label had requested demo tapes for 'the accountants' to listen to, which went against the way The Fall had operated since the days of Kay Carroll.

'Mark didn't work like that so he basically said, "Oh, fuck it", and they refused to renew the contract,' he says. After the Top 10 *Infotainment Scan* in 1993, Fall albums were no longer faring as well, and finances suffered. Wolstencroft also expands on Brix's suggestion that Smith was in poor health at the time and had suffered epileptic-type fits.

'There were a couple when I was with the band. I don't know if it was connected with the drink. He always liked a drink, Mark, but I just thought it was catching up with him. His vocals were getting worse, and I resigned in the end,' he explains, admitting he put his young family first. He still regrets that, after so many great years, he exited on a 'sour note'.

After leaving The Fall, 'Funky Si' added his funk to ex-Stone Roses' Ian Brown, although since then drumming work has been harder to come by and he's had to find other gainful employment, including driving a taxi. Oddly enough, not too long ago he ran into Smith, who was getting out of a taxi – not his own.

'He gave me a big hug,' he muses. Although he's been out of the Fall loop for some time, 'Funky Si' reveals he too has recently found himself drawn back to their gigs and is amazed how Smith has turned it around again. He acknowledges the Fall experience changed him and still feels the strange, unearthly pull. He'd even consider going back – 'I'd give it a go!'

'It did affect me,' he concludes. 'It wasn't really my kind of music, I was more into Motown and soul, but he [Smith] taught me to play in a minimal style. But generally I learned so much about people and life, just listening to him.' As with Adrian Flanagan, Wolstencroft seems to have gained an 'education' in The Fall.

He considers himself a good judge of character now – having seen a lot of them, some more extreme than most – which he wasn't before.

'I've developed a no-bullshit attitude,' he affirms. 'The thing I most admire about Mark is that he's got a way of looking at situations that's different from anyone and he's brought that into music.'

In 1997, with Wolstencroft out of the picture, Smith turned again to Karl Burns for what would be, fatefully, the last time. The next line-up – Burns, Steve Hanley, Edinburgh man Tommy Crooks and keyboardist Julia Nagle – would explode in pieces in New York.

CHAPTER 26

'He'd knock on the windows or sing through the letter-box!'

I've talked to Tommy Crooks, Steve Hanley and American fans, but I want to know more about the New York punch-up and, in particular, the circumstances which led Smith to jail. So, I track down Julia Nagle, who, reverting to her maiden name, is now called Julia Adamson and runs a publishing company, Invisible Girl. Nagle/Adamson is every bit the music industry professional. She is very approachable and friendly, but wary: although we communicate a lot she prefers interviews to be conducted via email – presumably so she can have a written record – and then retracts it all, but thankfully reconsiders. A very tough cookie to deal with: but after all, she has been in The Fall.

What I know about Nagle is this: she was born on 30 September 1960 in Ontario, Canada. Her family moved to Manchester when she was a child. She was a member of the St Winifred's School Choir, who scored a British

Number 1 with 'There's No One Quite Like Grandma', although Nagle wasn't on the single. Her first (punk) band were called Blackout, although she made a musical connection of a different kind when she married Chris Nagle – a producer whose studio career took off when he engineered Joy Division alongside the legendary producer Martin Hannett – and had a child, Basil. Basil provides backing vocals on The Fall's 1998 single, 'Masquerade'. After forming the band What? Noise and subsequently splitting with her husband, Nagle spent 1995 to 2001 in The Fall and co-wrote 'Touch Sensitive', the ridiculously catchy single used in the Vauxhall Corsa advert.

Uniquely, it would seem, Nagle joined The Fall after taking the trouble to send a CV to the group's office/label at Cog Sinister, but contradicts Dave Bush's account that she effectively stole his job.

'I wasn't aware Dave felt like that,' she insists, pointing out that, yes, she 'may' have mentioned Bush being disillusioned, but only after she had joined. Whatever the ins and outs, Nagle soon accustomed herself to The Fall's curious but effective working methods. She talks of Smith as 'brilliant', 'creative', 'shrewd' and a 'leader and employer', observing that brilliance and being difficult often go hand-in-hand.

Like many Fall recruits, she was dropped in at the deep end, playing her first gig on keyboards in front of 2,000 people in London. Although she was nervous, she confesses Brix (who was in her second spell) later told her if Smith hadn't taken her to task on anything, she was doing fine. She found the whole experience 'thrilling' – although was suffering with nerves enough to be sick on the bus as they drove back up to Prestwich.

She also became used to Smith's fabled amp-fiddling. Brix had told her how she loved it when Smith put a microphone to her amp, because this meant she was 'super-amplified'. But Nagle mostly found it funny. 'Occasionally, he'd drop instruments to the floor,' she adds, 'which didn't impress me, then I'd just walk off.' She soon realised these shenanigans were intrinsic to The Fall, along with various examples of Smith's unusual, psychological approach to musicians, such as instructing Simon Wolstencroft to play drums while standing on the drum stool.

'I didn't know what to make of it, as I was new,' she says, 'but I wouldn't put up with it. That sort of thing doesn't make me "perform". It just upsets me.'

She reveals that in her early days Smith tried to show her how to play guitar: 'He was pulling it aggressively. I just unbuckled the strap and let him keep it.' However, she soon understood the logic. 'He hates low-slung guitars because he thinks it looks like you're playing your sex organs and, when I thought about it, he's right.' Ever since, she's kept the instrument at hip height.

Other curious aspects of The Fall at the time included accommodation – one night they might find themselves staying at a posh Hilton, the next a Brighton bed-and-breakfast where the plumbing kept 'gurgling' all night.

Although it would be years before she'd share a room with Smith, Nagle's partnership with the leader had begun a decade earlier, when she'd engineered the *Bend Sinister* album. She barely remembers him in the studio and hardly made eye contact. Nevertheless, once she was in the group, something developed.

Almost a decade on, Nagle doesn't seem happy about the way history and biographies have cast her as 'Mark Smith's girlfriend'. She's particularly irked about the various enquiries she still fields from disturbed Fall fans asking about Mark E Smith. 'I've had a bloke ask me, "What's Mark's penis like?" Another said he wanted to "take me to bed and pretend to be Mark E Smith"!'

She insists they were an item for only eight weeks – she remembers she was very poorly afterwards but doesn't elaborate or apportion any blame. She does describe the process by which The Fall's latest office romance developed and gives some insight into Smith's apparent red-hot sex appeal. The appeal, it appears, is the same as it is to Fall fans – apart from those interested in the details of his penis. His 'voice and lyrics'. She witnessed the 'groupie experience' on tour, where 'practically all' the women wanted to 'shag the pop star', although she insists Smith should not be seen as some sort of Casanova, commenting that two divorces are difficult to deal with.

She should know. When Nagle joined The Fall, she was recovering from her own split from Chris Nagle and making her son a priority, not looking for a relationship. But she reveals how her resolve started to weaken once she started receiving Smith's voice and lyrics through unfamiliar means.

Apparently, the Fall boss would turn up at her house – often late at night

– and perform an unlikely serenade. 'He'd knock on the windows or sing through the letter-box,' she recalls. Eventually, Smith started knocking on Basil's window and she let him in to avoid disturbing the boy's sleep or, indeed, the neighbours'.

'He was seducing me, as well as telling a few fibs about his fiancée [Lucy Rimmer] moving out . . .' she says. Nagle felt 'unsure, but flattered'. Although they didn't date for very long, Nagle got close enough to throw a different light on Smith's drinking. She doesn't think Smith is an alcoholic at all. According to Nagle, The Fall rarely drank before gigs and insists she saw him go 'quite a few' days without drinking. She believes Smith uses alcohol – as fuel for conjuring up 'Lowry-esque' observations – rather than alcohol using him. Something else she is also keen to emphasise is that by the time of the fateful tour of America, they were again just 'colleagues'.

Nagle confirms Steve Hanley's portrayal of the backdrop to the 1998 tour being financial trouble. 'Skint', as she puts it. One of the problems was the group were in dispute with a label who she says owed her alone £12,000. But the biggest difficulty was the arrival of an unexpected VAT bill which meant Smith and Steve Hanley were on the brink of having their houses repossessed. 'They were quite desperate – under tremendous strain – and it was sad to witness.'

As we know, the strain and desperation erupted onstage, but I wasn't clear about how the scuffling had continued to the hotel.

'It was a bonkers time. The incident was distorted, and made out to be about Mark and myself, but there was a lot more to it.' The situation has often been portrayed as domestic violence, however, Nagle insists not only were her and Smith not 'together', but it was the hotel staff – not her – who called the police.

'Mark had been acting the goat all night,' she explains. 'I was in the room when they arrived, and they said, "Did he hit you?" When I said, "Yes", they said, "You should charge him if he has hit you." I said, "Okay", and they had reason to remove him without further ado.'

It's worth mentioning that Smith didn't target Nagle – according to her, he was lashing out angrily in all directions and it was unfortunate she was in the way. He could just have easily belted a nearby standard lamp or, indeed, the policeman.

Nagle suggests the whole thing – which still clearly troubles Smith when it is brought up in interviews, as it often is – was 'blown out of perspective'. After spending time in the cells – during which time he acquired a lawyer, a new suit and a haircut – Smith played on, following a restraining order aimed at keeping him from aggressive contact with Nagle which she says 'was meant as a warning to him, from which he has learned'.

In fact, she stayed loyal for another three years, until 2001, when she says she deliberately 'priced herself out' of being in The Fall because she needed a break and to spend time with her son. After the New York implosion, the other members fled to England – according to Nagle, taking the tour proceeds with them. When I put this to Steve Hanley he responds, 'We were only ever going to break even on that tour anyway . . . there weren't really any "takings" to take! I'm not saying this was anyone else's fault but mine, by the way.' It's significant that Nagle, who remains proud and loved being in The Fall, stood the boss's bail.

But, in 1998, for the first time in his career, Smith was on the brink of losing everything – his house and his group. It wasn't quite 'Me and yer granny on bongos' but The Fall were temporarily down to a two-piece. Smith's response – urged along by Nagle – was to perhaps sheepishly return to his feminist roots and unleash the intriguing prospect of an all-female Fall. I want to ask Nagle more about this period – in fact, lots more in general – but she proves increasingly elusive. She doesn't show up for one meeting – at a Fall gig, no less – but texts the next day to say things had become rather fuzzy after a friend kept giving her whisky. Other proposed get-togethers come to nothing and – partly because I don't want to push it or fall out, partly because emails go unanswered – communication fizzles out. Then again, this is not the only area in which I'm experiencing communication problems.

There's been an argument at home. Like a lot of arguments, I'm not really sure how it started, I just know Suzanne and I haven't spoken for a few days. I can remember this happening before in our years together but never for this long. The situation is further complicated by Suzanne having a really heavy cold and not even speaking to the dog. Almost immediately after stopping talking to me, she literally loses her voice. I wonder what to do and consider popping her autographed copy of *Look, Know* on the mantelpiece to cheer her up, but suspect it might not go down well with all the time I've been devoting to The Fall. In the end I buy a packet of Lemsip and place it by her side. The ice is broken but it's an uneasy peace. In the meantime, I'm shooting off over the Pennines once again.

CHAPTER 27

'So what do you do? Are you in a group?'

The choice of drummer to replace Karl Burns was Kate Themen, a Mancunian whom, typically, Smith had already spotted, before New York. He was in the audience when Themen's band, Polythene, played at Manchester University and he may already have been considering her for his 'subs' bench'. When the band gathered together in a city centre bar, Themen found herself and colleagues being given a 'group hug' by the passing Faller. Shortly after it all going off at Brownies, Themen got the call.

'I was basically asked if I'd do some gigs,' she recalls as we sit in drizzle outside Manchester's Atlas Bar. The female drummer who was handed the gigantic task of filling Burns' not inconsiderably-sized Doc Martens and place in Fall legend is a tiny, bubbly character with curly hair, distinctive teeth and a habit of unzipping and zipping her brown tracksuit as she talks, which may or may not suggest a nervous or at least excitable disposition. She zips and unzips it faster as she recalls 'the most bizarre phone call ever', then a typically surreal rehearsal as Smith demonstrated the drumbeat to 'Hip Priest' by tapping it out with a Biro.

Very shortly afterwards, the kid with the nervous zipping habit found herself delicately taking the stage in Camden as part of a three-piece miniature Fall, alongside Smith and Julia Nagle. She remembers the moment Smith walked onstage behind her kit as the one where her brain went 'Zap!' and she suddenly realised she was playing in a British institution. Themen's nerves weren't helped by not being able to hear anything onstage. The sound system was so bad she just had to hit the drums in some sort of time and hope for the best.

'I started playing one song and he [Smith] obviously decided at the last minute not to play it 'cause he walked up and slapped his hand down on my drumsticks,' she remembers, admitting she's never dared listen to the gig again on the freely available bootlegs. A further problem was the audience – having paid to see The Fall, they were not overly impressed with what had gone on in New York and the fact that their favourite band were suddenly down to a haphazard trio. Without warning, and with echoes of the very early Fall gigs when the 'Northern white crap that talks back' took on hostile audiences in WMCs, the audience turned against this not-so-Mighty Fall.

'I got pelted with cans,' remembers Themen. 'All sorts of stuff was coming over, landing on the drum kit. Something, a bottle, I think, was headed straight for my head, but luckily it hit the cymbal at the last moment. I didn't really understand the reasons. I'd had half an hour's practice in front of people who'd paid. It wasn't my fault what happened in America.'

Although Smith is no doubt aware such episodes fuel the Fall myth, Themen remembers his mood as being downbeat, perhaps one of those moments when – as he'd suggested in Malmaison – he really thought the game was up. Themen says he was unhappy with the gigs, so unhappy – and broke – that, as Nagle suggested, post-gig drinking was limited to a 'few beers' at the second gig following 'some sort of a do with Julia'.

Themen had a further insight into the odd band she'd joined when

Smith locked her in the dressing room and refused to let her out. Shortly before her third performance, at Reading, he shoved a wad of cash into her hand as the mini-Fall took the stage.

'About two grand or something,' she smiles. 'I wouldn't have dared steal any of it. So, there I was, playing with this enormous wad in my pocket and wondering what on earth would happen next!'

At this delicate point in their history, life around The Fall sounds more like a *Carry On* film than a legendary rock group.

Themen remembers Smith moaning at the sound man that the drums sounded like something 'made by [toy manufacturers] Chad Valley'. She relates how The Fall were in such chaos they had to use Polythene's rehearsal room and travel to gigs by phoning a man who lived up the road and had a minibus.

'And he was two hours late,' she grins. 'Three of us piled in this minibus with all the gear, we paid him in cash and rang him up later to fetch us back. I remember the driver said, "So what do you do? Are you in a group?" And Mark E Smith – without a hint of irony – said, "Yeah, we're called The Fall".'

On the bus, she remembers Smith catching her reading *New Left Review* and erupting with scathing laughter. 'He said, "I vote Tory".' To this day, she has no idea if he was joking – which must have first Fall drummer Dave/Steve, author of rejected Fall song 'Landslide Victory', spinning in his grave.

Despite the tomfoolery, Themen didn't last longer than three gigs, making her reign behind The Fall drum kit one of the shortest ever – if not as brief as Nick Dewey who lasted 45 minutes in 1999 (and who I've yet to find). Although Julia Nagle raves about Themen's drumming, the girl herself suggests she was growing 'more reticent' with each gig. And then Smith stopped phoning.

'I don't know if I could deal with being in The Fall,' she admits, candidly and reasonably enough. She suddenly looks wistful, toying with her orange juice and pondering what might have been. 'I think he knew that, even though it was unspoken.'

Smith's trusty antennae had served him once again. However, it was not her last experience of Mark E Smith. When Polythene subsequently played in America she found herself besieged by trainspotter Fall fans interrogating her about the spell in the group. One of them asked her to get something signed by the great man. She phoned him up and, where Steve Davies and others had failed, found herself in the rare position of being an ex-Fall musician allowed past Smith's front door.

She remembers a lot of whisky . . . and those blinds.

'The blinds! They are amazing!' she shrieks. 'They're like something your dad would have.' Fall trainspotters might like to know that at the time the Smith household contained very little except for two couches and an old Bush stereo.

'Really bizarre decor, as well,' she smiles. 'It looked like it hadn't been decorated since the 1980s.' Which it probably hadn't. As for Kate Themen, there haven't been too many changes in her life either. She's still drumming with Polythene, although she's currently finishing her PhD. She zips up her top for the last time as we stroll towards the station, her to go home and me to see yet another Fall gig.

'He just handed me a guitar. It had only five strings.'

Such was the chaos around The Fall at the time that at Themen's third gig – at Reading Alleycat, the last of the 'granny on bongos' concerts – they actually recruited a guitarist for one song. His name was Stuart Estell.

He plays 'traditional English music' – most recently in a now defunct band called The Village Wakes – and finding him is as simple as posting 'Are you Stuart Estell?' on the Fall forum. He sends me a photo – he is big, with cropped hair and a Roman nose – and emails me the story of one of the more peculiar Fall 'careers'.

An avid Fall fan – he knew Smith didn't like this in musicians but didn't let it put him off – he realised the group were in big trouble after America and offered his services on guitar or bass. 'I fired off an email a day or two before the gig. I was chancing my arm, really.'

He heard nothing back, but by a bizarre coincidence, which he doesn't think could possibly be connected, he was at the gig when Smith suddenly reached down and handed him a guitar, while he was in the audience.

'I was quicker to take it than anyone else who might have been within reach,' he says. 'It had only five strings on it though'. Even so, he thinks he did quite well.

'Yeah, fine,' he says, explaining that it took a few minutes to work out what The Fall were playing. 'I couldn't hear the vocals too clearly so all I had to go on was a skeletal keyboard part and the drums. So I guessed it was "Lie Dream of a Casino Soul" and happily played that for a couple of verses before I heard MES sneering, "Yeah, yeah, industrial estate . . ." and switched songs accordingly!' Which was certainly the first time in a couple of decades The Fall had played 'Industrial Estate' – or, at least, something resembling 'Industrial Estate'.

Estell didn't continue in The Fall. There was no follow-up, no phone call. 'If I'd had the call, I'd have said yes, without question. Who wouldn't? But I think I'd have lasted about half an hour – Smith would probably have shouted at me for being a "bloody muso" and kicked me out!' However, again demonstrating how small The Wonderful and Frightening World can be, he has subsequently collaborated with Julia Nagle.

With Estell and Themen gone, The Fall were again temporarily a two-piece. But, typically, as two were popping out, another was popping in. Ships in the night – a situation that seems to be spreading to my home life.

I do feel for Suzanne, and not just because of the outbreak of laryngitis. Sharing a house with a music journalist can't be an easy task at the best of times. For years, she's being slaving away at various nine-to-fives (or nine-to-eights) while I've been gallivanting off – usually at a moment's notice – around the North, and occasionally the world, in pursuit of rock stars. It's difficult to plan social occasions because I never know what I'm doing next week. It's probably a bit like being married to a policeman or paramedic. However, I think the bigger problem is when I'm at home – which is most of the time, cluttering up the house with CDs and slaving away at a computer to meet yet another stressful deadline. I love my job, but this aspect is definitely not glamorous or exciting. Even her mother struggles to grasp exactly what I do for a living: she often asks, 'Dave, when you say "reviewing an album", what exactly do you mean?'

But it's been worse these last few months, much worse. The daily task of music journalism is having to battle for my time with the increasingly all-consuming mission. I sometimes wonder if Suzanne – the love of my life – thinks I'm having an affair. I'm never home and when I am I'm buried in my office doing secretive things. Then there's the constant tiredness and moodswings; the mysterious phone numbers written on scraps of paper; phone calls at all hours and hurried disappearances, usually to Manchester. The hi-fi plays little else now apart from The Fall and on a couple of disturbing occasions I've even found myself addressing the dog in a pronounced Salfordian accent, much to Suzanne's chagrin. I remember Steve Hanley's words – 'After a while in The Fall, you're no longer normal' – and wonder if they apply to trailing The Fall as well. Still, Suzanne is a Fall fan. We've been together since 30 June 1989. I think she's just going to have to understand that things are going to be a bit weird until this is over. In the meantime, I have another appointment.

'It was like an out of body experience, or being in a movie.'

I meet Karen Leatham a few days later in another of Manchester's trendy watering holes. This time it's Dry Bar, once owned by Smith's arch rivals Factory Records, and the Fall musician bounds up wearing a long black coat, woolly hat and a Star of David. Now in her late thirties, Karen Leatham is as giddy as Kate Themen and laughs a lot – which is probably an understandable reaction to spending a very brief stay in The Fall. As she tells it, Nagle knew her from her days playing in a band called Wonky Alice and invited her into The Fall as a 'calming influence'.

There's a tiny snigger.

She remembers how Smith was 'getting anxious . . . about everything!' However, unlike Tommy Crooks, who joined pre-Brownies in the 'eye of the storm', Leatham perhaps brought the calm after the storm with her. She described being 'overwhelmed' at first but that there was an almost Dunkirk-type spirit in the group, of 'doing what we had to do'. Smith wasn't around much at rehearsals, where the group would be left to themselves. Leatham suggests his view was that musicians should 'sort the music out', although he gave them instructions such as, 'Do not play like Bon Jovi or Radiohead'.

By this point, the 'all-female Fall' finally fractured as Smith recruited drummer Tom Head and a pair of guitarists – Adam Helal and Neville Wilding, the latter of whom Smith had described to me as being 'at it with knuckle-dusters' with him before gigs. Leatham remembers Wilding as a great guitarist, very confident and a 'rock 'n' roll character', although she also describes a lot of violence around The Fall at this point. There is talk of van drivers being wanted by the police and unwanted visitors to the dressing room being despatched with kicks and punches – the violence didn't involve the group, but people around them.

'I'm not very rock 'n' roll,' she admits, 'so it was surreal. It was like an out-of-body experience, or living in a movie.' Which is why Leatham ultimately removed herself from the cast. After spending three months in The Fall, much of it working on the *Marshall Suite* album – an important comeback record containing 'Touch Sensitive', the Vauxhall advert song – things came to a head when bottles hit the stage in Bristol.

'I just thought, "That's it". I got in the van and drove home.' A decade on, Leatham – who now plays in Gabrielle's Wish (who occasionally support The Fall) and works as a manager of a mental health project for elderly gentlemen ('the stress levels are like The Fall') – has no regrets.

'I was 27 but a young 27,' she says. 'I'd handle it better now, but looking back it was a lot of fun. I'm glad I was involved with that album, my name's on it. I'm indelibly Marked.'

Isn't everybody? Before we say our goodbyes, Leatham relates a tale involving a visitor to her house while she was in The Fall – founding guitarist Martin Bramah. 'He came up to where I live and handed me a tape to pass to Mark . . . ideas for new songs. I asked Mark about it and he went, "Oh, I think I had it in my jacket, I appear to have dropped it down the toilet. Sorry about that." I didn't mention it again.'

The exciting prospect of a second Bramah return was unfortunately not to be, but there were plenty of other candidates lining up to join the ranks. From here on in, life in and around The Fall would get even more out of control. Meanwhile, I take a break from The Fall and head off with Suzanne and Guinness for a much needed country break. Quite why we're taking a country break when we live in the country is a moot point, but I suppose it's just become part of our routine from when we lived on the outskirts of the city. For the first few days I can't relax. A lorry driver dents my car before we even get there and I feel stressed out. But for the last two days of our week away, I do relax. We enjoy endless, sunny walks into the Peak District; a German tourist takes a photo of us together outside Sudbury Hall stately home. It's just like old times. I feel a long way from Prestwich and the Fall obsession. Then we drive home, and I set about finding a drummer who was in The Fall for 35 minutes.

> 'It was the sort of thing I'd dreamt of as a kid – the drummer being passed over the crowd's shoulders.'

I've started to wonder if any other employer in modern British business operates like The Fall. Searching around for comparisons only throws up the extremes of casual labour – strawberry pickers and the like – who can be recruited at an instant and don't require an interview or audition. You're just put out straight to work and probably last only a few days. But that kind of work is barely comparable to being around the 'Rorschach Test' of Mark E Smith.

In many ways, The Fall operate just like the mills in Victorian England. Smith hates being called a 'mill owner' but in 2003 he told the *Observer* how his grandfather owned a mill and would stand outside the local prison waiting for recruits. 'That's kind of how I recruit musicians,' he said. 'It's like, "You're on bass, so get cracking".'

But another historical comparison is creeping into my Fall-addled consciousness. Impressment was a notorious form of recruitment used by the Royal Navy in the eighteenth and nineteenth centuries, although as early as 1664 it was legally sanctioned by Edward I. The practice gave birth to the sinister term 'press gangs' – whereby groups of soldiers would scour the streets for employees in a not dissimilar way to Smith's psychic radar scanning the streets around Prestwich. To qualify for impressment into the navy, men had to be between 18 and 55, with little or no seafaring experience required. They would then be 'moulded' into sailors in the same way Smith 'brainwashes' The Fall. Although many press-ganged victims appealed to the Admiralty, they were usually unsuccessful. Tales persist of hapless men dragged off to sea without any warning. Similarly, if you think about it, to how people end up in The Fall.

I'm back in Malmaison's bar. This time, I've reverted to rock reviewing mode to cast a critical opinion over James Dean Bradfield, the Manic Street Preachers' frontman, who is about to play his first solo gig in the Roadhouse over the road. It's a side project he'd never be allowed in The Fall. The assembled gentlemen, ladies and illiterate scumbags of the press have assembled for a pre-gig meal and schmooze – the sort of thing rock journalists frown upon morally but otherwise lap up, as it's one of the few occasions where we're guaranteed a decent meal. Bradfield's PR girl, Gillian Porter, is running through the list of his musicians, when she suddenly announces, 'Drums, Nick Dewey'.

I know that name. I tell her as much, and she asks, 'You know him as manager of The Chemical Brothers?'

No, I tell her. For me, the name Nick Dewey can only mean Nick Dewey Who Spent An Afternoon In The Fall.

A couple of hours later, I'm in Bradfield's dressing room sharing stories with a tall, gangly 30-something who has the most wonderfully startled grin. Which you would if you were him and had been involved in one of the most demented Fall entrances/exits of them all. Dewey was in The Fall for eight songs, the duration of their set on 27 August 1999 at the famous Reading Festival, which makes him the second shortest-serving Faller ever. After Stuart Estell. But Dewey's story is even more bizarre.

As the grinning man tells it, he was at the festival with The Chemical Brothers. Everyone was hanging out backstage when this 'drunken bloke' came in who turned out to be Neville Wilding, the guitarist who Smith had told me was 'at it with knuckle-dusters' with him at that very festival.

According to Dewey, Wilding had been sent on a mission to find a drummer – not unlike a press ganger. The story Wilding was apparently putting about backstage – subsequently in doubt – was that The Fall were short of a sticksman after Tom Head had been abandoned at a motorway services station. Things were rather urgent, not least because they were due to play in front of a tent containing a thousand-odd people in an hour's time. Dewey reports that Wilding asked all manner of people if they would drum for The Fall that day, including Justine Frischmann who was headlining with Britpop superstars Elastica. When all Wilding's enquiries fell on deaf ears, he descended on Nick Dewey.

Fatefully, for Dewey, one of The Chemical Brothers remembered that many years before he'd been in a 'shoegazing' pop band called Revolver and played drums. Wilding's eyes lit up. 'Brilliant,' he slurred. 'Come and play drums in The Fall!'

The problem for Dewey wasn't only that he didn't know many Fall songs and really wasn't prepared to play such a high-profile gig: 'I said, "Look, I haven't played drums for ten years".' To which Wilding apparently responded, 'Don't worry about that, we're all pissed anyway'.

Wilding duly switched into press gang mode.

'He wouldn't take no for an answer,' says Dewey. 'He said he'd have a look around [for another drummer] but I saw him go into the bogs. Ten minutes later, he came back saying, "Nah, no one else can do it".'

Far from feeling he'd been press ganged – which he had been, in effect – Dewey considered it the 'sort of thing I'd dreamt of when I was a kid, the drummer being passed over someone's shoulders'.

Moments later, Dewey found himself being led onto a tour bus with blacked-out windows. Mark E Smith was on one of the tour bus benches, shirt off, 'passed out'.

'They'd obviously had a skinful,' roars Dewey, describing how Wilding tried to wake up Smith and couldn't rouse him, so punched him in the face. After two or three blows, Smith finally woke up to be informed by Wilding, 'Mark, this is Nick. He's going to be playing drums for us!'

Dewey describes how Smith put his face right up to his own and said, 'Right, let's have a look at you, cock!' while Dewey tried his best not to look like a prisoner-of-war about to face a firing squad.

Things became even more unreal when Wilding started to show him the songs, and Smith tried to stop him. 'They started fighting over the guitar,' says Dewey. Eventually, Smith got Dewey drumming on a guitar case with the instruction, 'No, don't look at him [Wilding], that's the only way you'll learn.'

Shortly afterwards, Dewey found himself setting up an unfamiliar drum kit in front of the Reading crowd and waiting for The Fall, who appeared 'at the very last second' before they were due onstage.

'They'd had another fight,' remembers the reluctant drummer. 'Mark E Smith's nose was cut open with blood everywhere. I said, "Are we going on, then?" and they ignored me. I grabbed the guitarist and said, "Tell me when the songs start and finish".

'He said, "Don't worry, mate. I'll be stood right next to you".' Dewey then recalls Wilding immediately disappearing to the other side of the stage. Unbeknown to Smith, though, Dewey transgressed the usual requirements – he was a Fall fan. He had 'tons' of the records. Sadly, this proved irrelevant because, as ever with The Fall, virtually all the set was made up of new material.

'I didn't know a single song,' he laughs. 'It was a mental experience. I was the last to end every song because obviously no one told me!' Smith spent much of the set fiddling with the keyboards and amplifiers, occasionally turning his attention to Dewey's drum kit. But the gig was a success, in a way, even if those who were there remember an 'excellent shambles'. The day-long Faller remembers it as 'an amazing, amazing experience' and something he relishes telling family and pals about to this day.

A year or so later, a mate of Dewey's bumped into Smith at a party, where the Fall leader had brushed it off saying, 'Yeah, I remember him. Quiet bloke. Didn't say much.'

Dewey is in hysterics. 'He's a genius!' he raves of Smith, still not knowing how he managed to be 'moulded' into pulling that gig off but realising he had a unique encounter with 'one of the great British characters'.

'He reminds me of Bob Dylan,' he says. 'You know he's in control, but his band members haven't a clue what song's coming next and are just waiting for that nod.' Dewey didn't get that nod again – Tom Head managed to get back for the festival's second leg at Leeds and The Fall's reluctant stickman returned to managing The Chemical Brothers, basking in the knowledge he would forever hold a special, if slightly unsteady, place among The Fallen. If Smith can take a musician in such circumstances and make him into a member of The Fall, surely he can do the trick with anyone? Maybe he could even do it with me.

I try to ask Tom Head about it but he seems to have disappeared. As usual, there is a further complication. Head isn't usually a drummer at all, but an actor who has appeared in *Coronation Street* and comedy horror series *The League of Gentlemen*, one of the few examples of art that is as surreal as The Fall. When acting, Head goes by the name of Thomas Patrick Murphy and I eventually track down his agent in Manchester. Alas, the agent says he hasn't been in touch with him for a long time. The agent kindly pops a letter through Murphy/Head's door, but neither of us hear from him.

CHAPTER 28

'It was like spontaneous combustion.'

I'd like to find out a bit more about the incident at Reading and run down Neville Wilding – the brother of boxer Spencer who lives in Prestatyn – to a street in London. Unfortunately, his neighbour says Wilding is 'in Guadalajara'. Fortunately, and because I am now knee-deep in The Wonderful and Frightening World, Wilding's neighbour was also in The Fall.

Adam Helal was the thirty-fifth disciple, a guitarist from December 1998 to February 2001, who also played at Reading. He says the Nick Dewey experience was one of his own most surreal experiences while in The Fall.

'He was very brave,' he says. '"This one goes like this." "This one goes like that." "Now play it." He was great!'

Helal's tenure in the group was hardly short of mad events – Reading was only one. He remembers bumping into his old English teacher, Charlie, at a gig in Cambridge and discovering he had been Smith's best man at his last three weddings.

There were jaunts like playing the piano in the Rover's Return at a *Coronation Street* party, or the gig in Holland where Smith did 'his Tasmanian Devil impression, there were amps and keyboards flying over'. It seems that after wreaking onstage destruction, Smith managed to tie himself up with whatever leads were left, before even reaching the first chorus.

Helal gives me another glimpse into Mad Mark's (as the neighbours had called him) peculiar life in Prestwich. Smith's house is apparently nicknamed The Vortex: 'Because once you go in, you'll be lucky to get out within five days'.

Like Dave Bush's experience before him, Adam Helal seems to have found being in The Fall a lot of fun. His route in was slightly different from the usual bumps, chance encounters and sudden career shifts from the road crew, but not that much. He was in a band with Wilding, and their soundman also took care of The Fall. One night, Wilding asked if he wanted to play a gig with The Fall . . . at the 3,000-capacity London Astoria. In 24 hours' time.

'Before I could think, the word "yes" fell out of my mouth,' he remembers. One sleepless night later, he found himself, like Dewey, playing unfamiliar songs in front of thousands of people. Helal had no idea why he'd been recruited but soon found himself being moulded. As he puts it, Smith has a 'PhD in manipulation' and being in The Fall could be like 'spontaneous combustion'.

'Brilliant, hilarious, elevating, tumultuous and shit' is how he describes the Fall experience, adding, 'I know most band members will probably identify with this but there's nothing so drastic as being in The Fall.'

Because Helal was, like Simon Rogers, based 200 miles from Prestwich, he often found himself without Fall transport. There were times when he found himself, as a member of one of the country's major bands, having to hitch-hike to their gigs in the same way my pals and I used to follow The Fall.

'Always a laugh,' he insists. The gigs themselves could be anywhere – churches, sweatboxes, festivals. Fall touring schedules never seemed to follow normal routes and he describes finding himself playing venues as disparate as London's respected Royal Festival Hall and a festival in a valley in Portugal which was on fire while the bands were playing.

Helal confirms that, amidst all the chaos of this period, creative freedom and spontaneity in the music were stronger than ever. One night in Southend, after a couple of weeks spent 'getting to know each other' had spawned various situations, Smith came up with the lyrics for a track called 'Ketamine Sun' off the top of his head in minutes, by rapping about his latest band mates and giving them names like 'Spliffhead' and 'Smart ass at the computer' (Julia Nagle). In the song, Smith tells about a drug addict who stole a television and nailed it to a jeweller's bench. Moments later, he's telling someone that their mother's moustache needs fixing and raging against training shoe culture on the grounds that someone wearing Adidas needs to visit a cobblers four times a month. Fantastic.

Predictably, Helal's time in The Fall came to a halt almost as abruptly as Nick Dewey's. It's widely believed Helal and Wilding were sacked for refusing to play, over a royalty dispute that ended in litigation. Helal says that there was a dispute, but with a record label, not with Smith or The Fall.

'We obviously weren't happy about that but I think litigation is a slightly over-imaginative interpretation,' he says. In fact, like many of The Fallen, Helal looks back largely without anger: he had a great time, the experience taught him to be more creative.

Since leaving The Fall, he's busied himself producing an album for Gigibaker, made music for adverts and PlayStation, and done sound design for the Whitney Museum of American Art in New York. He would never rule out returning to The Fall. He won't confirm Smith's story about phoning Wilding every month but reveals there has been 'sporadic' contact with the singer 'but no gigs so far'. With all this chaos going on, it's a wonder they made any music, but the two albums by the Helal-Wilding line-up were cracking returns to form. 1999's *The Marshall Suite* – containing 'Touch Sensitive' – and the following year's ridiculously innovative *The Unutterable* suggest 'creative tension' had paid off. A few weeks after speaking to Helal, I drop him a line to see if Wilding has returned. But the email address bounces back.

Maybe Adam Helal's now 'in Guadalajara' too.

CHAPTER 29

'I'm becoming a travelling minstrel.'

The list of remaining Fallen is growing ever shorter, but I'm still drawing a blank with Karl Burns. It's rather worrying. How can someone apparently so colourful simply disappear? Worrying about Burns doesn't just keep me up some nights but creeps into my days when I least expect it. One afternoon in Bowden, near Altrincham in Cheshire, I'm interviewing Johnny Marr from The Smiths when we get onto The Fall. It turns out the 'greatest guitarist of his generation' – as Marr is often called – is a Fall fan too. We talk about Fall guitarists we have loved – he is a particular fan of Craig Scanlon – and gigs we have seen. Marr reveals he used to follow The Fall almost as much as I did. Who would have ever thought the twangy Smiths' early singles or the darker terrain of later albums *The Queen Is Dead* and *Strangeways, Here We Come* could – somewhere in there – bear the DNA of The Fall?

Karl Burns crops up, because Marr is as mystified as I am. It transpires

Marr knew Burns quite well, before The Smiths, when Marr worked in the clothes shop run by Smiths manager Joe Moss. Burns was an erratic customer, obviously before the days when he toured America armed only with a pair of underpants.

'I sold him a leather jacket from the shop, probably about '81, '82,' Marr says. 'When I bumped into him ten years later he was still wearing that jacket.' I suppose the moral is: find the jacket, find the man.

I go home and decide to have another go at being Fallen Private Eye. Buried deep in an old *Directory of Enquiries* for Manchester is an address for one 'Karl E Burns'. It's worth a shot.

The address is in a rundown estate in Ancoats, just off the Oldham Road, which stretches from the city centre to Middleton and Failsworth. Because my Punto blew up on one of my many journeys to find The Fall, I've just invested in a new car – a green MG – that sparkles as I creep through the streets. Lovely car, but the last thing you want to be driving in an area like this, because it sticks out like a classical guitarist in The Fall.

The streets are strewn with litter. Half the houses are boarded up. I'm travelling at around five miles per hour because I'm struggling to find the street and feel like a kerb-crawler. And I'm attracting attention. Lots of attention. Some of it comes from the disturbingly young but worldly-looking kids who ride BMX bikes on the pavements – the traditional form of courier used by Manchester's drug gangs. But most comes from the police, who I notice in the rear-view mirror have taken up a similar pace directly behind my car. They follow me at five miles per hour and have just started to gaze even more intently when I decide to cut my losses and head off. If Karl Burns is there, he is safe from me. For now.

I haven't yet located Burns, but I have a phone number for another of the disappeared – Brian Fanning, the thirty-ninth person to join The Fall and a guitarist from 2001.

He joined shortly after Jim Watt, who lives in the same street – being neighbours and being in The Fall isn't confined to Helal and Wilding. I've been told Fanning is 'a bit eccentric' and under no circumstances must I phone before 2 p.m. What happens before then? Is he a vampire? Does he turn into a pumpkin?

'The last few days, I've been up all night jamming,' he mumbles, bang on 2.03 p.m., sounding as if he's been up for years rather than hours. He's not rehearsing for The Fall. He's planning a new career: 'I'm becoming a travelling minstrel.'

Fanning's in his early forties, which makes him older than most Fallers and almost of Smith's generation, something the singer has otherwise frowned upon since losing Karl Burns and Steve Hanley.

Fanning does not claim to be particularly good on guitar. He was working for The Fall as a guitar technician when he found himself being asked to do a gig in Greece. The gig never took place because a storm blew the stage down. But a week later, he made his debut with The Fall at a gathering of Hells Angels in Warwickshire known as The Bulldog Bash (the backdrop of an infamous biker shooting on the M40 in 2007). 'The Fall are very popular with Hells Angels,' he says.

Fanning found The Fall's relentless touring schedule particularly difficult. It wasn't just that the dates were Leeds, Newcastle, Edinburgh, Dublin, Belfast and Liverpool within his first week, but they were playing them in that order, which makes no logistical sense. When I'd asked Smith about The Fall's seemingly crazy schedules in Malmaison, he blamed a 'conspiracy'.

'I said to one of them [tour organisers], "What do you do, just get the fuckin' darts out and throw them at a map of Britain?" She said, "It's very co-ordinated, actually." I was a bit bad-mannered but I said, "Your dad wasn't a British army officer, was he?"'

Smith then adopted a perfect English upper-class female voice. '"Yes, he was!"' he howled. 'It's funny, the things you learn about people. It was a shot in the dark.'

But as we can testify, Mark Smith *knows*.

Brian Fanning tells me that after the frenetic jaunt round England the group went to Belgium, Germany and Holland – all within a few days. The situation was further complicated by Smith having his leg in plaster following the tumble that landed him in hospital, and Fanning remembers putting the legend of British music in a cart and wheeling him to the stage.

He felt honoured, though, to be of service. Like fellow local Adrian

Flanagan, Fanning grew up in awe of Smith and, like Eric the Ferret, says the more he worked alongside Smith, the more he recognised him as a genius – even though he seems unsure what that genius is.

He remembers arriving at rehearsals to be confronted with 'demented' instructions, but which seemed to work every time. Once, when they were recording a song called 'Gotta See Jane' – on the 2001 album *Are You Are Missing Winner* – Smith suddenly started shouting at the drummer, Spencer Birtwistle, that the music was all wrong, even though Fanning insists it sounded perfectly all right. Smith suggested a ten-minute break, during which Birtwistle started playing a different beat. Fanning picked up the bass and played along. Then Smith started rapping over the top – 'Spencer is a bastardo, he needs to go back to Rusholme' – before going on to sing the same song as before over the completely new rhythm.

'And it was perfect,' insists Fanning. 'Nobody else would do that, but that's the way his mind works.' Perhaps it wasn't all too perfect though. After two superb albums in *The Marshall Suite* and *The Unutterable*, *Are You Are Missing Winner* was the worst Fall album in years. Well, I thought that when I first heard it in 2001. But a remastered version in 2006 banished the sound quality problems of the original and revealed itself as a fine but flawed return to rockabilly.

If everything was so rosy, why did the budding minstrel leave after just three months?

According to Fanning, it wasn't anything to do with problems with the boss. Yes, Smith was 'volatile', but he understands that. 'People think he's a miserable bastard, but he's not,' he contests. 'He's just very good at winding people up. Anyone who knows Mark's temperament knows he can be explosive. But anyone with that artistic nature is entitled to be awkward.' He's another to suggest the hair-raising events are 'just part of the show'. He says it was the shows that were the problem – there were too many of them and, almost immediately after he joined, being in The Fall was wearing him out. 'It was a good laugh when we weren't getting on everyone else's nerves,' he says, 'but it simply got too much.'

Call yourselves bloody professionals?

For the apprentice travelling minstrel, The Fall 'weren't professional enough'. 'We were all a bit tired and emotional, pissed really,' he continues, explaining that after three weeks in Europe he didn't want to be around 'these people'.

'I still go for a pint with Mark, but I wouldn't go back,' he declares, unusually in both aspects. 'You hear these stories about Mark, but he's always been great with me. We're both Pisces, maybe that's why we get on.'

Fanning reveals he was one of the people who interviewed Smith for the *FC United* fanzine, and thus indirectly responsible for postponing my interview with Smith, by taking him to the pub.

He signs off with an ominous warning for the current line-up: 'He won't keep this line-up for too long. Most of them get sacked, left in motorway caffs or whatever. As soon as he detects a lack of freshness, they'll be gone.'

When I put this opinion to current guitarist Ben Pritchard, he suggests Fanning was fired himself – for banging on The Fall's hotel room doors.

CHAPTER 30

'Come on, cock, you can do it. We'll have a rehearsal before you go on.'

J im Watts lives on the same road as his 'eccentric' neighbour but is another kettle of cuttlefish entirely – a straight-up chap, large of frame and with a dusting of facial hair. He seems too normal, far too normal to have ever been in The Fall. Perhaps Smith suspected this and set about changing his condition.

As part of the boot camp process, Watts was required to make sure the

Fall backdrop was correctly positioned onstage – an intricate process that often involved moving it several millimetres while being 'colourfully' shouted at by the leader.

Like an army private, he was also given the duties of retrieving the group's intro music from the sound desk after gigs: 'I kinda fell out with Mark because I kept losing it,' he says. 'The thing is, it wasn't a proper intro. It was just a looped piece of music. At some gigs it must've gone on for hours.'

Watts' entrance into the group was a classic Fall baptism of fire.

In 2001, he was in a band called Trigger Happy with Dave Milner and Ed Blaney, who it turns out also lives in the same road as Watts and Fanning. Trigger Happy were meant to support The Fall. However, in the February following the Helal-Wilding meltdown, Trigger Happy were suddenly subsumed into The Fall. Watts remembers his induction – which has echoes of Nick Dewey's – as 'one of the most intense things I've done in my life'. 'It was a big crowd in Ireland. They [The Fall] hadn't rehearsed or anything. The night before I was packing my stuff – the first time I'd ever been abroad – and suddenly I get a call [from Blaney] saying, "You're playing bass in The Fall".'

Like Dewey, Watts protested, pointing out that he only knew four Fall songs, but he was similarly press ganged with the instructions, 'Nobody else can do it'.

It was 11.30 at night. The ferry taking The Fall to Eire was due to leave at six the following morning. Watts protested so much Smith even rang him up himself. 'Come on, cock, you can do it,' he told him, entering Cloughie mode. 'You'll pick it up. We'll have a rehearsal before you go on.' Inevitably, the promised rehearsal amounted to little more than 'a short strum'. The situation was made more complicated because Ben Pritchard – another recent recruit – had only rehearsed four songs too.

'We sort of struggled through seven or eight songs, but it was a big crowd and was very intimidating,' recalls Watts. 'There were about 800 people who'd all paid £20. After eight songs we went off, but people were going, "You've got to go back on!"'

He reveals that in the end Smith was literally shouting out titles and the band were making it up as they went along. 'We'd be going, "Uh? How does that go?" and he'd go, "It sounds like [Led Zeppelin's] 'Kashmir' . . ." I've done gigs before where things have gone wrong but to actually play for an hour where you've no idea what you're playing is trial by fire!'

To add insult to mental injury, he came offstage to be confronted by seasoned Fall fans asking, 'So, do you think you're as good as Steve Hanley?'

According to Watts, Ben Pritchard had joined the group by being on the subs' bench, and Smith had recruited him as 'additional guitarist' alongside Neville Wilding with a view to replacing the knuckle-duster man.

'Sometimes people get this idea that he [Smith] sacks people willy-nilly . . . which he does!' laughs Watts. 'But he was always planning to replace Neville Wilding.'

But why?

'His name says why. He was wild!'

Although Watts wasn't in The Fall with Wilding, he seems to have heard the tales. One of them is that Helal and Wilding actually left over a 'face-off' with Smith over money from The Fall or from the label. The pair apparently phoned Smith to tell him they'd left and were on a train to London – expecting him to back down. Instead, Smith called their bluff.

Watts suggests that the two guitarists probably thought they could get away with it because Fall guitarists are 'fired' all the time. 'It starts as a joke, although sometimes the laughing stops and that person isn't there anymore.' Watts' first exit was a sacking after Smith said he'd found out he was planning to play with a heavy metal band by 'intercepting' his phone calls.

'I've been fired every half an hour,' he grins. 'Then Mark will come over and say, "Obviously you're not fired, cock. Not yet!"' Watts gave up a lucrative job in IT to play in The Fall, relishing the break from nine-to-five employment, and was actually paid Fall royalties, although he admits he discovered 'a whole new world of pain'.

His second exit was due to 'the pain' of making records.

Like Simon Rogers in the 1980s, Watts says he found The Fall's recording process 'pretty odd' – in fact, he makes it sounds even odder than it was back then. He describes rarely entering the studio familiar with songs they'd be recording (a situation Smith told him he prefers); songs being credited to people who haven't written them and vice versa; weird commands like, 'Give me more of the fookin' top drums.' 'Mark, what are the top drums?'

Apparently, one of Smith's tricks in the studio is to assemble the controls into the shape of a 'big wave', then inform startled producers, 'That's the Fall sound'. The way Smith 'winds up' his musicians sounds odd too – bombarding them for hours with tapes of Bernard Manning or playing them a Dylan album with the specific instruction, 'This is what not to do'.

One of the more celebrated Fall fans is Frank Skinner, who opens his TV show with their 1982 song 'Jawbone and the Air Rifle'. According to Watts, Smith does not appreciate the honour and views Skinner – a multi-millionaire and hardly short of exposure – as somehow trading off The Fall.

Again, Smith seems impossible to second guess.

'Mark's difficult to get close to,' Watts ponders, implying the main reason for this is because Smith knows he'll eventually lose or sack them all. However, Watts found himself unusually honoured when his songwriting on the opening track of *Are You Are Missing Winner* was reflected in the title, 'Jim's The Fall'. While Watts says he was never privy to Smith's mythical 'secrets', he admits he worked some out after a while.

He describes seeing Smith 'screaming at people' and then trotting away, laughing. As for Smith's drinking, he says he's often seen people think the singer's drunk when he's actually been acting – a favourite trick of boozy actor Oliver Reed. Which makes me wonder whether he was putting on an act for musicians like Marcia Schofield, all those supposedly whisky-sozzled years ago. To freak them out? To trigger more creative tension?

'His stagecraft can't be underestimated,' concedes Watts. 'He's a stage person. He can go, "Move that amp four inches to the right and two inches back". He has a look at the stage to see how it looks visually. It's easy to think that he just stumbles around the stage. It's not staged but he is a consummate showman.'

Watts played on *The Real New Fall LP* – another storming example of later Fall – released in the UK in October 2003 and in the US in June 2004. It contains a *bona fide* classic – 'Theme from Sparta FC'. It's another football-themed Fall song (albeit about hooliganism rather than the game, a colourful account of Chelsea fans receiving a beating in Eastern Europe) which became a minor hit – Number 66 – on release as a 2004 single and grew in status when it became used as the theme music to the BBC's Saturday afternoon sports coverage, The Fall's first connection with BBC Sport before Smith was called on to read the football results. For Watts, however, the peculiarities of making the music finally got too much and he quit to enjoy life in a more straightforward world. He's currently leafleting for Salford Council – reliable employers who pay £1.75 per door – and planning to launch his own band which he says will sound 'absolutely nothing like' The Fall.

CHAPTER 31

'If you're a mate, you can tell him to fuck off!'

S hortly after saying good-bye to Jim Watts, I speak to the man who stepped into the breach when Watts was sacked the first time, although the circumstances of the interview are as odd as Watts' first departure. Over a crackling phone line from Saddleworth Moor, Steve Evets – who calls himself a 'Fall musician in emergencies' – relates how he's spent the day watching Myra Hindley and Ian Brady burying bodies. How lovely.

Luckily, both are actors – Evets is currently shooting scenes for *See No Evil*, a film where he plays 'David Smith . . . the bloke who was with Ian Brady when he axed [final victim] Edward Evans,' he says excitedly, although in fact the shocked Smith then made the call that led to Brady's arrest.

Acting and drama, it turns out, is Evets' usual profession, although he does have his own acid house band called, unsurprisingly, Dr Freak's Padded Cell, who, equally unsurprisingly, sometimes open for The Fall.

Evets is also one of Smith's few best friends, meaning he will step up to the plate when he really needs him – like when a bass guitarist has been fired or abandoned at a foreign airport. 'I first stepped up in Istanbul,' he says of the gig (5 March 2003) after Jim Watts resigned. It was 'cracking', but he'd never consider making the role permanent. 'You're joking aren't you?' he shouts. 'I value our friendship.' He believes the difference between being a mate and being a Fall musician is 'if you're a mate, you can tell him to fuck off!'

He laughs, and the phone goes dead.

I contact him again, and Evets expands a little on the difference between Smith at home and Smith in The Fall, suggesting that perhaps it's not quite '24-7'. 'We go for a pint and take the piss out of everything. He's got a great sense of humour. He just gets a bit stressed out when he's on the road.' In fact, Evets confirms what Smith said to me about getting 'nervous'.

'When he's relaxing in the pub he's fine,' he says. 'He gets bothered a lot on tour, y'know, sycophants,' and the line goes dead for good. I'm getting slightly paranoid now. Is MES briefing against me?

At least all this time on the phone is made slightly easier by no longer having to ferry Suzanne to and from work. She's been coming home later and later, and to make it easier for me has started cycling. I was Suzanne's Ben Pritchard, but in the chauffeuring department at least, it seems my services are suddenly no longer required.

CHAPTER 32

'It was all done very quietly, so no one knew I'd gone.'

In a way, interviewing a Fallen musician can be like being in The Fall –
you never know when you'll be cut off in full flow.

I get more of a sense of this, and a few more examples of cult-like
behaviour, from Simon 'Dingo' Archer, Watts' replacement and the forty-
third person to join The Fall.

What I know about Dingo is this: he was introduced to Smith by a mutual
friend, but as a sound engineer, not a bassist. He runs 6dB Studio in

Manchester, where he helped Smith record a solo album, *Pander! Panda! Panza!*, in 2002. Shortly after that, Smith asked him to remix some tracks from what eventually became *The Real New Fall LP*. Once Watts was gone, the man nicknamed 'Dingo' was given the job of 'watering down' or getting rid of Watts' parts on the record.

'So, I first played for The Fall then, in the studio,' he explains. As usual, Smith had realised Archer's suitability for the role when he'd seen him in a small role in the movie *24 Hour Party People* playing Sex Pistols bass player Glen Matlock.

'One night after a recording session, Mark asked if I would like to play bass for two gigs that he had coming up. I said "yes", obviously, and in typical Fall fashion, I didn't hear from anyone until about two days before the first show.'

As with Jim Watts, Archer's induction didn't involve anything as conventional as a rehearsal. Instead, Ben Pritchard was despatched to Archer's place to show him the music – but the guitar parts, not the bass. 'It was very much a case of winging it,' he says, fitting the classic bassist's profile – tall, with long arms that enable the instrument to be flailed around. He did well enough – if 'well' is a Fall concept – to be offered the job. He says that for him the only possible comparison between being in The Fall and being in any other group is the act of actually picking up the bass guitar.

'Working with Mark can take you to any extreme emotion you can imagine on any day of the week,' he says. 'That's the essence of it, that word "extreme". There are no "average" moments, no "typical" days. You can't take anything for granted and you definitely can't assume anything. If you think something is good, Mark will see it differently, and vice versa. There is room for creative freedom and it's encouraged, but you never get to embellish it, you watch it metamorphose into something else when Mark gets to work on it. It means you can't be precious about anything.'

Even The Fall. Archer was a long-term fan, though he wised up enough to keep quiet about it. He makes clear that 'all the stories and rumours are true', which makes me fret again about Karl Burns.

Even the psychic ability – sort of. When Archer joined, Smith whispered to his musicians that Australian singer Nick Cave was trying to poach his group. In fact, Archer was poached by singer PJ Harvey, former girlfriend and confidante of Nick Cave.

However, after a period 'on loan' – much like a football club might borrow a central defender – Archer returned, co-producing and playing on 2005's *Fall Heads Roll*. But something had changed. Shortly afterwards, he was taken to one side and quietly dispensed with – the way he describes it almost sounds as if he'd been shot.

'It was done kind of quietly and without any blazing rows, so no one knew that I'd gone,' he says. He hasn't joined the disappeared though – he's keeping very, very busy, but misses the 'lunacy' of The Fall.

'As much as it was never "right",' he concludes, 'the random nature of being in that band is highly addictive.' He makes me think: what will I do when I have found all The Fallen? What will I do next?

CHAPTER 33

'I found him barking like a dog.'

I'm nearing the end of the road. Shortly after speaking to Archer, I find Ruth Daniel, who spent a day in The Fall playing keyboards on 22 September 2002. Daniel is the forty-second. Unless Tom Head or Neville Wilding suddenly turn up, there's only Ed Blaney and drummers Dave Milner and Karl Burns left. I email Manchester University asking, 'Are you the Ruth Daniel who used to be in The Fall?' We eventually meet up in Manchester's Kro bar, over the road from where she works at the university on a project called In Place of War, investigating 'theatre performance in war zones' – which she assures me has nothing to do with The Fall. Now in her mid twenties, Daniel is a slightly-built, pretty girl with deep plum-coloured hair and an infectious, excited manner. Hardly a typical Fall musician but, then again, who is? She cradles a Corona lager as she tells her story, and it turns out that Nick Dewey isn't the only person to spend an insane day in The Fall.

Having played in bands for years, Daniel was fronting an all-girl band one night at Manchester's Night & Day Café, when up strode Jim Watts and Ed Blaney. The request from Fall manager/sometime member Blaney was simple but unexpected: 'How do you fancy playing with The Fall?' Daniel's parents are massive Fall fans and any doubt in her mind was immediately overruled as her father told Blaney, 'Yes, she'll do it.'

'So, then I said, "Er, yes, I'll do it!"' hoots Daniel. She was told to attend Manchester's Sankeys Soap club for rehearsals, which went very well. There was just one tiny problem. There was no sign of Mark E Smith.

'I kept asking, "When's Mark arriving?"' she says, 'and they kept putting me off. Then Ed took this phone call and the whole atmosphere in the room changed.' Blaney told her she'd have to leave immediately. Elena, Smith's then new wife, was playing keyboards, and no one had informed Smith there would be another keyboard player too.

Quite why The Fall needed an extra keyboard player is a moot point, although they were due to film a live DVD and Daniel suggests there might have been 'some question over the ability of the keyboard player from the other members'.

'Which was a big problem for me,' she says, realistically. 'Knowing what Mark's like, I couldn't turn up at his gig and start playing, knowing that his wife's going to hate me and that I'm probably going to get stopped by Mark.' She mentioned the problems to her father, who declared, 'That's fine by me! Even if you get fired, you'll have still been in The Fall!'

Daniel duly turned up at King George's Hall in Blackburn and despite being primarily a guitarist she'd written the songs on sheets of paper. By this time, Smith had apparently been informed that she was playing, as had Elena. Daniel suggests that, after all the apprehension, she 'bonded' with Smith's wife over keyboards, not least because Elena admired Daniel's set-up more than the 'little Casio keyboard she found on a skip, that had melted!' she was playing at the time.

Daniel was told 'under no circumstances' must she enter the dressing room and disturb Smith 30 minutes before the gig. Alas, she suddenly realised that she'd left all her notes in there and couldn't do the gig without them.

'I walked in and found Mark walking in circles yelping and barking like a dog, which is obviously how he warms up his vocals. I knocked on the door and he ignored me and just stood still in silence.' Daniel got her things, closed the door and walked away to the unmistakable sound of Smith barking away.

The gig was equally eventful. She remembers 'crazies' in the crowd – Ed Blaney leaping on for a drum solo and Elena playing all the wrong notes.

'I've never seen anything like it,' she grimaces. 'When does the manager play a drum solo?! It was bizarre to play a gig that unprofessionally but everyone was so into it and I have to say it was fantastic.'

After the gig, Daniel went up to Smith to thank him for letting her play and took her parents into the dressing room to meet the band. Smith closed the door and the three of them stood in silence for several minutes, Smith just staring and holding the door shut.

'It was like he was keeping us hostage. Then he opened the door and just went, "Ta very much".'

Daniel wasn't asked to play with The Fall again, but that same night she met the person who helped her set up her record label, Fat Northerner. A few hours in The Fall had changed her life.

CHAPTER 34

'I thought I was going insane. The only way I got through it was by taking up meditation.'

When I was a child, I used to while away hours doing jigsaws of things like dogs and trains. Now I'm doing a jigsaw of The Wonderful and Frightening World and, there, the pieces that will complete the picture can sometimes lurk where you least expect.

I'm back in the Peak District where I encountered Tony Friel and holidayed with Suzanne and Guinness. This time, I've journeyed to the rural New Mills in Derbyshire to find Dave Milner, drummer on *The Real New Fall LP* and custodian of the honoured, if precarious, drum stool from November 2001 to June 2004.

Milner's in his thirties now and a teacher of drums and music technology, so I consider asking him for a drum lesson – perhaps I'll be fined a fiver every time I hit the tom tom. I'm having trouble finding his house. He lives in a street where the house numbers follow no discernible logic – a street pattern that could have been designed by the architect of The Wonderful and Frightening World. Finally, I spot him loading suitcases into a car, as if he's about to make a hasty exit, but this turns out to be nothing more sinister than taking the wife and two kids on holiday.

We sit outside his terraced house on two stools. I can't help thinking how much Smith would hate this scene. A journalist-drummer interviewing a Fallen drummer. In the country. All I need is the dog.

'Those lyrics about hating the countryside were directly inspired by this place,' proclaims Milner, grinning. It seems the Fall van used to have to negotiate Snake Pass to pick the drummer up, at which point Smith would grumble, 'Where the fook are we going now?'

Milner is funny, thoughtful, and looks different to every other Fallen. In shades and shorts, he looks more rock star than worker – perhaps an act of quiet rebellion now he's left the cult. But perhaps the most unusual thing about Dave Milner is that I'm here with him at all.

In spoof 'rockumentary' *Spinal Tap*, the band's drummers keep disappearing in every which way, from bizarre gardening accidents to spontaneous combustion, but it seems genuinely like that in The Fall, to me. I've found drummers Paul Hanley, Steve Davies and Simon Wolstencroft, but people like Tom Head and, especially, Karl Burns seem to have gone up in smoke.

The non-disappeared drummer Milner has a theory – that people dream about being rock stars but The Fall is the worst band in which to have that dream. It's inevitable that 'the rug will be pulled from under you', especially if you're a drummer, in which case you disappear to lick your wounds. He says he avoided that fate because he was genuinely in it for the music, and his only regrets are that 'reasons in Mark's head' meant they didn't make any more music together than they did. Still, he may have been 'only the drummer', but Dave Milner will tell me as much as anyone about the curious workings of The Fall.

When he joined, the writer of modern Fall classic 'Mountain Energei' was actually a singer-songwriter as well as a drummer, but he was hurled in along with Blaney and Watts from the Trigger Happy band when Spencer Birtwistle quit (after another New York punch-up, this time with management, not The Fall).

Milner had an early trial by fire. After his first two gigs with The Fall, Smith started screaming that there was a problem with the drumming – but, true to form, addressed this complaint to the guitarist Jim Watts, not the drummer.

The following day, Milner chose the risky setting of a motorway café to ask Smith what he wanted and was informed: 'Keep it simple. When I want you to stop, stop.' He found this such an interesting concept that he decided to take it to the 'nth degree' – creating the most simple, minimal beats possible and stopping songs when told to, even if they were in the middle of the chorus. He loved it – he says the approach was 'two fingers up to the conventions of playing music'. Milner has more tales of inspired, if irregular creativity – the bulk of the colossus 'Theme From Sparta FC' was recorded with one microphone in a bedroom.

Milner soon realised that musical peculiarities were only the start when he found himself being asked to embark on a full-scale European tour. At the first gig, in Prague, he found himself staring at an empty stage because Smith had a 'fit' and missed the flight – although he subsequently made it there. As the tour progressed, Milner feared he would actually go insane and so took up meditation.

One of the challenges was that The Fall – The Mighty Fall, with 30 legendary years behind them – were actually touring Europe on trains. In this fashion, Milner underwent the 'crazy' experience of Smith (who, despite his job, 'doesn't travel well'), the musicians he hates, a manager, Ed Blaney, whom he was always arguing with, and a suitcase full of merchandise, hauling themselves around the Eastern Bloc on decrepit trains which sold beer 24 hours a day. They'd invariably get no sleep and then a van would arrive to take them from the railway carriage to the gig.

No wonder 'it got nuts'.

Milner reveals a typical instance in Portugal that perhaps puts a more comical angle on Smith's ability to predict the future. The Mighty Fall were employing road managers and crew whom Smith became convinced were trying to rob the band. He complained about this so much that two managers finally resigned in exasperation – taking some money with them. As payment, perhaps? Whatever, Smith has since explained that the pair quit after 'a piece of paper was thrown at them, like a plane or something'; the affair was later documented in the brilliant track 'Portugal', which consists of Pritchard and Milner reading out emails from the managers explaining their departure, over a powerful musical backing. These emails perhaps encapsulate what it can be like to actually work for The Fall.

We had two conversations with you. He would be paid more than he had in fact asked for. No real arrangements were made. Very standard industry procedure.

You were abusive, way beyond what anybody should have to deal with. Both myself and the crew were subjected to verbal and physical abuse.

Words fail me. How offensive a human being you are. They are a very professional crew. This complete debacle could have been avoided . . . Treat people as you want to be treated.

They were swearing, throwing newspapers with snotballs – band sing 'SNOTBALLS!' – and spit at us across the plane and physically slapping members of the band. I had to threaten him, and I told him that if this continued I would have to review my position.

At 10 p.m. the crew and myself went to our rooms after being out for just an hour and 15 minutes for a bite. We had not had any sleep . . . began banging on doors and then what sounded like throwing himself against myself and the crew's doors. This is becoming unbearable.

Milner regards this as a form of genius but suspects that Smith has got to the point where he actually doesn't know what's real. Either way, growing tensions erupted in Italy, where Smith and Blaney had a row that spilled out of the van into the road, along with all the band's equipment. Blaney quit on the spot, which prompted Smith to decide to get drunker and drunker.

'He got smashed,' sighs Milner, relating tales of Smith being escorted from bars while the musicians had to reassure worried promoters that the gig would take place. When Smith finally made it to the venue, he took one step onstage and landed on his face. Milner is almost awestruck in his description of – subsequently – one of the best gigs they ever played.

He was also thrilled to be at last rid of Blaney, describing being 'threatened' by the 'broker' and explaining that being on the road with him was like encountering 'two Marks'. He soon learned the only way to get through it was to laugh – and do even more meditation.

There was actually a lot to laugh about. He remembers one instance when The Fall were due to fly home but Smith made such a fuss about not being able to take a keyboard on the plane that airport staff refused to let him board the flight. The keyboard then made the journey – in the seat that had been reserved for Smith. Milner can reel off countless similar instances like snaps from a particularly barmy photo album: Smith greeting smiling venue staff with, 'Where's the fookin' gear, cunt?'; Smith catching Ben Pritchard listening to Eric Clapton and bellowing, 'What's this Clapton blues shit?'; Smith having an altercation in a car at 70 mph; another – with echoes of Nick Dewey's story about Nev Wilding – has a tour manager waking Smith to be told, 'If you come near me again, I'll stab you!'

'But people get used to environments,' muses the Fallen drummer. 'That's how they fight wars.' He reveals that one of The Fall's business team once told him he would survive boot camp because, perhaps due to the meditation, he had a 'Jedi calm'. If so, this calm was certainly tested. He tells how Smith tried to wind him up by actions like throwing his pizza on the floor. However, a bigger source of frustration was the time Smith had lined up a massive record deal and suddenly, irrationally, pulled the plug. 'I said, "Mark, do you not get a sense of momentum?"' He understands, but disagrees with, Smith's world view: 'If a record company's got a big name, they're "crap"! I'm not saying they're as pure as the driven snow, but they wanted The Fall to succeed. But he will not let people get that close. Either in a business sense or personally.'

Which makes Dave Milner different. He did get close. Very close indeed. As he tells it, the line-up that made *The Real New Fall LP* – himself, Archer,

Watts and Pritchard – had a closer bond with Smith than most line-ups because they would do anything for him. The drummer asserts that Smith needs it but paradoxically can't handle it because he needs the distance and control. Milner got close because he was frank with Smith and the boss respected that. Milner was also diplomatic and because he was older didn't fall for Smith's usual tricks, such as making musicians feel like paid employees whenever it suited. Yes, there were times when Smith hit Milner through frustration. However, they got so close that on one occasion he 'crossed the line' to the point where he could no longer be in the group.

Milner tells the story: The Fall were playing in Austin, Texas, and had hours to kill before the gig. The musicians, as usual, found a pool table. However, there had been an argument, and because of this Smith later began screaming about the songs the group had decided for the set list – a task the singer usually undertakes himself.

Because of the hangover from the argument, Milner declared, 'Mark, if you care that much about the set list do it yourself.' 'He threw a bottle of beer in my face. So I stood up, six foot one and a lot fitter then. And he cowered in the corner. It was so sad to see. I said, "What do you think I'm going to do?"'

Milner says he announced he was leaving – not The Fall, just the environment – and returned to do the gig.

As he walked off the stage Smith quietly whispered, 'I'm sorry, Dave.'

Later, he found himself alone in the dressing room with Smith and Elena. 'I just said, "Why mate, why? You've got a friend here." And he burst into tears and said, "I know, it's pathetic".'

Leaving Smith to get himself together, Milner later returned to find the singer had left him a bottle of whisky. The drummer who wanted to be Smith's friend but whom Smith could not allow to be his friend had seen something perhaps never witnessed in the history of The Fall. Vulnerability. Like Brian Clough, or any football manager, Smith realised the moment you show weakness to a player, one of you has to go.

Milner jokes about first becoming aware of his imminent exit via the 'Mafiosi-style' gesture of a fish's head outside his hotel room. I mention Dave Tucker's arsonist story and there's a knowing laugh. 'He's a man of extremes like that. These things start as a joke but he's testing you to see which way you'll take it. But if you think you know which way to react he'll take you to the cleaners.'

Milner has yet another angle on Smith's drinking, suggesting he runs on alcohol to the point where food would actually clog his system and that if he ate well he would be dead. It's an interesting take on things, although as Milner is a drummer, not a medical practitioner, it's probably likely to be pounced on by the NHS. 'When I see what he's put himself through, I am amazed,' he says, expressing concerns about those 'fits' which he says always coincide with the start of tours – perhaps confirming what Smith had said to me about getting 'nervous'.

He seems to understand the man more than most – he compares Smith to a Goon, a 'Spike Milligan figure', more than a Bob Dylan – so I find myself asking about Smith's father, a figure who has intrigued me since Tony Friel talked about how, in their teens, he'd be in an adjoining room in the pub, distant but watchful.

'That's one thing I was going to say,' replies Milner, who seems to have been anticipating the enquiry. 'There were definitely issues.'

He reveals that he used to talk to Smith about country life – 'It's great living opposite the park. I can boot the kids out' – and the singer would respond by comparing it to the days his father would boot him out of the house.

'From a few conversations I gathered that there was a lack of closeness with his father,' he suggests.

In childhood, his father seems to have been a detached but dominant presence: it was his scolding that sent his son to take refuge in the library and thus triggered The Fall. 'What you get with unusual people is a combination of events and circumstances that combine to create this person,' reflects Milner. 'He's got this natural intelligence combined with the way he reacted to his upbringing, and then at the age of 17 to be thrust into the limelight and very soon afterwards lauded as a wordsmith. That's a pretty unusual and strong kind of path.

'The way Mark's mind works . . . his growing up wasn't kicking a football around like a normal guy who craved attention from his dad. It was old school working-class. So, you've got a father who's a plumber and a son who's reading history books. I think he felt he was not the son his father wanted. I think he was enormously hurt by it.'

Milner says Smith once told him that one of his greatest moments was finding out his dad was proud of him. As he should have been; after all, Mark E Smith has carried on his very own Fall family firm. However, Milner adds that the first Smith knew of this was when his father's friends told him at the funeral. Is it coincidental that The Fall's revolving door and Smith's drinking seem to have intensified when Jack Smith died? Mark E Smith is from a generation and a class that never had therapy; he is his own ever evolving 'Rorschach Test'.

There's an eerie calm now and we can hear the bees in the garden. Neither of us wants to delve any more. I think we both know this is as close as we will go — or would want to go — towards understanding what makes Smith tick.

Milner offers me a drink, but I have to go and find another Fallen. Before we say our farewells, the drummer sheds more light on his own exit. There were family issues — his partner didn't like him much when he was in The Fall, because the 'state of mind' produces a certain arrogance. He also mentions he developed a foot problem which made it hard to play the bass drum — something of a career killer when you've already stopped hitting tom toms and cymbals. Crucially, he couldn't work with Ed Blaney, who he thinks 'manipulated' himself into The Fall inner circle by providing a Transit when Smith broke his leg.

'That leg break changed the dynamic,' he claims. 'If he hadn't broken his leg, I might still be in The Fall.'

Bur the detonator for the inevitable expulsion came when Milner had the 'temerity' to ask for his money, and was sacked. In a final joke, the execution warrant was delivered by Smith's sister, Caroline, who Milner compares fondly to one of the factory girls on *Coronation Street*.

'She phoned me . . . Mark was in the background,' he says.

'Erm, Dave, Mark's asked me to phone you, luv, because we really appreciate what you've done for us but we no longer require your services.'

'I said, "I appreciate that. If you ever need me again give me a bell."'

He's laughing.

'To be sacked by Caroline was funny and a Greek tragedy at the same time. But that's The Fall. Everyone leaves their mark on Mark and vice versa. It's got everything: it's a great comedy, a horror film and a pantomime all in one.'

I arrive home to an answering machine message from Ed Blaney.

CHAPTER 35

'My job was to stop the musicians having fun.'

'**E**re, I hear you've been looking for me,' he begins, sounding like something from an old James Cagney movie, albeit with a distinct North Manchester accent. I've been phoning different numbers for Blaney for months to no avail, but he explains that he's been difficult to track down owing to a spell 'offside' after serving two months for drunken driving. He hasn't seen Karl Burns.

Blaney – who's been at liberty for a few weeks – was part of Trigger Happy with Watts and Milner, although he says that Smith had originally heard his demos and asked him to be tour manager, which suggests Blaney was being groomed. He did a tour with 'Helal and Nagle and all them' but when they walked out he did the short notice gig in Dublin. 'I like a challenge,' he says, 'although that was a bit ridiculous.' Trigger Happy's guitarist, Tim Scott, didn't make it into the Fall like the rest of them: 'Probably because he was a Scouser.' Soon after, Blaney was asked to manage Smith – not The Fall, just Smith. He was offered ten per cent, stuck out for some more and they came to a deal. I wonder aloud what the precise difference is between managing Smith and managing The Fall. Blaney responds that Smith is a 'spiritual man' who should receive a knighthood, although he's heard the stories – like him sticking tapes up promoters' noses. He says that managing someone like that requires you to be 'Jack of 94 trades' but his biggest task – certainly the one demanded most by Smith – was stopping the musicians having fun.

I start to see why Milner and Pritchard don't like him. He says his role model was Peter Grant – the infamous Led Zeppelin manager who was known to carry a baseball bat. Blaney says a typical job was the one where Smith had spied the musicians 'stuffing their faces' in a restaurant and Blaney was instructed to cart them back to the hotel.

'Their heads have to be kept level,' he barks, suggesting that musicians had to be smart and 'well-turned out' and sounding like a sergeant major. The problem, he argues, is that band members become accustomed to being in a famous band and start 'thinking they're Oasis'.

'We soon put a stop to that,' he cackles, echoing Milner's description of 'two Marks' by explaining it was him and Smith versus the band. 'But in a friendly way. Methods of keeping the musicians in line ranged from sending them to addresses for 'celebrity parties' miles out of town which did not exist, having spies everywhere 'like the CIA' and feeding musicians so much misinformation they would no longer know what was real – which could explain the baffling and differing stories about Smith's drinking. Or some of them. But Blaney says his responsibilities extended to 'counselling'. 'I've had guitarists threatening to jump out of windows,' he says. 'I've said "Go on then, jump." They soon get their act together. Couple of whiskies and they're all right. It was my job to fire them up.'

I ask about the incident where Pritchard and Co. were supposedly dumped in Houston. Blaney replies that when he joined the tour, it was a 'shambles'. Smith was in a wheelchair and promoters weren't leaving him room to get onstage. The tour was pulled and the broker's responsibility was 'to get the boss and his wife home'. The musicians? 'They're grown adults. They were more interested in meeting their new friends off the internet in LA.'

Blaney certainly sounds as if he was devoted to his job. I ask about some of Pritchard's more extreme suggestions, like the one about the 'broker' fighting with promoters.

'Er, well, there was one night in Derby,' he reveals. 'The promoter offered us less money than we'd agreed. He was stood there with three doormen, one that had an eye missing. I wasn't scared. I gave one of the doormen a crack cos he went for me. There was a bit of a scene. We got full money.'

What about fighting with Fall audiences?

'There was one incident in Sheffield. The police were called. The bloke's uncle was an MP. The police said he was a tosser, that it would go no further. All I did was push him off the stage.

'You've got to be tough like me and Mark,' he says of life around The Fall. 'It's not Take That. You're on edge and that's the buzz. Everyone has their way of preparing for a show and sometimes he [Smith] lets a bit of tension out. If you're smart you'll keep out of the way.' He suggests the musicians were 'jealous' over his alliance with Smith. However, Blaney seems to have been on the end of the boot camp treatment himself. When I ask him about being ushered off in Stourbridge because it 'wasn't working', he insists it was 'mutual' – it was actually his guitar that wasn't working.

'My job was to come on and create chaos. Sometimes, I'd just get shoved on during a song I hadn't written and [was] expected to come up with lyrics. Mark likes spontaneity.' He admits he was always rowing with the singer – 'constructive arguments' – but they'd always sorted things out.

So, why did you part company with The Fall?

'Er, when?'

It seems there have been quite a few partings, and not just the occasion in Italy where they were shouting at each other in the road. It seems the final exit was the local difficulty encountered by drunken driving, which put him off the scene. He says he's owed money but they'll sort it out.

Of the wider confusion over royalties, he thinks The Fall have recorded so many songs people who collect the royalties 'make mistakes'. He says so many of them are Fall fans they start chatting about the band and get 'confused'. Then there are the 'people who think they wrote summat that they actually haven't'. I take up Dave Milner's suggestion that he was sacked for asking for his money. 'Overpaid, Dave Milner!' he laughs, suggesting the drummer's problem was that he 'wanted to be a singer'.

Like Smith, Blaney seems to regard ex-members with disdain, suggesting they never get over leaving The Fall and that being an ex-member is 'like an illness'. 'They're all on the internet under false names,' he says, and it's certainly true that some ex-members (Jim Watts and Julia Nagle, for example) post missives on the Fall forums. He believes few of them can accept the loss of income or that they've peaked – asserting that his biggest job in The Fall was keeping ex-members out of the dressing room because they are all 'stalking'.

I try to clear up the fate of one of them – Brian Fanning. I'm still not sure whether he leapt or was pushed.

'Oh, that,' shrugs Blaney. 'We were in the middle of nowhere and Mark suddenly asked the driver to stop and said, "Right, you, off the bus!" We were in Sweden, in the middle of nowhere. I think he got home in the end.'

And now it's my turn to try and get home in the end. I'm still perturbed by Karl Burns, but as the list of those yet to find is almost blank, I find myself thinking how far I've come. As an obsessed journalist-cum-private detective, I can hardly believe I've found all these musicians – most, if not all, of the 43 on the original list, with one or two alluring leads yet to be fully pursued.

But there's a parallel, much longer-lasting journey as well.

It's over 25 years since I stood on those university steps waiting for Smith and I wonder now how I would have reacted as a teenager if I'd known how far The Fall would take me, before I even started unearthing The Fallen. As a fan, The Fall have whisked me to smoke-filled working men's clubs and open-air festivals in the twilight. Sometimes, in quiet moments, when the phone is off and the computer is finally shut down, I see my Fall life as a series of snapshots: The Fall accompanying and even directing my rite of passage from boy to man, in what Craig Scanlon described as a 'very strange upbringing'. I see myself in 1980, the ridiculously naive schoolboy in Kevin Crotty's cellar about to hear 'Totally Wired' for the very first time. Then I'm in Carol's parents' tiny dining room, taking delivery of the holy *Grotesque* in the brown paper bag. There are all those gigs, those wonderful gigs: a spiky and predatory Fall at the Riley-Smith Hall in 1981; tense and all-pervading in the dusk at WOMAD Festival in 1985; those concerts with Victoria, a relationship that quickly blossomed and dwindled like a classic Fall line-up; Suzanne moving in with that record box; and moments – even one as recent as the Leeds Festival in 2006 – where we were together, watching The Fall, and nothing else mattered.

I wonder at what I've learned – never to take anything at face value and never assume the obvious path will be the one to take – and what The Fall have yet to teach me.

Finding The Fallen has been no less an education and has provided another very different series of mental snapshots. As I sat in Malmaison what seems like many moons ago, I had no idea I was about to embark on this quest, never mind where it would take me. I travelled from dark, police-patrolled streets in Manchester to deserted London streets and, above all, to Smith's hallowed Prestwich, a place I'd never been entirely convinced existed outside Smith's feverish imagination, until I went there and discovered what was real. I never made it to Guadalajara, on the trail of Neville Wilding, but I wouldn't rule anything out in what has often felt like my own personal shadow of the assault course musicians must undergo if they're to survive The Fall. I've probably developed psychological problems. I've wreaked havoc on my relationship. I've developed more intimate relationships with internet search engines than I have with friends. I've developed unusual ailments like ear infections and lost weight through not eating properly and wrecked my work and social structures. But compared to The Fallen, I've had it easy. Sometimes, in fleeting moments – as fatigue, stress, mental anguish and a sense of not quite definable achievement dovetail into each other – I've even felt something of what it must be like to be in The Fall.

But the question nagging me now is this: I've found all those musicians, but have I managed to find Mark E Smith? In fact, I've found many, as each

Fallen musician has given me a different insight to The Fall's absolute ruler, from Tommy Crooks' depiction of a crazed genius to Hanley's portrayal of a benevolent dictator. I've heard about Smith the disciplinarian father figure, English eccentric, unrivalled pop comic and prankster; the school bully, cruel factory owner and even arch-feminist. I've heard about the loyal friend; the understanding shoulder to cry on; the grafting tradesman; the myth-maker; the loving husband and vengeful lover; the damaged, deranged, out-of-control drunk; and the consummate showman and master craftsman vocalist.

I think, is Smith still driving The Fall or is the beast now controlling him? Is he really a drunkard? Or is he just someone who uses alcohol to its maximum limit, sometimes using what appears to be drunkenness as a smokescreen for yet more creative sleight-of-hand? Is Smith really cruel, or just insanely hard-working? Is he somehow indestructible or is he somehow ill? From talking to The Fallen, it seems that even to those who know him best – even an ex-wife – Smith remains truly elusive, as unknowable as any ghost. However close, or far from close, I have ventured, I sense that The Wonderful and Frightening World hasn't yet given up all its secrets.

It's New Year's Eve, 2005, and Suzanne and I have been invited to a family party, the sort of thing (with balloons and party hats) that's taking place across the nation. Except I can't relax. It doesn't help that I've got to stay sober – to drive home, and because I have a task tomorrow – but I'm still a world away, thinking of Prestwich and Karl Burns. While uncles throw nieces over their shoulders and people play hide-and-seek, as I've been doing these last few months among The Fallen, Suzanne and I end up in a room alone, experiencing again the familiar loneliness of the long-distance Fall fan. Sometimes, I wish we were like everybody else. I wish I could talk about golf and quantity surveying and throw a niece or two over my shoulder. But once you hear The Fall you're not like anybody else. I think, or at least hope, Suzanne knows this. Anybody else hasn't experienced the electrifying thrill of watching Smith onstage, or felt the almost primeval pull as the latest line-up power into the drumbeat or unveil a new song. For the Fall fan, an urban landscape is not a morass of black and grey but an unexplored fantasy land of evil flats, poisoned lager, rampant conspiracies and sinister city hobgoblins. Life is something not to be celebrated but suffered, on the way to some higher glory that can only be provided by the knowledge passed on by The Fall. Music isn't something to entertain you but to provoke, chide, dictate and inspire. If the price that must be paid to experience all this is to abandon the 'normal' world and submit to The Wonderful and Frightening one, then it is a price worth paying for as long as humanly possible. For me, though, it looks like it's time to stop, and I feel glad, in a way, to face the prospect of returning to something like normality.

Part of me doesn't want to leave the new psychological environment this quest has brought me, a land new to me. As a vegetarian I've always been fiercely opposed to fox hunting, but these last few months I've gained some insight into the appeal. Not that I've ever yearned to chase a Fall musician around a field accompanied by a pack of hounds – unless it's Karl Burns – but I've started to understand the meaning of the 'thrill of the chase'. There's the illicit pleasure of the unearthing of tiny secrets. But another feeling looms even larger: the feeling that, like The Fallen, I have been indelibly Marked. I can't put my finger on it yet, but I have this nagging sense that, somehow, things will never be the same again.

And I am scared.

Like a condemned man, I savour my last few hours. As the nation settles down to dinner and Suzanne disappears out with the equally long-suffering dog, I spend New Year's Day 2006 alone in my room, writing about The Fall and wondering if all this is really over, or ever will be.

It's 5 January 2006, and the piece is finally in the newspaper, spread across four pages with a fetching picture of Brix on the front cover. It gets a huge response – not just from within and without the paper but in my email inbox, which bulges with missives from The Fallen. Emails flood in from people as diverse as Marc Riley – who says he had a great time at the photo session meeting 'all those people!' from The Fall – and Dick Witts, their first manager in 1976. The first, and one of the nicest, messages comes from Tommy Crooks, the first one I tracked down many moons ago: 'I'm impressed by how you've managed to convey the weirdness and excitement,' he says. 'In fact, it's brought back feelings to the extent that I'll be frightened to answer the door today in case Mark's there! I've said to people before that it's impossible to conceive of the utter gravity of strangeness unless you'd been there. So well done.'

Marc Riley describes the weirdness of the photo session – when ex-members spanning four decades came together in a Manchester bar, some seeing each other after many, many years and some meeting for the first time: 'I had a very interesting conversation with a chap called Dingo.'

One of the stranger missives comes via the Fall forum from Ed Blaney, who rages, 'Where's the fuckin' money, cunt?' I'd normally be bothered but take the language as a form of tribute to The Fall's 2001 track, 'Where's The Fuckin' Taxi, Cunt?' – an account of an ill-fated Fall attempt to procure transport. In any case, Blaney mails again a while later to tell me about his new projects (he was managing another band, and has subsequently popped up on Salford City Radio) and says, 'All forgiven'.

Someone on the official Fall website – which will shortly become the unofficial website after a fallout with Smith – even claims to have spied Karl Burns at Manchester Piccadilly station.

Inevitably, the most bizarre response comes from Smith himself, who takes the rare step of releasing a 'statement' – like the ones from Downing Street – via Fall magazine *Pseud Mag*, in a way the publishing arm of The Wonderful and Frightening World.

Hiya cock,

A word for you to ponder on the state of British Journalism in the modern age.

Given the hatchet job carried out by a *Guardian* journalist on Fall members past and present yesterday; I would like it to be known that any future dealings with the press by The Fall will not be through the aforementioned publication, but through a more worthy journal of a much higher calibre . . . such as the *Daily* fucking *Star*!

Happy New Year.

MES

The *Daily Star* line makes me smile. Any other rock singer would have been delighted to have his band on the front page of a national newspaper for perhaps the first time in his career. But they would not be Mark E Smith.

It crosses my mind Smith may be feeling like he did when he saw that billboard of Marc Riley – 'all the people I've ever known flashing before my eyes'. Then I remember something Dingo Archer said: 'If you think something is good, Mark will see it differently and vice versa.'

I decide to take Tommy Crooks' advice: 'Go and take a break and stop listening to The Fall for a while, give your head a chance to recover.' However, within weeks, there's another earthquake in boot camp. The entire line-up has imploded in America yet again. On 9 May 2006, it emerges that all that remains of the latest Fall line-up is Smith and wife Elena. Precise details of the split are unclear; rumours blame an incident involving a banana. Even the ultra-loyal Ben Pritchard has allegedly departed, and two new names are added to my list: Spencer Birtwistle and Steve Trafford. I feel like a retired safecracker, called back into active service for that one, possibly final heist.

'You don't join a band, you join his world . . . That's us, thieving lying cunts!'

In the aftermath, Smith carries on their American tour using picked-up East Coast musicians, who subsequently record The Fall's twenty-sixth studio album, *Reformation Post-TLC*. The album gets noticeably less excited reviews than *Fall Heads Roll*, with some critics suggesting that turnover may be harming the music, not helping it. By this time, Smith is fronting not one but two Fall line-ups – the second being an entire British 'subs' bench' who fill in when the Americans are unavailable and will no doubt be on hand should he dispense with them entirely.

Shortly after these developments, I'm in a Manchester bar meeting Steve Trafford – bassist in the last, fateful line-up who, alongside Pritchard and drummer Birtwistle, has the no doubt temporary honour of being the last musician to exit The Fall.

Sipping coffee, denim-jacketed and in possession of a full head of hair, he looks relaxed and surprisingly healthy – neither of those being qualities too often associated with The Fall. But, of course, he is no longer in The Fall. He begins his first interview since departing by insisting, 'I'm not here to slag Mark off,' but it's obvious he has things to get off his chest. Later, he'll tell me of another strange induction into The Fall. He was in a toilet in Manchester when someone approached him, admiring his pinstripe jacket: 'This lad came in and said, "I love your coat, can I try it on? I'll get one of these for when I'm onstage." I said, "Are you in a band?" He said, "Yeah, I'm in The Fall." I said I was a musician. He went, "You don't play bass, do ya?"'

The lad was Ben Pritchard.

'I lied and said, "Yes",' laughs Trafford. 'I'd only played guitar. The next thing I knew, I was touring America.'

But I begin the interview by asking him what it was like in the cult, reminding him of an email he sent me when he was in The Fall describing it as being like 'the film *Full Metal Jacket* being made into a chess game – and you're one of the figures'.

'It was quite regimented in some ways,' he nods, sipping a cappuccino, but the problem with being a 'figure' now is the chessmaster's paranoia.

'That's the biggest thing to deal with in The Fall now,' he says of the singer. 'He's paranoid beyond belief. Ridiculous situations. But it was time for us to go. He [Smith] sent the record company bosses to the airport begging us to come back, saying he's really sorry, he's changed. He did everything he could to get us back, but we'd made our minds up.

'Have you seen that stuff he's been saying in the press?' he blurts. 'He's been saying that we were writing country and western songs! That he could see the writing on the wall, that the new band is tons better.'

Trafford suggests that far from that being the case – and, to be fair, fans and reviewers seem to support him – the last line-up had actually recorded an album that was 'miles better' than the hallowed *Fall Heads Roll*. They recorded '16 to 17 tracks and it was amazing'.

'That's what I'm most gutted about,' he sighs, divulging that at least two copies exist. He has one, along with producer Grant Showbiz, but Smith never finished adding vocals to it because the line-up split. According to Trafford, the opening track – 'Over! Over!' in which Smith darkly reproaches, 'I think it's all over now' – on *Reformation Post-TLC* is culled from those sessions, but Smith has 'done something to it'. Another revelation is that, contrary to popular opinion, the 'TLC' in the album title does not refer to Tender Loving Care.

'That's what you're supposed to think. That's us,' he says, referring to himself, Pritchard and Birtwistle. 'Thieving Lying Cunts!'

He at last allows himself a grin. He's used to this sort of stuff from Smith, soon reeling off familiar tales of being mis-credited for songs ('Blindness' – *Fall Heads Roll*'s best track – is built around his hypnotic bass riff but is credited to Spencer Birtwistle, the drummer).

'Anyone who hears that knows I should have got a credit on it. This is what it's like!' he says. 'Dave Milner somehow got the credit for "Open the Box", because he sang backing vocals on it! There's so many injustices and a lot of the songs are in dispute.' He suggests royalties for many Fall songs are currently bound up in litigation.

You never really know what to believe in The Wonderful and Frightening World but Trafford doesn't seem to have a particular axe to grind. Like many bass players – who have the task of anchoring a band's sound – the early 30-something seems solid and dependable.

In fact, like Dave Milner, he insists he and Smith actually became quite close – and that *Fall Heads Roll* track 'Early Days of Channel Führer' originally included a lyric about 'My best friend, Steve' before Smith suddenly wiped it prior to release.

'Mark's a great bunch of blokes and one of them I really liked,' he says. 'We had some great times. But he lost it.'

I want to get onto what happened in America, but first want to know more about something Ben Pritchard told me – that the last UK tour, prior to the fateful US visit, was the most stressful ever.

Why was that?

'Paranoia and general, unexplainable nastiness,' says Trafford, going on to describe a typical incident in Wales where Smith had taken exception to the bassist's sound equipment. After the gig, Trafford returned to the band's hotel to find the singer had stolen his suitcase.

'I spent two hours trying to get into his hotel room to get it back,' he frowns. 'When I got it back, he'd poured water on my clothes . . . We had to go.' He says that things around the band were getting 'violent'. It wasn't a case of Smith attacking his musicians, but if he'd carried on The Fall would have attacked the singer.

Despite the numerous bust-ups over the years, actual violence involving Smith is surprisingly rare. As Trafford says, the 'threat of violence' is yet another strategy of Fall boot camp to keep musicians on their toes: 'He takes everything to the limit, he'll take away any pleasure you have left.' On the grounds that they'd 'play better'.

I tell him that, as Smith told me, it works. The Fall were fantastic on that last UK tour. He agrees, but says that, when the musicians sound good, people tell them they sound good. And then, Smith suspects they'll begin playing worse because he thinks the band are 'getting above themselves'.

I tell Trafford something Pritchard told me: that no matter what happens, the current line-up would never leave.

'He said that?' He sighs. 'Ben had a full head of brown hair when he joined. He's prematurely grey. That moment when we left was the only moment of solidarity between us.' He says they were friends, but just like the Hanleys had told me, talking about the 1980s, in The Fall you get divided. Elena acts as Smith's 'eyes and ears. In the end it becomes every man for himself. So, walking out together was a great moment between us.'

According to Trafford, the problems in America started after the band mislaid the precious backdrops, which they'd been entrusted to transport to the States. 'That was really unfortunate,' offers Trafford. 'They got lost at the airport.'

And you got the blame?

'It's The Fall!' He suggests Smith actually took it well, but they suspected further trouble.

Kay Carroll in 1983. The punch-up in 1998. Why do The Fall have so much difficulty in America?

'It's like he can't handle it,' he replies. 'He gets stressed out.' According to Trafford, they first became aware something was looming in Tucson, when Smith lunged at Birtwistle in the dressing room with a corkscrew. He missed and everything blew over, but, by the time they got to Phoenix – it had to be Phoenix, The Fall do have a song called 'Bonkers in Phoenix', after all – things imploded.

For no obvious reason, the tour manager – he was 'really loyal', although Trafford admits Smith sees outsiders as a threat – had arrived at the top of Smith's fabled torment list. 'So, Mark was flicking cigarettes at him, pouring beer over him,' he recalls. Which wouldn't have been that bad if the tour manager hadn't been driving at 70 mph at the time. He left, taking the vehicle with him and leaving the entire band 'in the middle of nowhere'. Smith alludes to this incident in his autobiography and admits 'spilling' beer over the driver. However he says he did this because the fellow was asleep.

After a discussion, the musicians decided to leave too – Trafford was surprised Pritchard agreed but says 'everybody has their breaking point'.

Deciding that Phoenix would be their last ever gig, horror turned to comedy when a member of the support band assaulted Smith onstage with a banana. Trafford describes it as a 'hilarious farce', with Smith – who'd been 'drinking a lot' – chasing the offender right around the venue and into the car park.

The moment the gig was over, the Fall-ing trio fled, ignoring the record company people Smith sent to the airport.

Like most Fallen, he has mixed feelings about leaving, admiring Smith's 'almost supernatural' methods of coaxing performance, but says he doesn't miss it. He's now fronting a band called Tycoon's Follies and playing with The Beautiful South's Paul Heaton.

'I'm a lot happier than I was then,' says Trafford of his active service. 'There were a lot of drugs going on on that tour,' he says, not necessarily referring to within The Fall. He doesn't go further. 'Coupled with everything else going on, it wasn't a good mix. I'm happier now but I can look back on it as a great experience.'

I ask about the others. Birtwistle is apparently in a band called The Blimp while Pritchard – after a spell installing burglar alarms – is delivering for Parcelforce, sometimes to Dave Milner.

Ironically, in light of what I discussed with Milner, Trafford says he views Smith now as the ultimate Victorian stepfather, 'caring but cruel', who must be 'pleased' at all costs.

Our father who art in Prestwich.

I arrive home to more upheaval: this time in my own life.

CHAPTER 36

'You've got the curse of The Fall!'

It's the early hours of a Sunday morning and we've had a meal out with friends – a rarity since I started tracking down The Fall. It's been another eventful 24 hours and I've been on the move. I spent yesterday in Liverpool interviewing Spiritualized singer/mainman Jason Pierce, another mythical musical talent with a reputation for hiring and firing. He drank an inordinate amount during and after the interview, and I couldn't help laughing at some of his explanations for why he goes through so many musicians – admittedly, most of them are hired for projects, rather than group members. He complained that 'most of them seem to think they should be playing stadiums by now but that's not what it's about'. He sounded just like Smith.

Pierce was in Liverpool for 'Silent Sound', a performance/art installation by artists Iain Forsyth and Jane Pollard for which he was asked to provide the score. This is his first classical composition (a serenely beautiful melody which, because he doesn't read or write music, was hummed down the phone and transcribed, a three-hour 'operation' which sounds rather Fall-like). The show partly recreated an 1865 séance carried out by Victorian spiritualists, the Davenports. He said he didn't believed in ghosts but was starting to believe that life was all a giant cosmic prank. On the way back home, I'd taken another detour through the avenue all lined with trees but, once again, there was no sign of Smith being home.

So here I am, 24 hours later. It's two in the morning, I've had a bit of red wine but not so much that I couldn't drive home, and I'm lying awake thinking about The Fallen. I've spent the evening telling our friends what I've been doing for the last year and one of those friends was Bruce, who was with me at that very first gig at the Riley-Smith Hall all those years ago. In particular, I'm thinking about Karl Burns. I stare at the moon outside the window and I realise that Suzanne, the love of my life, is awake as well, so I give her a hug. She doesn't respond. She feels warm, but I feel a sudden chill. What's wrong?

'I'm leaving you,' she announces, there and then, after 17 years. 'I've stopped being close to you . . . It started when you were looking for all those people who were in The Fall.'

I'm speechless – we've been together most of our adult lives. She has seen me through poverty, success, a car crash and a beating (not Fall-related). For those 17 years there have been two predominant sounds in my life; the sound of The Fall and the sound of Suzanne's breathing as we lie side by side.

And now – because of one of them – the other will no longer be there.

For days, weeks, months, I am inconsolable. It's been difficult enough trying to work anyway, but now my life careers further into an abyss. It feels like Dad and Mum dying again, but at the same time. I feel like I have died.

The trouble with being a Fall fan in these situations is there are no songs to turn to. Smith's songbook is full of bile about break-ups, not tunes for wallowing in despair. For a while, I find I can't listen to The Fall and in a really low moment, find myself relating to the lyrics of 'Against All Odds (Take a Look at Me Now)' by Phil Collins as it plays on local radio.

At this point I wanted to express the pain I was going through by reprinting the lyrics to Phil's song about being parted from the only one who really knew him. However, Phil's 'people' feel that using the song here wouldn't express my heartache but in fact would be 'derogatory'. And they're right. Derogatory of me! What greater slur can a man carry than admitting to listening to Phil Collins?

Anyway, my own editor helpfully slips into Smith mode and gives me an aural clip around the earhole: 'Get a grip, man!' And I do, because as some form of clarity takes over, I realise what has happened. You see, for anyone not steeped in The Fall this would be the natural end of a relationship that's lasted far more than most and has probably run its course. But I am steeped in The Fall. So I know differently.

Suddenly, everything all makes sense: the car with the MES registration plate in the village; Brix's warning of Smith's words to an offending journalist, 'I fucking curse you! You've got the curse of The Fall'; Eric the Ferret's words to me, 'There is a cost, a cost to fronting The Fall.'

There is also a cost to finding The Fallen. I have gone in search of Smith's secrets and ghosts, and now I must bear the price, delivered from Prestwich within 24 hours of my latest sojourn outside Smith's front door. I have got the curse of The Fall.

Over the next few months, everything that can possibly go wrong does. I drive my new shiny MG car into a river. Leeds United are first relegated, then deducted ten points for going into administration, then deducted another 15 for the circumstances of it, and the club teeters on the brink of existence. Finally, I am struck down by a particularly nasty type of food poisoning called Campylobacter. I have surely been cursed as effectively as if Smith had delivered a fish's head to the front door.

And all the while, the ringmaster is mocking.

He gives a wonderful interview to *Stool Pigeon* music newspaper in which the subject of my article is raised.

* * *

I wanted to talk about the LP. He [me] kept going, 'What's happened to blah blah?' For two fucking hours! After two hours, he fucking cracked. [Mimes crying.] 'I've had about [enough] of this. I can't get anything out of you.' I'm saying, 'Have you heard the new LP or not?'

I gave him a few whiskies. Then I took him to the pub over the road and got it all out of him. What it was, his boss had said, 'Get the dirty on Mark E Smith.' The editor. Because he [me] used to have an office in London. Then they have a bit of a cutback. He was kept on but he had to go back to Yorkshire. They said, 'You've got to get a fucking scoop.' I'll tell you a funny story about that. As he was going back to the train station, by which time I'd got more out of him than he'd got out of me. But as we went in this fucking pub, I couldn't believe it. There was Karl Burns's mum! She's like, 'Long time no see.' And he gets his fucking notepad out! 'What's Karl Burns doing now?' 'Oh, he lives on the farm in the hills somewhere. Looks like that bloke out of Emmerdale [Shadrach Dingle?!]. Ha ha.'

I love this story, because as well as demonstrating that Smith still has a vibrant imagination – which I suggest in a friendly letter telling *Foggy Notions*, another magazine in which he makes similar claims, that Smith should remember I have a digital recording of the interview – it is another piece in my jigsaw. It illustrates perfectly how tiny pieces of reality distort and refract back through smoke and mirrors, and then either become lyrics or myths in The Wonderful and Frightening World.

Having said that, a lot of people *are* saying Burns lives on a farm in the hills somewhere.

Meanwhile, back in my own Wonderful and Frightening World, the curse exacts another cruel twist when I discover what the love of my life's new partner does for a living.

He does deliveries for their warehouse.

He is a lorry driver.

Yes, I have been dumped for a Container Driver. So I play my favourite

Fall song on my first and favourite Fall album for hour upon hour – relishing its gloriously malicious portrayal of the empty lives of truck drivers.

> They sweat on their way down
> Grey ports with customs bastards
> Hang around like clowns the
> Uh-containers and their drivers
>
> Bad indigestion
> Bad bowel retention
> Speed for their wages
> Suntan, torn short sleeves.
>
> SWEAT.
> BASTARDS.
> CLOWNS.
> BAD INDIGESTION.
> BAD BOWEL RETENTION!

I have never loved any song as much as I love this song right now. As I peer into the abyss of my once blissful rural life, the cruel but caring cult offers me a lifeline.

'Are they still doing "Bingo Master's Break-Out!"?'

A work email arrives from head office, but at the bottom it has a tantalising PS: 'A man called Johnny [sic] Brown called for you regarding ex-members of The Fall.'

And there's a phone number.

I stare at it in disbelief. It can't be? Surely this isn't Jonnie – not 'Johnny' – Brown, the near mythical bassist who lasted three weeks in 1978, who embarked with girlfriend Una Baines on that 'mad, drug-crazed' adventure? Who hasn't been heard of for 30 years and who I tried so desperately to find by ringing every Brown in Rotherham?

I ring the number. It is indeed the long-lost Jonnie Brown, who describes how he popped into his local pub quiz for the first time and there was a question about the number of people that had been in The Fall.

'And people were saying, "It's on the internet! In the *Guardian*! You're the long-lost Fall member!"' he says. He phoned the paper, and the paper has brought Jonnie Brown to me.

24 hours later, I'm happier than I've been for months, hurtling towards Rotherham, where I find the bassist in a very small flat above a newsagent. The walls are peppered with arty designs and an enormous tie-dye-pattern sheet – he was an art student, after all. There is a computer, and – just like Tony Friel – a solitary bass guitar. Standing amidst them all is a 50-year-old who looks a lot younger than Mark E Smith. Something tells me he hasn't really kept up with The Fall.

'Are they still doing "Bingo Master's Break-Out!"?' he enquires.

I don't know where to start, but try my best to fill him in on 30 years of Falldom. No, his old love Una Baines is no longer with them, nor is she dating Martin Bramah. 'Has she got loads of kids?' he asks, then changes the subject to Bramah. 'I always liked Martin. He was really good on guitar but he never had the energy for the business side.' It's a perceptive insight, which makes up for his thinking that Smith is married to an oriental violinist.

I'm worried that if we go much further down this road I'll end up telling him we've gone through several prime ministers and John Lennon is dead. Still, it's not just Brown who's suffering from misconceptions. I scan the flat for drug use but there is none and I feel guilty at being influenced by his old 'junkie' reputation.

'Oh, the drug thing,' he sighs, unhappy that it's in 'every biography'. He's carried that reputation for 30 years even though it was just a phase. The drug thing isn't the only thing the world has got wrong about Jonnie Brown – he spells his name Jonny but is actually called David. 'My dad was called David John but my mum wanted to call me Jonathan,' he explains, pouring some tea. 'So, I'm David Jonathan! But we switched it around to avoid confusion with the postman.'

He also says he was in The Fall 'a lot longer than three weeks, which everybody says. We rehearsed a set of 11 songs.' It turns out he designed the 'Bingo Master''s sleeve (a strange voodoo image). He didn't get paid. In fact, he didn't even get a copy.

So what did happen to Jonnie – sorry, Jonny – Brown?

As he tells it, he joined The Fall after seeing an advert in Virgin Records – making Yvonne Pawlett not the only one to join from an advert – and was supposed to be the guitarist, but by the time he got there the guitarist (Bramah) wasn't leaving but the bassist (Friel) had.

Brown said, 'I'll have a go.' He soon realised he wasn't joining a normal group. They were ridiculously hard-working, Smith was very 'into himself' and modelled himself on Elvis and Lou Reed, although their rehearsals included a version of The Troggs' 'Wild Thing'. They rehearsed for weeks on end although he only did one gig – at Huddersfield Polytechnic, supporting Sham 69 – where he remembers not being able to hear what anyone else was playing.

'We got some good write-ups,' he says, his South Yorkshire accent sounding incongruous among The Fallen, 'although we could have played owt!'

But then he got the sack. As Brown tells it, The Fall were in the habit of listening to John Peel's show religiously and one of the early rules was that they all had to be back at the Kingswood Road flat for the ten till midnight programme.

One night, Brown was in the pub with Baines and 'the next minute Una was on top of me'. Brown didn't just miss the Peel show but took Baines 'home, away from them' and so began their wild, drug-crazed adventure.

'Of course Mark used to go out with her,' he says with regret. 'My lifestyle at the time . . . I was into drugs and all sorts. Una came back, and she told Mark, and he took one look at her and sacked me. He got rid of me like that. But that's fair enough. It's his group.'

Nevertheless, Brown was devastated: 'I nearly cried when he told me,' he confesses. 'I shut the door and it really hit me hard. It was worse than your best girlfriend finishing with you.' And not long after that, he lost Una as well. In all these years, he never knew Baines had a breakdown. He seems concerned and asks if she's all right now.

But that wasn't quite the end of Jonny and Una, nor of David Jonathan Brown and The Fall. A while after being booted out he went to see them play in Sheffield but found himself stumbling into the road and falling on his face into the path of a taxi. He missed the gig.

Many years later – when his mum got the internet – he found the Fall website and sent a message to Smith saying, 'Hello. It's me!' But he didn't hear back. He finished his degree and liked Manchester so much he stayed another year. He remembers going to the opening of the Hacienda when Smith's favoured comic Bernard Manning played.

As for the drug use, it 'faded away'. 'I don't know if I was experimenting,' he considers of heroin, a drug which Smith has disapproved of since 'No Xmas for John Quays'. 'I think I was just free of my degree and wanted to go mad. Kids do it today. Probably worse.'

He moved to London and started squatting, which in those days was 'the thing to do'. He stayed for ten years during which time he almost joined Siouxsie and The Banshees, but his friend John McGeoch (the legendary Scottish post-punk guitarist who played with Magazine and PiL) got the job. He wasn't aware McGeoch – whose extraordinary, driven, angular fretwork lit up Magazine's classic *Real Life* and *Secondhand Daylight* albums, the Banshees' high watermark of 1981's *JuJu* and helped define the post-punk style that resonates through many of today's groups – is dead now and seems moved.

There were also spells in Sheffield – at one point playing in a punk band – and during one of them he went to see Baines and Blue Orchids play in a pub that had been bombed during the war and was supposed to contain buried bodies. He says Baines ended up coming back to where he was staying in Sheffield. 'And that's when it started up again.' Not just the thing with Baines, but Brown actually joined the Blue Orchids – rehearsing with them, at least – until one day he just walked away and never saw Baines again.

'Not on purpose, but it was a hell of a long way to go for practice!' he laughs.

I can't help liking Jonny Brown and understand exactly what Baines saw in him. He's perceptive rather than super-intelligent and has an almost child-like enthusiasm that is utterly infectious. Now he has his own two children – aged six and 21 – although he's no longer with their mothers and one of them 'ran off with someone else'.

As for work, he was until recently a jeweller – his speciality at art school – but is currently unemployed. He grumbles about kids throwing milkshakes at the window but becomes animated when he remembers seeing Smith on television, in a famously incomprehensible interview on *Newsnight* the night John Peel died.

'Had they messed about with it?' he asks engagingly. 'I wouldn't like to be seeing myself on telly. Bloody 'ell!'

His excitement switches to something else: 'I've got a new bass, look. I've blown a speaker with this. It's got a battery in it which gives it a better tone. Isn't it beautiful? I got it from Cash Converters in Rotherham.' It turns out he's still playing music – most recently in a covers band called Nexus who do songs by The Stones and Thin Lizzy. But nothing by The Fall. It seems they're having problems with drummers too. 'Go through one every other week,' he says. I check that none of them was Burns.

We go to the pub. The pub where he did the pop quiz. The pub that brought him to me. We sit, and we drink. Brown tells me how much those few weeks with Una Baines still influence his world view.

'I'd never looked at adverts and seen [them] as a woman selling a product until she told me about it, but even to this day I can see it like that.'

As we drink up, David Jonathan Brown has a question of his own. 'Can you put me back in touch with Una?'

And I promise I will.

* * *

'Who wants to know?'

I've gone back, right back to where it started for me. Not the Riley-Smith Hall but the hallowed landscapes of *Grotesque* and, specifically, the track 'English Scheme', which plays on repeat in my car as I drive, in which Smith sings about armchair rebels who talk of Chile while driving down the poky, quaint streets of Haslingden, and points out that if Britons were smart, they'd emigrate.

I am driving through Haslingden, which lies in the hills above Manchester, but I am not talking about Chile, I am looking for Karl Burns. The Steve Trafford connection hasn't come through, so I'm down to my last remaining leads, one of them being that Kay Carroll thinks that he lives here. Except it's bigger than I imagined, much bigger, a largely Asian area these days by the look of it, with scores of shops offering things like 'family footwear' and, presumably, corrective shoes. He might have emigrated, but if Burns is here, I'll never find him.

I turn the car around and head for the other destination that comes up more often – the farmland around Rossendale, a mile or two up the road, higher in the hills near Burnley. Here, I watch a sparrowhawk stalking its prey – obviously an emissary from Smith – then drive into a desolate village like something from *Village of the Damned*. There are two pubs. I head for the first, armed with a tiny photograph of Karl Burns. I order a shandy and do it like *The Sweeney*.

'I'm looking for this man,' I say. 'He might be older-looking now, possibly with a beard. He's called Karl. Plays drums . . .'

There's a deathly silence in the pub. The barman – big beard, leatherclad, if he was a bit older he might actually be Karl Burns – looks at me suspiciously. He remembers how they do it in *The Sweeney* too.

'Who wants to know?' he asks, fixing me with a beady stare.

I lie like I have never lied before, making up some unbelievable story about once being in a band with him – wish fulfilment, probably.

'Nah, mate. Not 'ere.'

I drink up and head for the other pub, which lies at the very top of the hill. It's called The Deerplay, an obvious code for 1982 Fall song 'Deer Park'. This must be the place. Crack the code and find the drummer. Except it's shut down, doesn't look like anyone's been here for days.

The wind is blowing over the hills. I feel like Clint Eastwood in *The Good, The Bad and The Ugly*, especially when I become aware of being watched. I turn around slowly. There are two of us in the car park. Just me and him: hairy with weird, staring eyes.

Except it is not Karl Burns.

It's a sheep.

The painful truth dawns that I will probably never locate Karl Burns, but I realise that that might not be a bad thing. Whatever terrible fate has or has not befallen The Fall's missing drummer, I've become obsessed with the myth. One of my few clear memories of my father was one night before Christmas, when he sat me at my bedroom window, pointing at the sodium lights of distant street lamps which he said were 'fairy lights' which would guide Santa's sleigh to my bedroom. And I believed that because I wanted to, like my adolescent fascination with the myths of Lord Lucan and the Loch Ness Monster. And now I believe in the myth of Karl: the greatest unsolved mystery of The Mighty Fallen.

I came in search of The Fall's lost drummer and found a sheep. I came in search of 'God' and found a human being. But I discovered something else. I discovered the motivations and travails of musicians, and the art of survival and deep enduring love and obsession, and what it means to make music in intolerable conditions. I honestly have no idea how close I've got to Smith – every time I think I've cracked him there are 25 times when I fear I got nowhere near at all.

And what of The Fallen? Right at the start of this journey, Steve Hanley said something in the pub: 'Mark's had all these talented people in the band, but not many have done anything without him. He must have something . . .' Which he has, but they have done something, all of them, whether it's Marc Riley on the radio or Ruth Daniel with her record label or Una and Jonny with their various children. All of them have done something none of us will ever come close to doing. They have survived The Fall. When I began all this, Mark E Smith was my hero. They are all my heroes now.

EPILOGUE

'I can't tell you any more. I'd have to kill you.'

It's never over. In the Wonderful and Frightening World, there is never an end, just another new beginning. No sooner have I finished the hardback edition of this book than there is more Fall upheaval, with the departure – unannounced – of the 'Dudes', the American Fall line-up which Smith recruited in May 2006 after the implosion in Arizona and he used to record 2007's *Reformation Post-TLC*. However, tracking the Dudes down doesn't involve trips into the American desert – one of them is performing a few miles from my house. His name is Orpheo McCord, a drummer, and I find him playing with US songwriter Cass McCombs. When we hook up before the gig, both are enjoying a curry, a disgustingly wholesome state of affairs which you'd never encounter with The Fall. But then again, McCord and pals –bassist Rob Barbato and guitarist Tim Presley– were not a regular Fall line-up. They weren't hired from the support band or plucked hurriedly from a pub.

They were called by Emmett Kelly – a musician, not the clown – on behalf of The Fall's American label, Narnack, and were pitched into the fray. McCord suggests that because 'Mark knew we were helping him out' there wasn't as much pressure, and Smith seems to have treated them differently from previous line-ups. There were no abandonments at airports or suitcases filled with water. In fact, McCord describes them all 'hanging out', practically friends. Although Smith is well-versed in America and Americans, there was enough of a cultural gap to make both parties interested in each other. McCord uses un-Fall-like words like 'team' to describe their bond. Not that the Dudes committed the cardinal Fall sin of getting ideas above their station.

'We were there to back him up,' admits McCord, who clearly wasted no time in acquiring the Fall state of mind. 'We weren't there to say "Hey, we are The Fall". Because there have been so many members I really feel that Mark is The Fall. It was about backing Mark and making it rock so hard that he could do his thing, and if we wanted to back off, we could do that. I think that's why he didn't react to us like he has with some line-ups. We never got pissed before shows. And I think that's a difference between being an American. I mean, I know about The Fall and their significance to rock music, but I'm still this guy just coming in'. There was another difference, perhaps, between the character of these LA Dudes and former laddish recruits from Prestwich. They weren't dour Northerners burdened by Fall history. They were 'excited, very positive people'. However, otherwise, their first days in The Fall were typical.

They were required to learn eleven songs on the first day alone, implausibly downloading the *Fall Heads Roll* album from iTunes. McCord – an accomplished drummer often found playing afro beat – wasn't fazed. 'Because it's The Fall they're repetitive,' he smiles, 'It wasn't as if they're super complex.' The only instruction, as ever, was 'keep it minimal'. He complied, and wasn't fined a fiver.

McCord remembers that at the first gig –in San Diego –Smith was 'quiet'. 'I think he was nervous, you know, his band's left him. He may have been a bit upset about that.'

But soon enough, Smith was in his element. He decided he wanted to play the 1988 Fall song 'Wrong Place, Right Time', which the group were unfamiliar with, and simply whistled out the melody. 'We did a version that was totally different from the recorded version,' laughs McCord. His understatement is wonderfully American: 'I think Mark's a very spontaneous person.'

McCord loved his year as a Fall musician, and Smith responded to their 'professionalism' by paying them generously and – on the rare occasions when tempers frayed – making an effort not to take it out on us'. The only real problem was geography, but Smith's solution was the same as it had been for Londoner Simon Rogers all those years before: the Dudes would come and live in Prestwich.

McCord remembers surreal nights with bandmates (who had never left the States before) suddenly finding themselves holed up in 'proletarian' Prestwich B&Bs. Their regular home was the Rocket Club, where Smith housed them so they could be close to him and Elena. Most nights, the Dudes and the Smiths would be found touring Prestwich hostelries, with Smith operating as tour guide,perhaps occasionally having to step over a discarded ex-Fall guitarist in a bar. Along the way, McCord noticed something else which no other Fallen musicians have commented – on directly – the powerful bond between Smith and his young wife.

He describes Elena as 'very maternal . . . always running around. "Is anybody hungry?" Stuff like that. She loves Mark, that is really obvious'. But Elena's cuisine didn't generally reach the mouth of the leader. 'I don't think I ever saw him eat," McCord chuckles, echoing Dave Tucker's observations years before.

'But they make a good match and she looks after him. If Mark wants something doing a certain way she does it. Nobody stands in front of him.'

The Dudes line-up seems to have been something otherwise unthinkable: a friendly Fall. There doesn't even seem to have been much of the fabled Fall 'creative tension'. Even when they tired of Prestwich and moaned that they wanted to be 'nearer the action', Smith relocated them to the Salutation, a hotel near the university and city centre. It provided the setting for an unlikely development.

With Barbato and Presley busy with their other, Los Angeles-based group Darker My Love, and McCord also having other commitments, the geographical problems got too much. The Dudes bade a friendly farewell to The Fall with their last gig on 1 June 2007 in Barcelona. Smith even arranged a parting gift, one a bit more tender than a fish's head. They rolled off the tour into the Salutation to find a camera crew in their room. There, the chuckling Dudes and Smiths filmed a video for the track *Reformation*.

'It was fun, and that was our farewell memento,' smiles McCord, to date the only Fall drummer ever to part on genuinely good terms.

Later, as he's drumming with McCombs, I notice a very un-Fall-like quirk. He's drumming barefoot: 'I like to feel the pedals,' he explains. 'I don't think Mark noticed.'

I'd love to talk to the other Dudes when Darker My Love hit the UK, but their entire tour is suddenly cancelled, perhaps another victim of the Curse Of The Fall. But an email from Rob Barbato fills in a few more details about the Dudes, such as the fact that the Darker My Love pair had suddenly become available to tour with The Fall because the Darker My Love drummer broke both his arms in a bicycle accident. Almost exactly as I'm reading this, I receive another email from previous Fall guitarist Adrian Flanagan, explaining that he too has broken both his arms in a bicycle accident. Things like this just seem to happen around The Fall. Barbato also reveals another facet of Smith's curious musical psychology. Often, they'd be expecting a long soundcheck and find themselves hauled off after half a song, Smith's logic being that 'it's good and to go back stage and wait to play'. But he confirms that the Dudes never asked—and were never told – what had happened to the previous line-up.

'It was like a *Twilight Zone* episode. Once we were in the band, they didn't exist.'

Intriguingly, both Dudes say they will 'definitely' be working with Smith again, which must be alarming for the current Fall.

I'm finding other new names to add to the list of The Fallen in my own personal Twilight Zone. It turns out that Smith's old squeeze Lucy Rimmer did more than contribute backing vocals to an encore, and in fact played at least four gigs. Thus, her name is added to the roll call, although the St. Helens born, sometime DJ (and one-time Choir Singer Of The Year) hasn't been heard of since being spotted working in a Manchester city centre shoe shop. Similarly, Mike Bennett (producer of *Cerebral Caustic* and *The Light User Syndrome*) emails to say that he too played live, in both the UK and Europe. Bennett's inclusion takes the number of Fallen to a mammoth fifty. But others already on the list are still proving elusive.

I'm given an email address for Tom Head a.k.a. Thomas Patrick Murphy – the drumming TV extra notoriously 'abandoned at motorway services' before the 1999 Reading Festival – but don't get a reply. I'm told that he lives in Rochdale and when anyone tracks him down, he claims to be his brother – who it turns out is Steve Evets, who was also in The Fall. I'm given an unpublished interview with Head (done by Dave Bromwich for now defunct Fall fanzine *The Pseud Mag*) in which he suggests the motorway services incident (as described to Nick Dewey to convince him to join The Fall for that gig) never happened. As Head tells it, he was waiting for the tour bus outside Smith's house, with his car window down. The singer came up and 'smacked' him in the face. Following a 'scuffle', the drummer refused to do the festival. The following day, he went to the Leeds leg of the event to pick up his drums, saw Smith and was asked to play. 'Why not? I'm here!' he replied, only exiting the Fall much later, tiring of paying for the train to gigs in London only to find that he had nowhere to stay.

Another one of The Fallen, Martin Bramah, suddenly agrees to break decades of silence, but just hours before we're due to meet I receive the following mysterious email, headed 'Ms Bramah regrets':

Hello Dave,

I think you can guess what's coming – I can not do this interview after all.

I have received a serious threat from a certain entity in the service of persons who must remain unnamed.

Since the publication of SR's *'Totally Wired'* [Simon Reynolds's collection of post-punk interviews, which features an old interview with the Fall-turned-Blue Orchids founder], it has been made clear to me that my lips must remain sealed.

It is however, my belief, that the truth will out in the end.

I have nothing more to say until such a time as this ban can be lifted.

In "(!)" we trust,
"ALL HAIL THE MIGHTY FALL!"
LAMF NGAGPA

Meanwhile, I'm still troubled about Karl Burns.

Weirdly, an entry on *Wikipedia* suggests that Burns is running a bistro in the south coast seaside resort of Lyme Regis, 'with his wife, Linda,' which Steve Hanley can't imagine at all. 'Knowing Karl he'd poison someone,' he says. However, one night I arrive home to a message from QTarquin on The Fall forum, regarding 'urgent news re. missing members'. He's found The Fall's long-lost drumming legend. Except it's not Burns. It's Mike Leigh, the near mythical 'Teddy Boy'drummer last heard in 1980.

I'm directed to the website of a roofing company based in Blackburn, apparently 'the first name in lightweight roof tiles'. Halfway down the page, under the heading 'northern region salesman' is Mike Leigh. There's even a mobile number. Moments later, I'm talking on the phone to one of The Fall's ultimate lost legends, who played drums on the *Dragnet* album's 'Fiery Jack' and 'Rowche Rumble', wore Edwardian/Showaddywaddy drapes and often played while standing at his drum kit. It turns out he now lives in Hatfield, near Glossop, where they filmed *The League Of Gentlemen*, which occasionally starred Tom Head.

A few days later, we hook up at the not inappropriate location of a motorway services. A huge stack of a man –twice the fellow he was in 1980 –Leigh is immensely likeable and still instantly recognisable. The rocker side-burns are long gone and the drapes have been replaced by a salesman's leather coat, but it turns out he wasn't a Teddy Boy at all.

'I'd been drumming in Rocking Ricky and The Velvet Collars,' he explains, smiling. 'We were a professional act, seven days a week, all over the country. Sometimes I'd wear a Lurex waistcoat or a leather tie, and I kept the outfits when I joined The Fall. I was always an extrovert. I used to leap over the drum kit. Once the kit collapsed but because I'd done judo I managed to do a forward roll. The audience thought it was part of the act.'

Leigh's 1979 entrance came about in typical madcap fashion. His best mate Ian was engaged to Smith's sister, Barbara. One night Ian came round and mentioned that Barbara's brother was stuck for a drummer. At the time, Leigh was taking three weeks off from The Velvet Collars. The next day, Smith called and invited him round to the flat. They had 'a chat' and Leigh took his drums to the TJ Davidson warehouse, where The Fall rehearsed. He was provided with *Live At The Witch Trials*, 'Bingo-Master's Break-Out!' and 'It's the New Thing', and then they had a 'practice'.

'A couple of hours later Mark called and said, "You've passed the audition,"' Leigh remembers. '"Audition? What do you mean?" They wanted me to join permanently. I thought stuff it, count me in!' As Leigh tells it, making the leap from The Collars to The Fall was a no-brainer. For the now travelling salesman (which began, in best Fall drumming tradition, with selling insurance), it was the chance of a lifetime. The Collars were always touring, mainly playing the cabaret circuit, but The Fall were a recording band, who played as far afield as America. Leigh's intended three weeks helping out ended up being two years. He loved those days, where he wasn't just a musician but – because he had a van – was often responsible for ferrying the group around. Once, they were dropping Craig Scanlon off and saw a police roadblock ahead, not the thing you want to see when the van is filled with dope smoke.

'I could hardly breathe in the van for the fumes, and thought "Bloody hell we're in for it"', the drummer chuckles. However, as the policeman slid back the van doors, Leigh noticed that the air outside was acrid with smoke from a fire in a warehouse. 'So they couldn't smell what was in the back of the van!' he shrieks. 'They said, "There's a diversion Sir!"' The dope smoke had been nothing to do with Leigh in any case. Another unusual thing about the lost drummer is that he has never taken drugs – not illegal ones, at least.

However, Leigh was chemically-fuelled in a different way. At 17, he was diagnosed with epilepsy and put on tablets. He's not had an attack since 19 but takes the tablets to this day.

'But I never did drugs, partly because of that and also respect for my parents. I've never even smoked. But I had to take drugs to lead a normal life.'

Leigh tells how he suffered from the same grand mal epilepsy as tragic Joy Division singer Ian Curtis, who committed suicide after depression which his surviving bandmates attribute to his medication. 'That happened with me at first,' says Leigh, slightly shuddering. 'The first thing that happens psychologically is you get a chip on your shoulder. "Why me?? Why am I epileptic?"' Leigh recalls how doctors 'experimented' with his tablets.

'At first I was on 19 a day. They stopped the fits but they made me really depressed. Then they gave me Valium and I felt fantastic but I had two fits a day. I went to Manchester Royal and they put me on these others and I was right as nine pence, and I'm 53." Curtis was just 23 when he hanged himself at home. Leigh remembers Curtis fondly – Joy Division and The Fall watched each other play at Altrincham Bowden Vale Youth Club in 1979,and thought he was a 'lovely fella'.

'God, I didn't know that about Ian,' he sighs. 'If he'd have talked to me about it I could have helped him, cos I had it under control.' The drummer is soon back to his cheery self with a happier memory of that night–of The Fall and various associates piling out of his van into his Mum's house. Martin Bramah was 'out of his face'and ended up sliding down a wall and landing on the floor in front of Mrs. Leigh. 'My Mum still talks about it,' says Leigh. 'She's 77.'

Even though he abstained when the other members dabbled in narcotics, Leigh was very much a part of the Fall unit. He particularly loved Smith, 'like a brother', even though the Fall leader was 'on a higher mental plain'. They bonded because they were both 'comedians', and Smith introduced the drummer – two years Smith's senior – to music like Can, The Velvet Underground and The Doors (whose 'Light My Fire' Leigh has as his mobile ringtone to this day). Together, they formed one of the most formidable Fall partnerships. Leigh remembers the fabled gig at Bircoats Leisure Centre, Doncaster in 1979, immortalised on *Totale's Turns*, where Smith addresses the audience with the words, 'The difference between you and us is we have brains'.

'The promoter was a right tosser,' he begins. 'A local band supported us and the promoter was big on this band, he treated us very disdainfully, very cavalier and I don't take bad manners from anybody. If it riles me I play harder. And Mark's singing "The promoter is a jerk! The promoter is a jerk!" on 'Rowche Rumble'. I was pissing myself laughing. It was warfare some of the time. Mark was really against the bands that he said sold out. Do you ever watch *Boston Legal*, with William Shatner who's playing a lawyer who "never lost a case, never will"? Mark has never sold out, never will.'

After 28 years, he's still steeped in Fall dictum, and enduring respect for Our Leader.

'Every time I drove him anywhere he'd always say "Thanks for the safe journey, Mike." Every time. And he meant it as well.'

But Leigh was more than just the drummer-driver-footsoldier. His introduction coincided with one of The Fall's most important musical developments – the infamous 'Northern rockabilly' sound. When Leigh was in the group, The Fall sound changed. He's never thought about this before and says that if that's the case, it was a total accident. Because he'd been playing with The Velvet Collars, his drumming was still steeped in rock 'n' roll.

'"Fiery Jack" came about because I started doing a rockabilly beat on drums,' he remembers. 'Craig came in with that diddle diddle guitar riff, Steve got the bass line and before you knew it we had "Fiery Jack". "Flat of Angels" was a weird beat too where something came into my head.' Leigh didn't play on the recording of another Northern rockabilly classic, 'Container Drivers', but was involved in its creation. He is a genuine legend of The Fall.

Like McCord, drumming 26 years after him, Leigh remembers creativity but not too much tension, suggesting that it can be that way. The only time he witnessed 'aggro' was at New York's CBGB, where Kay Carroll praised Leigh for his playing but then suddenly threw a pint of lager in Steve Hanley's face. When Hanley announced he was quitting, the solid, non-drinking, non-drugging Leigh acted as pacifier. 'I said, "Don't do anything rash". He stayed another two decades.'

Leigh insists that he hadn't played any better that night, and as much as he loved Carroll, 'drugs alter the perception. People hear things that aren't there'. Leigh has other recollections of Fall line-ups from many years ago – insisting that Yvonne Pawlett (who he describes as 'a lovely girl, very cool, confident, very trendy, not out of her depth at all') really left because she'd fallen for Nightingales singer Robert Lloyd, and that her exit shocked them all. Another story details the night in Wakefield when a Hells Angel 'put his hand on Una Baines's bum'.

'She chucked a pint in his face. So he slapped her, Martin Bramah jumped in and they smashed a bottle over his head and kicked seven shades out of him. Martin insisted on doing the gig, covered in blood. But we went on and had an absolutely incredible gig. That was one of my first gigs and one of Martin's last.'

But after playing at Manchester Polytechnic on 20 March 1980, Leigh was out as well. The hardworking cabaret veteran had simply become bored. He'd been used to playing every night, not playing random tours, as they had started doing, and then twiddling his thumbs for weeks while Smith prepared new lyrics. So he quit, and like others, has regretted it ever since.

'If I'd thought about the long-term and not been so stupid I might still be in The Fall now," he sighs, unusually wistful. 'Because I was everything he was looking for in a drummer. Nothing fancy.' He can replay their gigs in his mind like a video, the way each musician would walk offstage one by one until he was left alone, ending the gig with a drumbeat. All these years later, Leigh still dreams about Smith, and has a recurring hope.

'Hopefully before I die I'll get a chance to play with them onstage again. Just one number,' he smiles. 'It probably won't happen but that's my dream'. The big, happy man looks suddenly overburdened with real sorrow.

'I miss the laughs we had.'

Leigh went back to cabaret, joining the band Stroller, whose female keyboard player was sleeping with the guitarist and would often refuse to sing whenever they'd had a tiff.

'We used to do "Strut That Funky Stuff" and one night she refused to sing her bit . . . so it would be 'Strut that funky stuff . . .'then silence. I've never been so embarrassed in my life.'

He carried on, starting insurance sales after failing to land a job spraying cars. After five years selling domestic heating, he got into roofing and has got rid of his drum kit. But he has a new outlet for his optimistic energy.

'The Fall is an attitude not a band,' he says. 'It's also like being in a special club . . . which is why I joined the Freemasons." Reaching for his mobile phone, he shows me a picture of himself – as extrovert as ever – not in Teddy Boy drapes, but multicoloured Masonic regalia.

'I can't tell you any more, I'd have to kill you,' he says, and I *think* he's joking. After we part, I put him back in touch with Carroll, Marc Riley and Steve Hanley - and they've picked up where they left off as friends. 'I can't tell you how good it feels to be back together,' he says as we meet up once again and share a coffee. He's even thinking of buying some electronic drums.

There's less camaraderie emanating from Salford, where Smith gives the *Liverpool Daily Post* his opinion on *The Fallen*, and its author. 'I hate that fucking twat. I've just burned the fucking thing!' he rages. When the interviewer comments on how The Fallen have actually been quite affectionate towards their former boss, and he sometimes comes over as (gulp) 'cuddly', his disgust explodes.

'You're right,' blasts Smith. 'That's why I burned it!'

Meanwhile, other ghosts from Fall past are rattling their chains. The fabled Craig Scanlon emails to say that he has bought a new guitar and is writing songs for the first time in a decade.

There are even developments with Burns. The Burns rumour mill is suddenly alive again with stories. One suggests that Burns (or someone posing as Burns) posted a message on an internet message board claiming 'Mark E. Smith is a dead man'. Weirder still is the sadly unprintable story involving Burns, Smith's sister, Smith's mother and a wardrobe. One night, I get home to even more eyebrow-raising news.

Burns has been in touch.

Out of the blue, The Fall's Lord Lucan has rung Steve Hanley, having heard about *The Fallen* and grumbling that people have been saying he's 'living in the wilderness'. Not only is Burns alive, but he is married, and working, although nobody seems sure where. Hanley provides me with an email address and phone number, which I'm told he never answers. My emails go unresponded. I pass the number onto Martin Bramah, who has known Burns since the age of 12 but who similarly fails to get a response.

Suddenly, after some weeks, I receive an email.

Dave,

I have heard favourable reports about your book from Kay and Steve, however I would like to make my own mind up. Please send a copy of your book for evaluation to . . .

And there's an address, with the bizarre warning.

Please note this is not my address!

Weirdly enough, the address supplied is in a small town in the Rossendale hillsides, a stone's throw from where I almost tracked him down.

I can assure you that this will receive my special attention and I will e-mail you to make arrangements for further contact.
Best wishes for the x-mas hols,
Karl.

I send the book, but again receive no reply to further emails, including a final request that if he doesn't want to break his silence and tell all, could he just tell me why he walked away. But again Burns disappears. Eventually, I go in search of the address and find a tiny terraced house. The house doesn't even have a number. After about an hour parked nearby I hear the sudden roar of a motorcycle—but it isn't a Harley Davidson, nor is it Karl Burns.

I've gone full circle —from ringing round Browns in Rotherham to becoming a real life stalker – and suddenly, the true madness of what I'm doing hits me. Whether The Fall's Lord Lucan lives here or not, I decide to leave him to his privacy. I can't help feeling that I've fallen at the final hurdle, but perhaps there are some things in the Wonderful and Frightening World that must forever remain a mystery.

As for me, unless or until Burns breaks his silence, it's time to take a sojourn from the Wonderful and Frightening World. I've got a fabulous new girlfriend, and it's time to rebuild my life somewhere where there are no Fall albums, no motorway services, no weird 1 am phone calls and no ghosts from my own past. Somewhere, in fact, like Rossendale.

Who knows? I might yet run into Karl Burns

ACKNOWLEDGMENTS

This book would not have been possible if it were not for the faith of the *Guardian*'s Charlie English, and his willingness when arts editor to allow me the time and space to go with the original idea. I am also enormously grateful to Jamie Byng and all at Canongate Books for proposing that my journey could be turned into *The Fallen*. Thanks to my Fall-obsessive editor, Andy Miller, who has been brilliant to bounce ideas off and with whom I have enjoyed many – probably far too many – conversations about The Fall. Thanks also to Canongate editor Dan Franklin, who has followed the path of what I hope will be a typical reader, from someone who had vaguely heard of The Fall to someone who is now, like we all are, drawn by the unearthly pull of The Wonderful and Frightening World. Thanks also to copyeditor Alison Rae, who did a wonderful job and confirmed that violinist Kenny Brady does indeed have a glass eye.

I am grateful to all at The Fall's (now unofficial) website/discussion forum, The Fall Online, especially Conway Paton, for contacts and help on what has been a very strange but fascinating trip. I am grateful to all the Fall fans who post on the forum, for allowing me to quote on occasions and for providing stimulating reading over breakfast. I thank The Fall Live Gig Repository for providing information on gigs I sadly missed, and Rob Waite for the generous donation of handfuls of live CDs. I thank Dorothy Howe for arranging my interview with Mark E Smith, and Fall producer Grant Showbiz for providing me with my first contacts for former members of The Fall. Also in this respect I thank *Hip Priest* author Simon Ford, and *Guardian* colleague Helen Pidd, whose journalist ex-boyfriend Neil Cooper put me in touch with Kenny Brady after bumping into him in a club. I am grateful to the array of internet sites and publications which have made it possible to do endless research into The Fall and events around them, from Margaret Thaler Singer's book *Cults In Our Midst* to *NME*, *Stool Pigeon* and *Loaded*.

I am, of course, grateful from the bottom of my heart to The Fallen, the former members who have been so generous with their time and reminiscences, whether for my original *Guardian* article or this book. I have nothing but respect for them all. I would particularly like to thank Marc Riley, and his mysterious pal Moey, for leading me to the holy grail of Craig Scanlon; the inestimable Steve Hanley, for similar contacts; Simon Rogers for access to his personal photographs; and Kay Bateman, née Carroll, who has been a continual source of enlightenment and amusement and never once lived up to her reputation as 'Mother Carroll From Hell'.

Thank you, Kevin Crotty, for first playing me The Fall, and thank you Carol Stubbs, for giving me my first Fall album. Thank you to Suzanne Underwood for cups of tea and helping edit down my original *Guardian* article on what was a very hectic New Year's Day, 2006, and to her, Bruce Paget, Alan Bilson, Susan Ackroyd and Victoria Cullen for accompanying me to Fall gigs over the years.

Last but not least, whether he welcomes it or not, I would like to extend my sincere appreciation to Mark E Smith, for giving me such an exhaustive interview in the first place and for getting the beers in. And, of course, for leading The Fall on such an idiosyncratic course for the last 32 years, without which this book would never have been possible, and without whom we'd have all led quieter – but duller – and far less enriching lives.

Dave Simpson, the wilds of North Yorkshire, February 2008

PHOTOGRAPHY CREDITS AND PERMISSIONS ACKNOWLEDGMENTS

Page 15: Mark E Smith by Christopher Thomond. Copyright Guardian News and Media Ltd, 2006

Page 29: Tommy Crooks, courtesy of himself

Page 39: Dave Simpson with his father (holding chisel), courtesy of the author

Page 41: Setlist from a Fall gig at Cleopatra's Club, Huddersfield, Friday, 12 September 1980

Page 47: Steve and Paul Hanley doing their impression of the Krays

Page 57: Ben Pritchard and Mark E Smith, courtesy of Dave Milner

Page 67: Author's father as Bingo Master. Tony Friel played on 'Bingo Master's Break-Out!', released in 1978

Page 75: Kay Bateman, aka Kay Carroll, courtesy of herself

Page 87: Brian Clough with assistant Peter Taylor, 1981. Courtesy of Action Images/Sporting Pictures

Page 91: Una Baines, courtesy of herself

Page 99: Martin Bramah, photo taken by author at a Fall gig

Page 103: A ferret

Page 109: Steve Davies by Christopher Thomond. Copyright Guardian News and Media Ltd, 2006

Page 117: Marc Riley, courtesy of Stephen Wright/Redferns

Page 139: 'Welcome to Prestwich' sign by the author

Page 145: Brix Smith onstage, courtesy of Simon Rogers

Page 157: Marcia Schofield, courtesy of herself

Page 165: Mark E Smith with hearse, courtesy of Simon Rogers

Page 169: Simon Rogers, courtesy of himself

Page 179: Kenny Brady, courtesy of himself

Page 183: Charlotte Bill by Christopher Thomond. Copyright Guardian News and Media Ltd, 2006

Page 185: Dave Bush, courtesy of himself

Page 193: Craig Scanlon, courtesy of Simon Rogers

Page 201: Brix Smith, courtesy of Simon Rogers

Page 213: Keir Stewart by Natalie Curtis. Copyright Natalie Curtis 2008, www.16apr79.com

Page 217: Simon Wolstencroft with Steve Hanley, courtesy of Simon Rogers

Page 223: Julia Adamson aka Julia Nagle by Christopher Thomond. Copyright Guardian News and Media Ltd, 2006

Page 229: Kate Themen by Neemo. Copyright Neemo, 1994–2008, all rights reserved, www.acomfortableplace.co.uk

Page 232: Stuart Estell, courtesy of himself

Page 235: Karen Leatham, courtesy of herself

Page 237: Nick Dewey, courtesy of himself

Page 243: Adam Helal, courtesy of himself

Page 247: Travelling Minstrels

Page 253: Jim Watts by Jon Super. Copyright Guardian News and Media Ltd, 2006

Page 259: Ian Brady

Page 261: Simon Archer, courtesy of himself

Page 265: Ruth Daniel, courtesy of herself

Page 269: Dave Milner, courtesy of himself

Page 279: Ed Blaney, courtesy of himself

Page 287: Steve Trafford, courtesy of himself

Page 293: Dave and Suzanne at Sudbury Hall by Helga Totale

Page 298: Jonnie Brown, courtesy of the author

Page 302: Karl Burns with Mark E Smith, courtesy of Simon Rogers

Page 305: Mike Leigh, courtesy of the author

Epigraph on p.1 by AC Grayling reproduced by kind permission

Lyrics on p.41 from 'The Legend of The Fall' by Jeffrey Lewis, reproduced with kind permission

THERE'S A RIOT GOING ON

PETER DOGGETT

Between 1965 and 1972, political activists around the globe prepared to mount a revolution, from the Black Panthers to the Gay Liberation Front, from the Yippies to the IRA. Rock and soul music supplied the revolutionary tide with anthems and iconic imagery; and renowned musicians such as John Lennon, Mick Jagger and Bob Dylan were particularly influential in the movement. This is the definitive account of this unique period in modern history; a compelling portrait of an era when revolutionaries turned into rock stars, and rock stars dressed up as revolutionaries.

'An extraordinary book . . . Grab a copy – By Any Means Necessary.'
***** *Mojo*

'A fascinating history of pop's relationship with politics, examining the establishment's skill at assimilating rock'n'roll rebellion into the mainstream.' *Independent*

'Meticulously researched, scholarly and often gripping.' *Sunday Telegraph*

£12.99

ISBN 978 1 84767 114 1

THE MOJO COLLECTION, 4TH EDITION: THE ULTIMATE MUSIC COMPANION

BROUGHT TO YOU BY THE MAKERS OF *MOJO* MAGAZINE

- The greatest albums of all time . . . and how they happened!

- Over 700 albums reviewed by more than 50 of the world's finest music journalists

- Each entry comes with recording and production details, release dates and chart histories, full personnel and track listings, further listening and reading suggestions

- Revised and expanded, with dozens of new entries

Spanning seven decades, *The MOJO Collection* presents an authoritative and engaging guide to the history of music via hundreds of crucial albums. From The Beatles to James Brown, from Elvis Presley to Pink Floyd, from Aerosmith to The Arctic Monkeys, each record is dissected in detail, offering new insights into some of the finest music ever created and enhancing your listening pleasure.

The MOJO Collection is an essential purchase for those who love and live for music.

£18.99

ISBN 978 1 84195 973 3

www.meetatthegate.com